T0192174

Communications in Computer and Information Science   1666

More information about this series at https://link.springer.com/bookseries/7899

Fernando Ortiz-Rodríguez · Sanju Tiwari ·
Miguel-Angel Sicilia ·
Anastasija Nikiforova (Eds.)

Electronic Governance with Emerging Technologies

First International Conference, EGETC 2022
Tampico, Mexico, September 12–14, 2022
Revised Selected Papers

 Springer

Editors
Fernando Ortiz-Rodríguez 🆔
Autonomous University of Tamaulipas
Ciudad Victoria, Mexico

Sanju Tiwari 🆔
Autonomous University of Tamaulipas
Ciudad Victoria, Mexico

Miguel-Angel Sicilia 🆔
University of Alcalá
Alcalá de Henares, Spain

Anastasija Nikiforova 🆔
University of Tartu
Tartu, Estonia

ISSN 1865-0929   ISSN 1865-0937 (electronic)
Communications in Computer and Information Science
ISBN 978-3-031-22949-7   ISBN 978-3-031-22950-3 (eBook)
https://doi.org/10.1007/978-3-031-22950-3

This Springer imprint is published by the registered company Springer Nature Switzerland AG
The registered company address is: Gewerbestrasse 11, 6330 Cham, Switzerland

Preface

A trend toward improving the public sector has emerged in many countries in recent years. Some demands are adding to the need for efficiency, transparency, and overall better performance, and some are trained by the innovation wave that originated with the adoption of the Internet and web-based services by, and care of, the private sector, boosted by smartphones and tablets. With the potential administrative revolution and feeling the need to reduce the existent gap between the private and public sectors, an increasing number of governments have adopted e-government strategies to support development.

There have been increased efforts to utilize advanced electronic and mobile services for the benefit of all. But fixed and wireless broadband subscriptions have increased unevenly across regions. A major effort is required to ensure universal access to the internet in the least developed countries. Countries in all regions are increasingly utilizing new information and communication technologies to deliver services and engage people in decision-making processes. One of the most important new trends is the advancement of people-driven services - which reflect people's needs and are driven by them. Disparities remain within and among countries. Lack of access to technology, poverty, and unequal society prevents people from fully taking advantage of the potential for information and communications technology (ICT) and e-government for sustainable development.

During the last decade, the role of emerging technologies in governments and public administrations has grown significantly. In addition, online communities and the rise of blockchain networks have resulted in new ideas and forms of governance inside communities with a degree of autonomy and self-organization. Decentralized autonomous organizations (DAOs) are examples of those forms of organization and governance that transcend national and geographical boundaries. As enabled by blockchain, decentralization is the critical element that allows for algorithmic coordination procedures that are the framework of DAOs.

Emerging technologies are enablers for these new forms of governance and novel applications to traditional governance functions. Concretely, artificial intelligence and the processing of large volumes of data are reshaping the knowledge-based economy. The number of experimental and theoretical findings is increasing rapidly due to many successful emerging technologies. The role of those technologies has been witnessed across various domains, including health care, education, tourism, and industry, among others.

This volume contains the main proceedings of the first International Conference on Electronic Governance with Emerging Technologies (EGETC 2022). EGETC has been established as a yearly venue for discussing the latest scientific results and technology innovations related to emerging technologies supporting electronic governance. It aims to provide a forum for academics, scholars, and practitioners to share and exchange recent developments in the domain of e-government and governance of digital organizations and to shed light on the emerging research trends and their applications. The first edition took place in Tampico, Mexico, during September 12–14, 2022.

The main scientific program of the conference comprised 17 papers: 15 full research papers and two short research papers selected out of 54 reviewed submissions, which corresponds to an acceptance rate of 31%.

The General and Program Committee chairs would like to thank the many people involved in making EGETC 2022 a success. First, our thanks go to the four reviewer chairs and the 49 reviewers for ensuring a rigorous and open review process that, with an average of three double-blind reviews per paper, led to an excellent scientific program.

Further, we thank the kind support of the team at Springer. We finally thank our sponsors for their vital support of this edition of EGETC 2022. The editors would like to close the preface with warm thanks for our supporting keynotes and our enthusiastic authors who made this event truly international.

September 2022

Fernando Ortiz-Rodríguez
Sanju Tiwari
Miguel-Angel Sicilia
Anastasija Nikiforova

Organization

General and Program Chairs

Fernando Ortiz-Rodríguez   Autonoma de Tamaulipas, Mexico
Sanju Tiwari   Autonoma de Tamaulipas, Mexico
Miguel-Angel Sicilia   University of Alcalá, Spain
Anastasija Nikiforova   University of Latvia, Latvia

Reviewer Chairs

Emmanouel Garoufallou   International Hellenic University, Greece
Eric Pardede   La Trobe University, Australia
Patience Usoro Usip   University of Uyo, Nigeria
Christy Fernandez Cull   MIT, USA

Publicity Chairs

Samir Sellami   ENSET Skikda, Algeria
Victor Lopez Cabrera   Universidad Tecnologica de Panama, Panama
Sarra Ben Abbes   ENGIE, France
Rim Hantach   ENGIE, France

Tutorial Chairs

Antonela Carbonaro   University of Bologna, Italy
Antonio De Nicola   ENEA, Italy

Special Session Chairs

Rita Zgheib   Canadian University Dubai, UAE
Gustavo de Assis Costa   Federal Institute of Education, Brazil
Praveen Kumar Shukla   Babu Banarasi Das University, India

Program Committee

Alexandros Gazis   Democritus University of Thrace, Greece
Amed Abel Leiva Mederos   Universidad Central de las Villas, Cuba
Carlos F. Enguix   Independent Researcher, Peru
Charalampos Alexopoulos   University of the Aegean, Greece

Csaba Csaki	Corvinus University, Hungry
David Martín-Moncunill	Universidad Camilo Jose Cela, Spain
Edgar Tello Leal	Universidad Autonoma de Tamaulipas, Mexico
Emmanouel Garoufallou	International Hellenic University, Greece
Eloy Gil-Cordero	Universidad de Sevilla, Spain
Eric Pardede	La Trobe University, Australia
Esther García-Río	Universidad de Sevilla, Spain
Francisco Edgar Castillo Barrera	Universidad Autónoma de San Luis Potosí, Mexico
Gerard Deepak	Manipal Institute of Technology, India
Gerardo Haces	Universidad Autonoma de Tamaulipas, Mexico
Hugo Eduardo Camacho Cruz	Universidad Autónoma de Tamaulipas, Mexico
Jose L. Martinez-Rodriguez	CINVESTAV, Mexico
Jose Melchor Medina-Quintero	Autonoma de Tamaulipas, Mexico
Jude Hemanth	Karunya University, India
Katerina Tzafilkou	Freee IKE, Greece
MA Jabbar	Vardhaman College of Engineering, India
Manuel Pedro Rodríguez Bolívar	University of Granada, Spain
MP Gupta	Indian Institute of Technology, Delhi, India
Nina Rizun	Gdansk University of Technology, Poland
Noella Edelmann	Danube University Krems, Austria
Onur Dogan Izmir	Bakircay University, Turkey
Otmane Azeroual	Deutsches Zentrum für Hochschul- und Wissenschaftsforschung GmbH, Germany
Pedro Baena-Luna	University of Seville. Spain
Pedro Palos-Sanchez	Universidad de Sevilla, Spain
Petar Milić	University of Priština - Kosovska Mitrovica, Russia
Rajan Gupta	University of Delhi, India
Ricardo Matheus	Delft University of Technology, Netherlands
Sailesh Iyer	Rai University, India
Saibal Pal	DRDO, India
Shikha Mehta	JIIT Noida, India
Serge Sonfack	Toulouse INP, France
Sourav Banerjee	Kalyani Government Engineering College, India
Stavros Kourmpetis	European Banking Institute, Greece
Stuti Saxena	Graphic Era University, India
Sukumar Ganapati	Florida International University, USA
Sven Groppe	University of Lubeck, Germany
Thomas Lampo	Itshammer Danube University Krems, Austria
Vasylevska Halyna West	Ukrainian National University, Ukraine
Victor Menendez-Dominguez	Universidad Autónoma de Yucatán, Mexico

Yulong Liu   Massey University, New Zealand
Yusniel Hidalgo   Delgado Universidad de las Ciencias
                                       Informáticas, Cuba

Contents

Deep Learning Based Obstructive Sleep Apnea Detection for e-health
Applications 1
   E. Smily Jeya Jothi, J. Anitha, Jemima Priyadharshini,
   and D. Jude Hemanth

Deep Learning and Sign Language Models Based Enhanced Accessibility
of e-governance Services for Speech and Hearing-Impaired 12
   R. Jennifer Eunice and D. Jude Hemanth

A Blockchain Enabled Trusted Public Distribution Management System
Using Smart Contract 25
   Rajdeep Roy, Paranjay Haldar, Debashis Das, Sourav Banerjee,
   and Utpal Biswas

Administration of Vaccine Mechanism for COVID-19 Using Blockchain 36
   Shipra Ravi Kumar and Mukta Goyal

Cyber Security Strategies While Safeguarding Information Systems
in Public/Private Sectors 49
   Alya Al Mehairi, Rita Zgheib, Tamer Mohamed Abdellatif,
   and Emmanuel Conchon

The Spatial Relationships of Meteorological Data for Unmanned Aerial
System Decision-Making Support 64
   Yuliya Averyanova and Yevheniia Znakovska

HIAS: Hybrid Intelligence Approach for Soil Classification
and Recommendation of Crops 81
   S. Palvannan and Gerard Deepak

Education 5.0 Maturity Index: Concept and Prospects for Development 95
   Volodymyr Skitsko and Olha Osypova

Interpretability of AI Systems in Electronic Governance 109
   Antonella Carbonaro

An Automated Stress Recognition for Digital Healthcare: Towards
E-Governance 117
   Orchid Chetia Phukan, Ghanapriya Singh, Sanju Tiwari, and Saad Butt

Emergency Supply Chain Management 126
  Volodymyr Skitsko and Mykola Voinikov

Public Budget Simulations with Machine Learning and Synthetic Data:
Some Challenges and Lessons from the Mexican Case 141
  David Valle-Cruz, Vanessa Fernandez-Cortez, Asdrúbal López-Chau,
  and Rafael Rojas-Hernández

Open Data Hackathon as a Tool for Increased Engagement of Generation
Z: To Hack or Not to Hack? 161
  Anastasija Nikiforova

Data Visualization Guide for Smart City Technologies 176
  Teresa Cepero, Luis G. Montané-Jiménez,
  and Gina Paola Maestre-Góngora

A Machine Learning-Based Mobile Chatbot for Crop Farmers 192
  Patience U. Usip, Edward N. Udo, Daniel E. Asuquo,
  and Otobong R. James

Urban Data: Sources and Targeted Applications for Urban Planning
Indicators Modelling 212
  Stéphane Cédric Koumetio Tékouabou, Jérôme Chenal, Rida Azmi,
  El Bachir Diop, and Hamza Toulni

Understanding KlimaDAO Use and Value: Insights from an Empirical
Analysis 227
  Miguel-Angel Sicilia, Elena García-Barriocanal,
  Salvador Sánchez-Alonso, Marçal Mora-Cantallops,
  and Juan-José de Lucio

Author Index 239

Deep Learning Based Obstructive Sleep Apnea Detection for e-health Applications

E. Smily Jeya Jothi[1], J. Anitha[2], Jemima Priyadharshini[3], and D. Jude Hemanth[2(✉)]

[1] Avinashilingam Institute for Home Science and Higher Education for Women, Coimbatore, India

[2] Department of ECE, Karunya Institute of Technology and Sciences, Coimbatore, India
judehemanth@karunya.edu

[3] Immanuel Hospital, Chennai, India

Abstract. The lack of oxygen caused by constricting of the upper respiratory system causes Obstructive Sleep Apnea (OSA), which mainly manifests as low concentration, sleepiness during the daytime, and irritability. Human lives can be saved and treatment costs can be reduced when OSA is detected early. OSA can be quickly detected by computer-aided diagnosis (CAD) using Electrocardiogram (ECG) and Photoplethysmogram (PPG) signals. Deep Learning (DL) has attracted dramatic attention due to its uses in biomedical applications and its efficiency in classifying OSA events. In this study, Convolutional Neural Networks with Long-Short Term Memory (CNN-LSTM) and Densely Connected Long-Short Term Memory (DC-LSTM) networks are used to detect apneic events using ECG and PPG signals. The study involves 200 recording of ECG signals and PPG signals collected from publically available apnea database. DC-LSTM network achieved accuracy of 98.2%, sensitivity of 97.4%, specificity of 97.5%, and Kappa coefficient of 0.92. In terms of performance, the algorithms employed here are comparable with those that are fully automated. This methodology can be easily incorporated with wearable medical devices, which makes it useful for e-health monitoring of OSA at home.

Keywords: OSA · ECG · PPG · LSTM · CNN · Densely connected LSTM

1 Introduction

A person is considered to have OSA if their nasal or oral respiratory amplitudes are reduced by 90% or more during sleep, for a period of 10 s or more. The OSA patients suffer from sleep fragmentation and repetitive airflow restriction, which reduce their sleep time and degrade their quality of sleep [1]. Sleep apnea occurs when breathing stops during sleep. It takes about 10–20 s between episodes of apnea. In the end, a reduced heart rate is caused by the inadequate supply of oxygen to the heart. ECG signals, which indicate the amount of oxygen that is carried by the heart, are the easiest way to monitor heart rate performance. When the amount of oxygen in the blood is low, the heart rate will be reduced, since the amount of oxygen is not sufficient to maintain the heartbeat.

F. Ortiz-Rodríguez et al. (Eds.): EGETC 2022, CCIS 1666, pp. 1–11, 2022.
https://doi.org/10.1007/978-3-031-22950-3_1

ECG signals can provide information on the oxygen delivered to the heart and are the easiest method for monitoring heart rate performance. An average case of apnea lasts approximately for 10–20 s and there may be more than 15 episodes in a severe case [2].

The ECG signal can be generated by connecting electrodes to the skin, producing an affordable and accurate simulation of heartbeats. Several studies have examined the possibility of detecting apnea by analyzing ECG signals. An ECG signal can be used to determine the performance of a heart condition. ECG signals typically have a low amplitude of 0.5 mV at an offset level of 300 mV, with a frequency range of 0.05 to 100 Hz. An electrocardiogram is a mark of electrical activity in the heart over a time period. Waves (P, Q, R, S, T, U) and intervals (S-T, Q-T, P-R, R-R) make up the complete ECG signal. Heartbeats' duration and amplitude are calculated using intervals in order to process or classify them [3]. Figure 1 illustrates the ECG intervals and waves. Standard ranges of these waves are shown in Table 1 [4, 5].

The PPG device has a number of unique properties that make it a very interesting part of the rapidly evolving and popular field of medical wearable devices, particularly its capacity to capture autonomic nervous system modulations during sleep. In addition to home-based detection of sleep disoriented breathing, long-term monitoring of insomnia, circadian rhythm, sleep disorders, and treated sleep disoriented breathing are all potential medical applications of PPG. Future wearables could benefit from new contact sensor combinations, particularly those that measure brain activity [6].

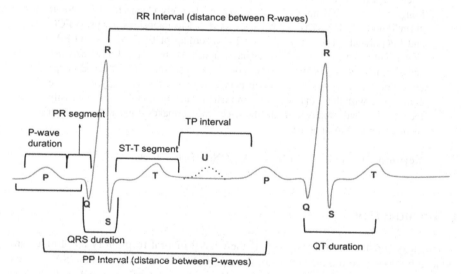

Fig. 1. Components of ECG waveform

Photoplethysmography (PPG) is a device that measures numerous physiological functions in an unobtrusive manner. PPG identifies changes in arterial blood pressure and breathing patterns during sleep, as well as abnormal breathing patterns, because sleep follows a common cardiovascular and respiratory pattern. In order to apply these data extraction processes clinically, mathematical models must be tested, trained, and validated before they can be applied to data [7]. Through the recorded ECG and PPG signals from the patients, the proposed system can direct users to distinguish between OSA patients and normal individuals.

Table 1. Range of ECG waves

ECG waves	Duration (s)	Amplitude (mV)
P wave	0.08–0.1	0.25
T wave	0.16–0.2	>0
QRS complex	0.08–0.1	Q < 0, R > 0, S < 0
R-R interval	0.6–1.2	–
P-R interval	0.12–0.22	R > 0
S-T interval	0.2–0.32	Isoelectric
Q-T interval	0.35–0.45	–

The sections in this paper are as follows: Sect. 2 discusses sleep apnea and CAD in relation to each other relating to various research works. The methodology is outlined in Sect. 3. The results and analysis of the obtained results are presented in Sect. 4. Following that is a discussion of the limitations, conclusion and future work.

2 Literature Survey

In order to determine the presence of OSA in an individual, the ECG signals are analysed to identify the heart rate and the RR interval. Analyses of the main components of the QRS complex are used to measure the increased sympathetic activity during apnea. The data between the heart rate and respiration are extracted using orthogonal subspace projections. Machine learning algorithms are trained on the extracted features. Researchers concluded that the use of ECG sensor values is sufficient to detect sleep apnea accurately [8].

By acquiring signals from a single-channel ECG, an automated OSA detection method based on CNN is proposed. 82 subjects participated in the study, and the data has been divided into training phase and testing phase [9]. A three-step procedure is used to detect OSA from ECG signals: (i) automatically segmenting the signal instead of using equal-length segmentation rules, (ii) removing RR intervals in the segmented signal using local median filters, and (iii) analyzing the ECG signals based on the severity index for OSA. An average accuracy of 97.41% is achieved using the Physionet Apnea ECG database in this study [10].

During the training of the deep learning network, seventeen features are extracted from airflow signals. The binary classification is originally used with AHI cut-off indices. A cross-validation technique of 10 folds is used, and the accuracy of the proposed method is significant at three different cut-offs −5, 15 and 30 (83.46%, 85.39%, and 92.69%) [11]. An apnea disease diagnosis system based on CAD is developed. The method has been designed in three steps: firstly, notch filters are used to reduce noise in ECG signals, secondly, nine features are extracted from the signal, and thirdly, 13 machine learning algorithms and four deep learning methods are used to classify sleep apnea from ECG data [5]. Deep Neural Network (DNN) is used for sleep apnea detection by analyzing the heart rate variability and respiratory rate variability values of Polysomnography (PSG) signals. Support Vector Machine (SVM) classifiers are fed with samples of segments every 2 min. PSG signals are normalized using Covariance Normalization, which strips away many features without affecting the patient details. The DNN proposed achieved 88% accuracy rate [9].

Two deep learning methods are utilized in order to detect OSA events automatically: a bidirectional long short-term memory (BiLSTM) network and a temporal convolutional network (TCN). In the convolutional layer, three different scaling features are discovered. An ECG signal with a single channel is processed through CNN to detect OSA. LSTM algorithm is used to analyse OSA transition rules. A 10-s sliding window is used to segment the ECG signal for detection of OSA events. A kappa coefficient of 0.92, a specificity of 96.2%, and an accuracy of 96.1% are achieved with the proposed model. A limitation of the study is that the proposed method could not identify hypopnea events, and transition epochs could not be scored accurately [6].

3 Methodology

3.1 Dataset

ECG: ECGs are collected from the human body by using an electrical impulse applied to the heart [11]. The dataset used for this study comes from Physionet's Apnea ECG database [12], which is publicly available. 70 records are in total, divided equally between a learning set and a test set of 35 records. For each patient, the total ECG duration is between [25,200, to 36,000] minutes. Data in this dataset is intended for determining apneic and regular ECG events lasting for one minute, based on which signals have been categorized as normal or OSA-affected. Due to the obstruction of the airflow, the ECG signal with OSA is less stable and consistent than the normal signal. Brain signals to muscles are interrupted when the mind stops sending them, so airflow is reduced. Shortly, the amount of oxygen is lacking, which results in an abnormal heart rate.

PPG: Patient-related BIDMC PPG and Respiration Dataset collected from hospitalized critically-ill patients at Beth Israel Deaconess Medical Centre in Boston, Massachusetts, USA, is made publicly available in Physionet [12]. The impedance respiratory signal was manually annotated by two annotators for each recording. 53 recordings in the dataset are each 8 min long, and contain:

- Signs representing bodily functions, such as the PPG, impedance respiratory signal, and electrocardiogram (ECG), which are sampled at a frequency of 125 Hz.
- Heart rate, respiration rate, and blood oxygen saturation level are physiological parameters. These parameters are sampled once per second.
- Fixed variables, like age and gender, can also be recorded at the same time.
- Breaths can be annotated manually (Fig. 2).

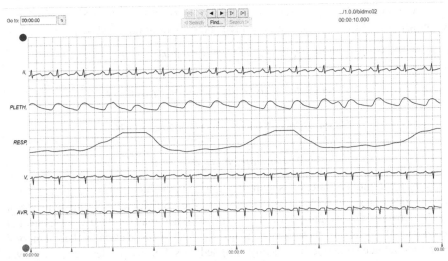

Fig. 2. Sample waveform from BIDMC PPG and respiration dataset

3.2 CNN-LSTM

In the CNN-LSTM, layers related to Convolution, LSTM, Pooling, SoftMax and Fully Connected (FC) are used. Neuron j net input is defined as follows in layer l:

$$Y_j^l = \sum_{i \in M_j} w_{j,i}^l * x_i^{l-1} + b_j^l \qquad (1)$$

where M_j represents the input map selection, $w_{i,j}$ denotes the filter or weight corresponding to the connection between neurons j and i, x_i^{l-1} is the signal output by neuron i in layer $l - 1$, b_j^l is the bias of the neuron j, and * denotes convolution. The training performance of a rectified linear unit (ReLU) is robust when compared to other activation functions. To achieve the desired output maps, we used ReLU as the activation function. A pooling layer follows the convolutional layer. Using this layer, successive layers can be reduced in dimension, network parameters, and computation cost. By considering the average value or maximum value, specific functions are used to summarize subregions. As a result of the pooling layer, the CNN could also learn scale-invariant features or those that are associated with orientation variations [13–15]. A window is drawn across the previous feature map during the pooling process. The convolutional layer is activated first, followed by max pooling. Finally, a dense layer is fully integrated with the outputs of all previous layers, which typically is used in the final stages of CNN-LSTM analysis.

3.3 LSTM

In an LSTM or Long-Short Term Memory network, the cell state is managed by three gates, namely the forget gate, the input gate, and the output gate. The gate units are fed with the output features of the previous dense layer of the CNN network. Each LSTM cell updates its state by activating the gate units, which are controlled by a continuous value between 0 and 1. After each t steps, the hidden state (h_t) of the LSTM is updated. As shown in the Eqs. (2)–(4), there are three gates: input, forget, and output.

$$Input\ gate\ =\ sigmoid(W_i x_t + W_i h_{t-1} + b_i) \tag{2}$$

$$Forget\ gate\ =\ sigmoid(W_f x_t + W_f h_{t-1} + b_f) \tag{3}$$

$$Output\ gate\ =\ sigmoid(W_o x_t + W_o h_{t-1} + b_o) \tag{4}$$

$$Hidden\ state,\ h_t\ =\ o_t . \sigma_c(c_t) \tag{5}$$

where h_t is the hidden state, σ_c is tanh function, x_t is the input, h_{t-1} is the input from the previous timestep LSTM, o_t is the output of the LSTM, and c_t is the cell state of LSTM network. The weight matrices (W_i, W_f, W_o), and bias (b_i, b_f, b_o) are not time-dependent. By detecting these feature maps, the LSTM layer extracts their temporal information. Such layers are specifically designed for solving dependencies arising over the long term. This skill is less hard than that of RNNs, namely remembering long-term information. In this study, 100 hidden units are used in the LSTM layer.

3.4 Densely Connected LSTM (DC-LSTM)

The module consists of multiple LSTM layers as illustrated in Fig. 3. For the first layer of LSTM, the input signal sequence is

$$\{x(w_1), x(w_2), \ldots, x(w_s)\} \tag{6}$$

and the output of the initial layer is

$$y^1 = \left\{ y_1^1, y_2^1, \ldots, y_s^1 \right\} \tag{7}$$

The input signal sequence is represented by x, weights by w, the output by y and the last layer of the network as s. For the second layer, the concatenated output from the previous layer is taken, formulated as,

$$\left\{ \left[e(w_1); y_1^1 \right], \left[e(w_2); y_2^1 \right], \ldots \ldots, \left[e(w_s); y_s^1 \right] \right\} \tag{8}$$

and the output is

$$y^2 = \left\{ y_1^2, y_2^2, \ldots, y_s^2 \right\} \tag{9}$$

In the third layer, the input is formulated as,

$$\left\{ \left[e(w_1); y_1^1; y_1^2 \right], \left[e(w_2); y_2^1; y_2^2 \right], \ldots \ldots, \left[e(w_s); y_s^1; y_s^2 \right] \right\} \tag{10}$$

The rest of the layers process similarly. Considering that there are L dense layers in LSTM network, the average pooling value is formulated as,

$$y^* = average\left(h_1^L, h_2^L, \ldots, h_s^L \right) \tag{11}$$

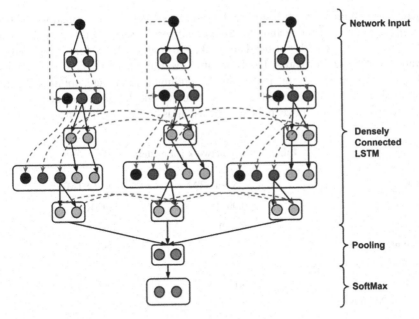

Fig. 3. Architecture of DC-LSTM

It consists of a simple soft-max classifier that takes a list of features, y^*, as features, and predicts a probability distribution over all labelled sentences.

The advantages of densely connected LSTM are,

- Trainable even with a very deep network. For each RNN layer, the outputs are directly sent to the last RNN layer as inputs, so vanishing gradient is alleviated because there is an implicit deep supervision.
- Better parameter efficiency is achieved. By reading the original input sequence directly, the system does not have to transfer all of the information to the network; it just adds it to the network. This means that the DC-LSTM layers are very thin (10 hidden units per layer).

In Fig. 3, black node denotes the input layer. Yellow-, green- and purple-coloured nodes are the hidden layers, the orange-coloured dotted lines indicate the average pooling between the layers and operation of copying. The blue-coloured node denotes the class. Solid lines represent the connection between layers.

3.5 Experimental Parameters

There are 70 ECG signals in the Apnea database, of which 35 are used for training and the rest for testing. Database for PPG signals included impedance respiratory signal, ECG lead II signal, and PPG, as well as heart rate and pulse rate. Signal data for 212 patients is listed along with the patient ID, ventilation status, and recording condition (critical or normal). A total of 282 measurements are taken, with data augmentation being done to increase the sample size for testing and training. Geometric transformation, rotation, and flipping are among the techniques used to enhance the data in this project. Of the total signals considered 80% of the data is taken for training, 15% for testing, and 5% for validation. Table 2 provides details about the learning parameters of the proposed model. There are several factors in this table, including: learning rate, optimizer, hidden units, number of fully connected layers, LSTM units, epochs, and activation function. There are no differences between the models as far as comparison is concerned.

Table 2. Deep network parameters

Parameters	CNN-LSTM	DC-LSTM
Learning rate	0.0001	0.0001
Optimizer	Adam	Adam
Hidden units in LSTM	100	100
No. of fully connected layers	2	2
Dropout	0.15	0.15
No. of LSTM units	512	512
Epochs	30	30
Activation function	ReLU, SoftMax	ReLU, SoftMax

4 Results

The purpose of this study is to compare two deep learning models for classifying sleep apnea with the help of ECG and PPG signals. Using hyper-parameter settings enables the classification method to tune its parameters to reduce error and hold onto the optimal settings for internal parameters. Our method is evaluated by using the Kappa Coefficient (KP), a statistical measure of inter-rater agreement. Further, Accuracy, Sensitivity, Specificity, Positive and Negative Predictive Values, are calculated according to epoch-by-epoch analysis,

$$Accuracy = \frac{TP + TN}{TP + FN + FP + TN}\% \tag{12}$$

$$Sensitivity = \frac{TP}{TP + FN}\% \tag{13}$$

$$Specificity = \frac{TN}{TN + FP}\% \tag{14}$$

$$PPV = \frac{TP}{FP + TP}\% \tag{15}$$

$$NPV = \frac{TN}{TN + FN}\% \tag{16}$$

Table 3. Performance of the proposed model for detection of OSA

Study	DL	KP	Acc. (%)	Sen. (%)	Spec. (%)	PPV (%)	NPV (%)	F1 score (%)
E. Urtnasan et al. 2018 [3]	CNN	–	96	96	96	–	–	95
L. Chen et al. 2015, [5]	SVM	–	97.4	–	–	–	–	–
N. Banluesombatul et al. 2018 [7]	CNN	–	79.45	77.6	80.1	–	–	–
Sheta A et al. 2021, [8]	CNN-LSTM	0.89	86.25	–	–	–	–	–
Vattamthanam, S et al. 2020, [9]	RNN		88.03	–	–	–	–	–
Zhang, J et al. 2021 [10]	CNN	–	96.1	96.1	96.2	–	–	96.2
Proposed model	DC-LSTM	**0.92**	**98.2**	**97.4**	**97.5**	**98.2**	**93.8**	**97.5**

True positives, true negatives, false positives, and false negatives are denoted by TP, TN, FP, and FN. The experiment is implemented using MATLAB R2021a. Different datasets, features sets, and classifiers have been used in different studies, making it difficult to compare various methods of automatic OSA detection. Comparing classification performances between existing methodologies and the proposed model is shown in Table 3, so that a fair comparison can be made with existing research. The proposed model performed better than the models in the previous studies, as shown in Table 3. Prior research primarily focused on the PPG or ECG signals; this study combined the two signals. Several factors contribute to the high level of accuracy achieved by the proposed deep learning method based on the table. Further, our method can be used with wearable medical devices, which makes it useful for monitoring OSA from home.

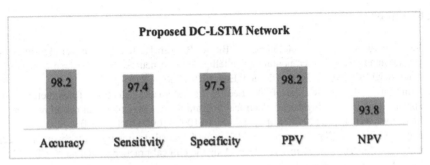

Fig. 4. Performance of proposed DC-LSTM model

Using deep learning methods, a CAD-based OSA detection method has been developed in this study. Figure 4 shows the performance of the proposed DC-LSTM network. Sleep apnea can be diagnosed using electrocardiograms and polysomnography recordings. With a sensitivity of 97.4%, specificity of 97.5%, accuracy of 97.3%, and a Kappa coefficient of 0.92, the proposed network model is as good as other research findings in detecting normal and apneic events. Traditional machine-learning methods require researchers to spend a lot of energy on feature extraction in sleep data, but neural networks do a better job in solving these problems. With increasing network depth, a CNN and LSTM are one of the most popular structures in deep learning. Group convolution and LSTMs are used at both levels in the structure, which enables us to maximize feature extraction capabilities, increase memory, and decrease network parameters, resulting in a faster training time for our network.

4.1 Limitations of the Study

Learning alone does not provide a complete understanding of output, which involves classifiers. In order to accomplish such tasks, convolutional neural networks are used. Network training is limited by the fact that it takes a longer time. Deep learning networks cannot be selected according to a standard theory. A better understanding of machine learning and deep learning is required for both the training and assessment of the results.

5   Conclusion

A lack of sufficient oxygen supply led to a persistent sleep disorder, OSA. Detecting OSA in its early stages can save lives. An innovative Densely Connected LSTM (DC-LSTM) is proposed in this paper for the detection of OSA. With DC-LSTM, vanishing gradients are alleviated, and overfitting can be effectively addressed even when networks have as many layers as dozens. Despite its robustness and automation, the proposed approach can be easily adapted for the analysis and prediction of other physiological signals. Experiments show that the proposed model is significantly better than traditional LSTMs and gets promising performance when compared to state-of-the-art approaches based on ECG and PPG signals.

References

1. Varon, C., Caicedo, A., Testelmans, D., Buyse, B., Van Huffel, S.: A novel algorithm for the automatic detection computational intelligence and neuroscience of sleep apnea from single-lead ECG. IEEE Trans. Biomed. Eng. **62**(9), 2269–2278 (2015)
2. Urtnasan, E., Park, J.-U., Joo, E.-Y., Lee, K.-J.: Automated detection of obstructive sleep apnea events from a single-lead electrocardiogram using a convolutional neural network. J. Med. Syst. **42**(6), 1–8 (2018). https://doi.org/10.1007/s10916-018-0963-0
3. Kapur, V.K., et al.: Clinical practice guideline for diagnostic testing for adult obstructive sleep apnea: an American Academy of Sleep Medicine clinical practice guideline. J. Clin. Sleep Med. **13**, 479–504 (2017)

4. Chen, L., Zhang, X., Song, C.: An automatic screening approach for obstructive sleep apnea diagnosis based on single-lead electrocardiogram. IEEE Trans. Autom. Sci. Eng. 12(1), 106–115 (2015)
5. Sheta, A., et al.: Diagnosis of obstructive sleep apnea from ECG signals using machine learning and deep learning classifiers. Appl. Sci. 11(14), 6622 (2021)
6. Zhang, J., et al.: Automatic detection of obstructive sleep apnea events using a deep CNN-LSTM model. Comput. Intell. Neurosci. 2021 (2021)
7. Lakhan, P., Ditthapron, A., Banluesombatkul, N., Wilaiprasitporn, T.: Deep neural networks with weighted averaged overnight airflow features for sleep apnea-hypopnea severity classification. In: Proceedings of the 2018 IEEE Region 10 Conference, Jeju, Korea, 28–31 October 2018
8. Banluesombatkul, N., Rakthanmanon, T., Wilaiprasitporn, T.: Single channel ECG for obstructive sleep apnea severity detection using a deep learning approach. In: Proceedings of the 2018 IEEE Region 10 Conference, Jeju Island, Korea, pp. 2011–2016, October 2018
9. Vattamthanam, S., Mrudula, G.B., Kumar, C.S.: Sleep apnea classification using deep neural network. In: Proceedings of the 2020 IEEE International Conference on Distributed Computing, VLSI, Electrical Circuits and Robotics (DISCOVER), Karnataka, India, 30–31 October 2020, pp. 133–136 (2020)
10. Christensen, B.: Normal Electrocardiography (ECG) Intervals. Medscape Hear. Drugs Dis. 2014, 20 (2020). http://emedicine.medscape.com/article/2172196-overview. Accessed 29 Nov 2020
11. Vulcan, R.S., André, S., Bruyneel, M.: Photoplethysmography in normal and pathological sleep. Sensors 21, 2928 (2021). https://doi.org/10.3390/s21092928
12. Goldberger, A., et al.: PhysioBank, PhysioToolkit, and PhysioNet: components of a new research resource for complex physiologic signals. Circulation 101(23), e215–e220 (2000)
13. Gaurav, D., Rodriguez, F.O., Tiwari, S., Jabbar, M.A.: Review of machine learning approach for drug development process. In: Deep Learning in Biomedical and Health Informatics, pp. 53–77. CRC Press (2021)
14. Tiwari, S., et al.: Applications of machine learning approaches to combat COVID-19: a survey. Lessons from COVID-19, pp. 263–287 (2022)
15. Raoof, S.S., Jabbar, M.A., Tiwari, S.: Foundations of deep learning and its applications to health informatics. In: Deep Learning in Biomedical and Health Informatics, pp. 1–28. CRC Press (2021)

Deep Learning and Sign Language Models Based Enhanced Accessibility of e-governance Services for Speech and Hearing-Impaired

R. Jennifer Eunice and D. Jude Hemanth[✉]

Department of ECE, Karunya Institute of Technology and Sciences, Coimbatore, India
judehemanth@karunya.edu

Abstract. Sign Language is the basic building block to communicate with the hearing and speech impaired. This can be made easy by developing a robust system to transcribe real-life spoken language sentences into its sign language sequence video and contra wise. Such a system is built with both a sign recognition unit and a sign translation unit. In this paper we provide an in-depth analysis of the existing proposed models to develop such a robust system, discussing their pros and cons. In addition to that, we evaluate the performance of those models based on the quality outcome from the video generation unit. We also brief the future scope in establishing real-life SLP communication models build with advanced deep learning architectures for the hearing and speech disabled thus paving the way to impart education and employment among the hearing and speech impaired.

Keywords: Sign language translation · Sign language production · Generative adversarial networks · Transformers

1 Introduction

We all humans communicate with each other through some verbal or non-verbal mode of communication. Language paves the way to establish a social relationship with society and exchange knowledge, thoughts, experience, Idea, etc., Language is an arbitrary system of symbols or code employed to express and receive a communicated message. But what in the case of people with hearing and speech disabilities? How do they interact with their near and dear ones? And if their basic rights of interaction itself is a question then how will they pursue their dreams? Their only mode of communication is through sign language. Sign language is the basic and more vital mode of communication among the hearing and speech impaired. It is observed that most of the hearing and speech impaired people live in middle- or low-income countries. India contributes a majority of the deaf and mute population with 63% of 466 million worldwide says [1, 2]. These people seek the help of professionally trained Interpreters to translate sign language into their local language and vice versa. But the demand for a professionally trained interpreter is very high since there are only a few professionally trained interpreters for the population of 7 to 13 million hearing and speech impaired people in India. Also,

F. Ortiz-Rodríguez et al. (Eds.): EGETC 2022, CCIS 1666, pp. 12–24, 2022.
https://doi.org/10.1007/978-3-031-22950-3_2

considering the current pandemic situation having professionally trained interpreters as a mediator between the normal and the disabled to transcribe sign language into its local language is not possible. With the advent of deep - learning in computer vision and Human-Computer Interaction it is possible to develop a system for this disabled community.

Over the years there have been so many works put through in the field of Sign Language Recognition for the development of the hearing and speech impaired community. The technology has developed to an extent that they have understood the challenges faced by this community in their everyday life and have developed multiple software packages for this community to enable teaching and understanding of sign language [3, 4]. Sign Language Recognition has two categories Static and Dynamic. The majority of the works have been carried out in recognizing static hand signs. The future directions in this field are moving forward from Static Sign Language Recognition to Continuous Sign Language Translation and Production. Rather than Static sign language recognition, continuous sign recognition and translation are challenging since both spatial and temporal features are needed to be extracted from the signing sequence videos. A fully connected Convolution Neural Network (CNN) with gloss feature enhancement for the betterment of sequence alignment without pre-training the model [5]. Overcoming the pretraining complexity in Continuous sign language is addressed by iterative learning in [6].

An end-to-end sign sequence information extraction from continuous sign language video is proposed by [7]. The sign sequences from the continuous sign language sentences are extracted with the help of CNN, Bidirectional Long-Short-term Memory (Bi-LSTM), and Connectionist Temporal Classification (CTC) without the need for Sign Boundaries. Initially, this technique trains its model with static sign sequences to perform better while recognizing continuous sign sequences. A hierarchical LSTM Network for sign language translation is proposed by [8] where the word and frame level alignment that occurs while extracting linguistic details from videos are addressed using Connectionist Temporal Classification (CTC). The shuffled words that are extracted from different frame sequences can be brought to a proper alignment using this Hierarchical LSTM Network. Later, a non-autoregressive approach to generating realistic pose from continuous sign sequence was proposed by [9]. This model efficiently generates all the tokens of sequences from the continuous video input sequence and utilizes Variational Autoencoders (VAE) for self-supervised learning on sign poses. Though these non- auto regressive SLP models are faster than auto-regressive models, generated pose sequences are of low accuracy. However, with the advent of Generative Adversarial Network has a generator and discriminator, and it can learn complex distribution in data and are widely used in Video Synthesis [10]. The 2D and 3D-CNN have their proven efficiency on heterogeneous data and complex models. Despite the deep generative models are very powerful and have gained a lot of attention in many applications. Besides their data distribution ability, the utility of such networks in SLR and SLT is very minimal.

In this paper, we perform an analysis based on lingual evaluation metrics in the existing proposed generative network and Transformer models and their successful contribution towards continuous sign language recognition. Also, we have discussed the future scope and directions towards Sign Language Production and Translation.

2 Related Works

On the contrary sign language is a multidimensional communication that includes hand, facial expression, lip, and body movements leading to multiple challenges in computer vision. Extracting the spatial and temporal features from the sign language and transcribing it into its local language is quite strenuous. Whereas spoken language is linear, only one sound is processed at a time.

Sign Language Recognition. Sign language recognition is a computational task of identifying or recognizing gestures and actions from performed signs. Sign languages can be categorized into Isolated (Static) and Continuous sign language recognition (Dynamic). A fully Connected CNN was proposed for online continuous Sign language was proposed by [5]. This technique extracts spatial and temporal features from the weakly annotated video sequences and is limited only to sentence-level annotations. The recognition part includes the extraction of gestures and features from the input modality and translating the identified extracted gestures in the form of voice and text excluding the underlying linguistic features of sign language. CSLR is relatively more challenging than isolated sign language recognition [11]. Since the simple progression of static signs may not produce meaningful interpretations.

Sign Language Glossing. In automatic sign language processing glossing refers to transcribing a particular sign or sequence of signs into its corresponding word with the appropriate label associated with the sign. In other words, gloss refers to labels that don't form any appropriate sentences unlike spoken sentences [12]. The glosses generated from the input sequences will not have a properly aligned sequence of sentences. While transcribing the continuous sign language into its spoken language Glosses stand as an intermediate representation.

Sign Language Translation and Production. Recently with the advent of deep learning, sign language translation created curiosity to venture into the field of continuous sign language recognition. Considering the state of art in sequence to sequence modeling [13] developed deep learning-based Neural Machine Translation that was trained to learn the hidden spatial-Temporal representations of signs also, this approach concentrated to understand the language models, the underlying relations between the generated sign with spoken or written language using vision and tokenization methods. A bidirectional Sign language translation system was proposed in [14] with Unity3D as a mobile application. Automatic sign language recognition has started to evolve from lab generated to real-life data [15]. Koller *et al.*, disclose their proposed system trained with two large public corpora SIGNUM Database and RWTH-Phoenix Weather database is suitable for real-life applications.

With the onset of adversarial techniques, conditional image generation can be done using Generative Adversarial Networks [16]. GANs are extensively used for image generation and image-to-image translation. Iso *et al.* [17] use pix2pix software to study and solve the underlying issues in the image-to-image translation. The outcome of this model is a high-resolution image. Wang *et al.* [18] proposed a network model which accomplished generating high-definition images from semantic label maps. He proposed

Table 1. Recent works and contributions towards continuous sign language recognition and production.

Ref.	Dataset	Objective	No. of Signer	Proposed Technique	Issues Addressed	Contributions	Results
[19]	SIGNUM, RWTH-PHOENIX-WHETHER 2014T	ASLR	Multiple signers	Constrained maximum likelihood linear regression	Signer Dependency	Tracking Features, Signer Dependencies, Visual and Language Modelling	Single Signer: 10.0% /16.4% (WER) Multiple Signer 34.3% / 53.0% (WER)
[20]	Self-Generated	Gesture Recognition	Single Signer	CNN+ DCGAN	Overfitting of model	Expression Recognition, Text output, better Results	CNN: 90.45% (accuracy) CNN+ DCGAN: 92.7% (accuracy)
[11]	PHOENIX-WHETHER 2014T, ASLG-PC12	SLT	Single Signer	Spatial-Temporal Multi Cue Network	State-of-art in gloss to text	Novel STMC Transformer for video-to-Text generation	21.0% (WER)
[21]	PHOENIX-WHETHER 2014T	SLP	-	RNN+ DCGAN	End-end Realistic sign language synthesis	NMT-based continuous text-pose network, Generative Network Conditioned on pose and appearance	BLEU-4 score of 16.34/15.26 (dev/test)
[18]	Self-generated Gesture data, CK & Jaffe database for facial expressions, Mandarin Conversation	Gesture and Facial Recognition	Single Signer	DCGAN+ LSTM+ Average Voice Model	Includes facial expressions recognition along with gesture recognition	Facial recognition, Emotional speech synthesis and Gesture recognition	96.01% (Recognition accuracy)
	PHOENIX-WHETHER 2014T	SLP	Multi-signer	RNN+ Motion Graphs+ GAN	Discards the use of costly motion capture or an Avatar	Continuous text to pose translation	BLEU-4 score of 16.34/15.26 (dev/test)
[23]	RWTH-PHOENIX-WHETHER 2014T, CSL and GSL	SLRGAN	Multi-signer	GAN+ BiLSTM + Transformer	Easy extraction of spatial & temporal features without the need of other visual cues	Leveraging Contextual Information	23.4%, 2.1% & 2.26% (WER)

a GAN model which incorporated a convolutional encoder, and convolutional decoder, a residual block followed by an enhancement network to improve the quality of the generated image.

3 Dataset Details

It is observed from Table 1 that the most frequently used dataset in previous literature studies related to sign language production and translation is using RWTH-PHOENIX WHEATHER 2014T [19], SIGNUM [20], and NYU hand shape dataset. RWTH-PHOENIX WHEATHER 2014T is an extended version of the CSLR benchmark dataset also called PHOENIX2014T. Since Transcribing a Spoken language into its sign language requires a huge amount of data and many available databases lack spoken sentence to sign sequence alignment. The first two datasets are signer-dependent ASLR with defined recognition and multi-signer setups. It is more definite that they are created extensively for pattern recognition.

RWTH-PHONIX 2014T. The PHOENIX 2014T is a publicly available corpus that holds the recorded videos of naive German sign interpreters on weather forecasting aired by the German public PHOENIX tv-station on daily basis perfect for sign language translations and production. This corpus uses gloss annotation for transcribing. Also Signing is performed right in front of the stationery-mounted camera, the person performing sign language is wearing dark clothes with a grey background. This dataset is a multi-signer database with all videos 25 frames and a size of 210×260 pixels/frame (Fig. 1).

Fig. 1. Sample frames from PHOENIX 2014T corpus

Hand and face tracking ground truth and ground truth labels are the available transcriptions and labels in this corpus. The database consists of 5356 sentences, 45760 running glosses 1200 signs, and 600k frames. When it comes to tracking the ground truth, the ground truth positioning with respect to face hand have been annotated in 39,712 images featuring all signers. Whereas in the case of ground truth labeling 38 facial landmarks in 369 images featuring all signers have been annotated to extract the facial expression (Fig. 2).

 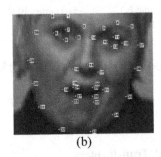

(a)   (b)

Fig. 2. a) Sample image of hand and face tracking ground truth annotation b) shows the sample ground truth labels Phoenix 2014T corpus.

SIGNUM Database. This corpus has both static as well as continuous utterances of various signers. The corpus holds the sequences of frames from the recorded video for quick random access to the individual frame. It is a German Sign Language corpus that consists of 450 basic signs, with 780 sentences with 25 naïve signers. It holds 5,970,450 images and 33,210 sequences. The time duration of the corpora is about 55.5 h and has an image resolution of 776x578 p/f (Fig. 3).

Fig. 3. Sample frames of multi signers from SIGNUM corpus

NYU Hand Pose Database. This is a video corpus that has 8252 test sets and 72757 training set frames of RGBD data with hand pose ground truth. Each frame of RGBD data is provided 3 views (i.e.) 1 frontal and 2 Side views (Fig. 4).

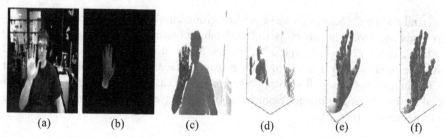

Fig. 4. Sample NYU dataset a) signer b) RDF segmented image c) ground truth labeling d) front view (e) & (f) side views.

4 Proposed Model Framework

In this section, we focus on the frequently used models for sign language Translation/Production.

4.1 NMT Transformers

Transformers are the backbone of any translation model. The sequence-to-sequence translation is eventually done with the RNN where both encoders and decoders are RNN. The classic RNN models were the center of attraction ever since they were introduced in 2014. Here the English to French translation was carried out with a multi-layered LSTM network one for mapping the input sequence to the vector dimensionality and the other one to retrieve the target sequence from the vector dimensionality. The dataset used here is WMT'14 English to French. Despite their progress towards the field of SLP, there still exist certain limitations in seq2seq modeling using RNN.

4.2 Generative Networks

The image generation concept is used in the Cascaded CNN refinement network, Pixel CNN generating images conditioned on vectors, feature embeddings, or image tags from semantic labels RNN for image generation. All these techniques suffer from blurred outcomes, a requirement for spatial information, and semantic labels. With the emergence of generative networks, widely used for image generation have paved the way for better outcomes than previous techniques. Later generative models using deep learning approaches such as Variation Auto Encoders (VAE) and Autoencoders (AE) generated comparatively good outcomes in video and image generation.

Conditional generative Adversarial were proposed to feed conditional information on both the generator and discriminator since unconditional information is out of control on different modes of generated data. Further DCGANs were introduced where the model architecture combined conditional GANS and the outcome of this architecture produced photo-realistic images. Further many extended versions of DCGANs were implemented by fusing the Conditional GAN Model in the DCGAN's architecture.

5   Translation Networks

The sign language production and sign language translations follow some evaluation protocols. The Evaluations are performed on the publicly available database PHOENIX 2014T and SIGNUM Since, these two databases have a large vocabulary of CSLT corpus primarily used datasets for CSLR and SLP over the recent years. They contain gloss annotations, sign language videos, and their translation suitable for validation and tests in SLP, CSLR, and SLT.

Sign 2 Text. The key goal of sign language translation is to translate the incoming sign video into its text or spoken sentences without any intermediate glosses. They perform continuous sign language recognition.

Gloss 2 Text. This is a sentence-to-sentence translation where the system has to transcribe the ground truth sign glosses into its spoken language sentences. The perfect sign translation in NMT is done with perfect understanding to ground truth gloss annotations. Also, while solving the transcription issues one should know that the glosses are imprecise and they are the information bottleneck in any translation model therefore the *Sign2Text* model must outperform *Gloss2Text*.

Sign 2 Gloss 2 Text. This protocol makes use of CSLR models for extracting gloss sequences from the sign videos and then addresses the sentence – to – sentence translations using CSLR predictions.

Sign2 gloss → Gloss 2 Text. This network first generates the Glosses from the sign language videos in its first setup. Then the best performing G2T network model is used to generate the written text sentence sequences.

Gloss2Skeleton Prediction. The model goal is to generate Human Skeleton pose sequences from the corresponding Sign Glosses or Spoken Sentences glosses. For generating skeleton poses from gloss sequence the arm position facial and body expression including the Torso positions are considered.

5.1   Evaluation Metrics

BLEU Score
A metric called Bilingual Evaluation Understudy (BLEU) score is a metric used for the automatic evaluation of machine translation. The score generally varies between 0 and 1. The score is awarded 0 if the outcome has no overlapping similarities or any sequence of similar words when compared with the reference translation. The perfect match score 1 is provided for a perfect overlapping outcome with the reference translation. The mathematical representation for BLEU Score evaluation is,

$$BLEU = min(exp(1 - \frac{ReferenceLength}{OutputLength}))(\prod_i^4 precision_i)^{1/4} \qquad (1)$$

$$Precision_i = \frac{\sum_{sent \in cand.corpus} \sum_{i \in sentence} min\left(m^i_{candidate}, m^i_{reference}\right)}{w^i_t = \sum_{sentence' \in candidate\ corpus} \sum_{i' \in sentence\ corpus} m^{i'}_{candidate}} \qquad (2)$$

where,

$m^i_{candidate}$ is the count of *i-gram* in candidate sentence overlapping the reference sentence.

$m^i_{reference}$ is the count of *i-gram* in reference sentence.

w^i_t is the total number of *i-grams* in candidate translation.

N-gram overlap counts the *n-gram* ($i = 1, 2..4$) match in the reference translations.

ROUGE Score

This metric is also used in and in machine translation ASLR for evaluating Automatic text summarizations. The Term ROUGE refers to recall Oriented Understudy of Gisting Evaluation. ROUGE-N is used to measure unigram, bigram, etc., up to higher order N-gram overlap. ROUGE-L is for measuring the longest overlapping sequence of words. The mathematical representation of the ROUGE Score value is,

$$ROUGE = \frac{No.\ of\ overlap\ words\ btwn\ cand.sent\ and\ ref.sent}{Total\ number\ of\ words\ in\ reference\ summary} \qquad (3)$$

Word Error Rate

A metric to evaluate the machine translation is mainly based on substitution(S), Deletion (D), and Insertion (I). This metric evaluates the word alignment by comparing the spoken sentence with the reference sentence using dynamic string alignment.

$$WER = \frac{S + D + I}{N} \qquad (4)$$

where N refers to the totals number of words in the reference sentence ($S + D + C$).
C refers to the number of correct words.

6 Performance Analysis

This section elaborates the performance analysis on existing proposed SLP/SLT models based on the evaluation metrics. The majority of the SLP models are trained using the PHOENIX2014T dataset since this is a large-scale dataset with multi-signers, gloss annotations for spoken sentences, and Ground truth annotations. From Table 2 it is understood that the network model presented in [11] outperforms well with BLEU 4 values of 22.43 and 21.65. The precision of the model refines based on the recall value. Based on the ROUGE Score value of 48.42 and 48.10 both in validation and Test, the SLRGAN with Transformer proposed by Stoll *et al.* gives outstanding performance for generating the sign video from the spoken or written language sentences.

Table 2. Comparative analysis of different network protocols concerning evaluation metrics.

Dataset: PHOENIX 2014T					
Network model	Ref	Dev Set		Test set	
		BLEU-4	ROUGE	BLEU-4	ROUGE
S2G2T	[13]	18.04	46.02	18.13	45.45
G2T		20.16	31.80	19.26	31.80
S2T		9.94	43.76	9.58	43.45
S2G → G2T		17.86	44.14	17.79	43.80
G2T	[11]	**22.23**	45.74	**21.65**	40.47
T2G	[21]	16.34	**48.42**	15.26	**48.10**

6.1 Evaluation of G2T in PHOENIX 2014T

The evaluation is done based on BLEU 4 score value since it is the widely used metric in Neural Machine Translation. The transformer proposed in [11] outperforms well for G2T and the model is trained on the publicly available benchmark dataset PHOENIX 2014. The proposed transformer has 6 layers since the particular network protocol is only chosen for evaluation the transformer model generates a maximum BLEU 4 score in layer 2 achieving a score of 22.23. The justification for its best performance achieved with only a 2-layer transformer is that a particular network protocol is only evaluated using the proposed transformer and the model is trained only with the ground truth gloss annotations which is a very small portion of PHOENIX 2014T (Fig. 5).

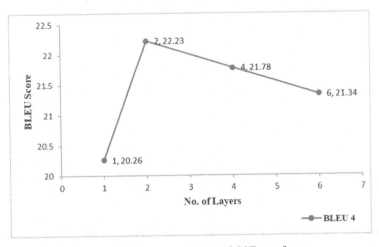

Fig. 5. Performance evaluation of G2T transformer

6.2 Evaluation of Models Based on BLEU and ROUGE Score

It is observed from Fig. 6 a) Transformers especially STMC transformer and Self-attention mechanism transformer achieves the best BLEU Score values. Thus, the evaluation of a complete SLP/SLT model can be done based on the evaluation of ROUGE Score values. From that point of view, SLRGAN with Transformers and Progressive Transformers are the best choices for Sign language Production.

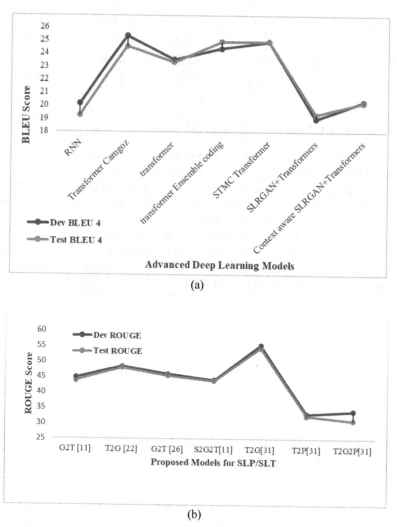

(a)

(b)

Fig. 6. a) Evaluation of model based on bLEU 4 score value. **b)** Evaluation of models based on rouge score

7 Discussions

This paper gives a detailed analytical approach to the recent advanced deep architectures used in sign language production and Translation based on lingual Evaluation Metrics. NMT is the best suitable deep learning model used for language modeling. Various Generative models and transformer models are analyzed and their performance evaluation is done. Though many efforts have been previously taken to improve the SLT/SLP, some challenges need to be focused on to improvise Sign Video generation. One major issue is the lack of a dataset to train the models. The NMT and NLP models are data Hungry, the performance of the models will improve only with a large vocabulary. For time being many research works are undertaken with PHOENIX Whether 2014T, How2Sign dataset, Dicta Sign, ASLVDD, and SIGNUM are the available large vocabulary benchmark dataset. The other drawback that SLP faces is the multi-signer issue when implementing real-time applications. Further, the Videos generated by the proposed model face resolution issues. Thus, the use of pretrained transformers along with generative networks can be a better replacement for SLP models.

8 Conclusion and Future Directions

In this paper, we have discussed various deep learning models proposed in the development of SLP/SLT and presented the state-of-art in SLP/SLT. A quantitative analysis of different models for translating a spoken language to sign language video generation was performed. The performance evaluation was based on linguistic evaluation metrics. A thorough investigation on generating Sign video from the spoken sentences based on different network protocols was conducted. After our analysis, we found that the techniques for real-time sign language production still need to improve. There still exist some challenges to break the communication barrier and paving the road for communication for the hearing and speech impaired community with this society. The quality of the generated video does not meet the expectations in existing models also there is a lack of large vocabulary since the existing large vocabulary sticks to German spoken sentences and German Sign Language. Fusing Multimodality is challenging. With this recent advancement in SLP, bringing a real-time and real-life communication device for the hearing and speech impaired is necessary.

References

1. Khan, M.A., Kim, J.: Toward developing efficient Conv-AE-based intrusion detection system using heterogeneous dataset. Electronics **9**(11), 1–17 (2020). https://doi.org/10.3390/electronics9111771
2. Krishnamurthi, S., Indiramma, M.: Sign language translator using deep learning techniques. In: 2021 Fourth International Conference on Electrical, Computer and Communication Technologies (ICECCT), pp. 1–5 (2021). https://doi.org/10.1109/ICECCT52121.2021.9616795
3. BSL SignBank. https://bslsignbank.ucl.ac.uk/spell/twohanded.html. Accessed 15 Mar 2020
4. American Sign Language|Complete 3-Level Course|Start ASL. https://www.startasl.com/. Accessed 15 Dec 2021

5. Cheng, K.L., Yang, Z., Chen, Q., Tai, Y.-W.: Fully convolutional networks for continuous sign language recognition. In: Vedaldi, A., Bischof, H., Brox, T., Frahm, J.-M. (eds.) Computer Vision – ECCV 2020. LNCS, vol. 12369, pp. 697–714. Springer, Cham (2020). https://doi.org/10.1007/978-3-030-58586-0_41

6. Cui, R., Liu, H., Zhang, C.: A deep neural framework for continuous sign language recognition by iterative training. IEEE Trans. Multimedia **21**(7), 1880–1891 (2019). https://doi.org/10.1109/TMM.2018.2889563

7. Sharma, S., Gupta, R., Kumar, A.: Continuous sign language recognition using isolated signs data and deep transfer learning. J. Ambient Intell. Humaniz. Comput. (2021). https://doi.org/10.1007/s12652-021-03418-z

8. Guo, D., Zhou, W., Li, H., Wang, M.: Hierarchical LSTM for sign language translation. In: 32nd AAAI Conference on Artificial Intelligence AAAI 2018, pp. 6845–6852 (2018)

9. Hwang, E.J., Kim, J., Park, J.C.: Non-autoregressive sign language production with Gaussian space. In: British Machine Vision Conference (2021)

10. Wang, T.C., Liu, M.Y., Tao, A., Liu, G., Kautz, J., Catanzaro, B.: Few-shot video-to-video synthesis. In: Advances in Neural Information Processing System, vol. 32 (2019)

11. Yin, K.: Sign language translation with transformers, *CoRR*, abs/2004.00588 https://arxiv.org/abs/2004.00588 (2020)

12. Yin, K., Read, J.: Attention is all you sign: sign language translation with transformers. In: European Conference on Computer Vision Work on Sign Language Recognition, Translation and Production, pp. 1–4 (2020)

13. Camgoz, N.C., Hadfield, S., Koller, O., Ney, H., Bowden, R.: Neural sign language translation. In: Proceedings of IEEE Computer Society Conference on Computer Vision Pattern Recognition, pp. 7784–7793 (2018). https://doi.org/10.1109/CVPR.2018.00812

14. Kanvinde, A., Revadekar, A., Tamse, M., Kalbande, D.R., Bakereywala, N.: Bidirectional sign language translation, pp. 1–5 (2021). https://doi.org/10.1109/iccict50803.2021.9510146

15. Koller, O., Forster, J., Ney, H.: Continuous sign language recognition: towards large vocabulary statistical recognition systems handling multiple signers. Comput. Vis. Image Underst. **141**, 108–125 (2015). https://doi.org/10.1016/j.cviu.2015.09.013

16. Goodfellow, I.: NIPS 2016 Tutorial: Generative Adversarial Networks (2016)

17. Isola, P., Zhu, J.Y., Zhou, T., Efros, A.A.: Image-to-image translation with conditional adversarial networks. In: Proceedings of 30th IEEE Conference on Computer Vision Pattern Recognition, CVPR 2017, vol. 2017, pp. 5967–5976 (2017). https://doi.org/10.1109/CVPR.2017.632

18. Wang, W., Yang, H.: Towards realizing sign language to emotional speech conversion by deep learning. In: 2021 12th International Symposium on Chinese Spoken Language Processing (ISCSLP), pp. 1–5 (2021). https://doi.org/10.1109/ISCSLP49672.2021.9362060

19. Forster, J., et al.: RWTH-PHOENIX-weather: a large vocabulary sign language recognition and translation corpus. In: Proceedings of the Eighth International Conference on Language Resources and Evaluation (LREC' 2012), pp. 3785–3789 (2012)

20. von Agris, U., Blomer, C., Kraiss, K.-F.: Rapid signer adaptation for continuous sign language recognition using a combined approach of Eigenvoices, MLLR, and MAP. In: 2008 19th International Conference on Pattern Recognition, pp. 1–4 (2008). https://doi.org/10.1109/ICPR.2008.4761363

21. Stoll, S., Camgoz, N.C., Hadfield, S., Bowden, R.: Text2Sign: towards sign language production using neural machine translation and generative adversarial networks. Int. J. Comput. Vis. **128**(4), 891–908 (2019). https://doi.org/10.1007/s11263-019-01281-2

A Blockchain Enabled Trusted Public Distribution Management System Using Smart Contract

Rajdeep Roy[1] , Paranjay Haldar[1], Debashis Das[1]([✉]) , Sourav Banerjee[2] ,
and Utpal Biswas[1]

[1] University of Kalyani, Kalyani 741235, India
debashisdascse21@klyuniv.ac.in
[2] Kalyani Government Engineering College, Kalyani 741235, India
mr.sourav.banerjee@ieee.org

Abstract. Nowadays, a large population of hungry people still exists in many countries. The government body of most countries in the world tries to provide food security to every citizen. They have implemented many rules to provide food safety for citizens. They also run many Public Distribution Shops (PDS) to distribute food products and essential commodities at low prices. But existing systems face many challenges in terms of low accessibility like buying items from the same PDS, transaction transparency, PDS trust, centralized system, and much more. So, to overcome these limitations, a Blockchain-enabled trusted public distribution framework has been proposed using smart contracts. The design and development of smart contracts will not only provide food security but can deliver transparency in the system, which leads to building trust in the system. Therefore, the concerned authorities of the distribution system can build trust with each other efficiently and reliably. In the proposed framework, people can also buy commodities from different PDS creating high accessibility to the system. The proposed work also provides secure communication among authorities and transparency and security of the management data.

Keywords: Blockchain · Smart contracts · Public distribution system · Food security · Decentralized PDS

1 Introduction

The goal of providing food security [1] to every citizen is possible due to the establishment Public Distribution Shop (PDS) [2]. PDS sells food items and essential commodities at a subsidies price. In the past few years, lots of complaints arrived against the PDS. The complaints are mainly about mishandling and unavailability of food items and essential commodities in PDS, and low accessibility of services as anyone can buy others allocated items. With the help of advanced technologies, many public distribution systems have been designed and developed to overcome these limitations.

With the assistance of Radio Frequency Identification (RFID) [3] and biometrics methodology [4], the allocated items of the user are given only to the user. The problem

F. Ortiz-Rodríguez et al. (Eds.): EGETC 2022, CCIS 1666, pp. 25–35, 2022.
https://doi.org/10.1007/978-3-031-22950-3_3

of low accessibility of PDS is resolved using a unique number that is stored in the RFID card. Now, using this card, users can buy items from different PDS. But all these systems are centralized in nature. The data stored in the server can be manipulated and accessed by an unauthorized party. The food department supplies items to the PDS, but there is no way to verify the number of items stored in the shop by the end-user.

A public distribution system should be transparent by having trust in that system. A secure and efficient public distribution system can be designed and developed using Blockchain technology [5], which can provide transparency, security, and trustworthiness. Due to its distributed ledger technology, anyone can see the distribution transaction. Due to this property, anyone can check the reserve status of the food items and essential commodities in the PDS. The immutability nature of the ledger makes it almost impossible to alter the information once it's written into the Blockchain ledger. Since all nodes are connected through a Peer-to-Peer (P2P) network [6], there is no single point failure in the system.

A Blockchain-enabled food and essential commodities distribution management framework have been developed using smart contracts. Using the proposed framework, the government can control all PDSs for food distribution and monitor transactions for each PDS. Therefore, citizens can get their foods and essential commodities without hesitating much more by the associated PDS. The proposed framework is also proper for any dispute handling.

The rest of the paper is organized as follows. Section 1 presents the introduction. Related works are discussed on the performance of PDS and their limitations. Section 3 presents the system overview of the proposed framework and the overall implementation procedures. The outcomes of the experiment are shown in Sect. 4. Section 5 explains a comparison analysis of the proposed work with other existing works. Finally, Sect. 6 concludes this research work by giving some future work related to this research work.

2 Related Works

This paper describes the PDS using Blockchain technology. There are some existing works on this public distribution system using different methods that are discussed below.

Sonawane et al. [7] developed a ration card system using RFID and biometrics methodology. This system collects the user's data with the fingerprint and stores them in a centralized database. In case of any change in user data, this change can be done only by the government authority. The ration shop will scan the card and check the recognition of the user using the fingerprint scanner. If the validation is successful, the user is allowed to take ration.

Kurkute et al. [8] proposed an advanced automatic Ration material distribution system using an ATmega328 controller [9], which can be used for user authentication, validation, and sending notifications. Users' data stored in a server can be accessed only by the admin upon successful login into the system. Users need to provide personal information and fingerprint to register at a fair price shop. The RFID card of a unique number is provided upon successful registration. The controller will validate the fingerprint with the fingerprint stored in the database. Upon successful validation, the user will be permitted the purchase of ration. If the verification is unsuccessful, a notification will be sent to the cardholder and the distributor.

Sengar and Chakrawarti [10] proposed a public distribution system under a cloud environment with improved security and transparency in the JAVA development environment. The proposed scheme has a user model, a distributor model, and a governmental model. In the user model, the user needs to provide their personal information. The system generates a unique id using that personal information. The personal information gets encrypted using this unique id and stored on the server. In the distributor model, the data is retrieved from the server and deciphered during utilization using the user id. In the governmental model, all the information is retrieved from the server and decrypted to get the distributor list, user list, tracking of stocks, and complaints.

R et al. [11] developed the RFID-based smart card for ration distribution. The RFID card holds a unique Aadhaar identification number with the type of cardholder. ARM7 LPC2148 [12] is used in this system to carry out all the computational activities. Out of the three serial communication ports of the processor, one port is used for RFID to scan the smart card, another port is used for the fingerprint module to check biometrics, and the last port is used for GSM SIM 800L to send SMS. The cardholder needs to scan the fingerprint at the time of shopping. Once the fingerprint is matched, the GSM SIM 800L will send an OTP to the registered number. The RFID card is scanned after getting the correct OTP. Therefore, the cardholder is allowed to input the items and their quantity. If the fingerprint is not recognized, an alarm will be triggered. If the OTP entered is wrong three times, an alert message will send to the card- holder. If the ration is already taken by the cardholder, a message will be shown. If the RFID reader doesn't recognize the card, a message will be sent, and the process will be terminated.

Manufacturing of drugs requires lots of hard work for developing and testing. The automation of the developing process will reduce the time of development. Mainly aim to increase the effectiveness of the drug development process [13]. With the advancement of technology in the field of artificial intelligence, there is much research carried out in the food sector. Different methods have been explored using Convolutional Neural networks for food recognition and nutrition assessment using different images [14, 15].

3 Proposed Methodology

This section mainly deals with the proposed distribution of foods and essential commodities using Blockchain technology and smart contract [16]. The proposed framework uses the distributed ledger technology [17] and smart contract to provide transparency, trust, and high accessibility to buy goods from PDS.

3.1 System Overview

The proposed framework monitors the distribution of goods and essential commodities through PDS. In this framework, all the entities are connected through peer-to- peer (P2P) connections of the Blockchain network. The entities are Food Distribution Agency (FDA), Food Distribution Unit (FDU), PDS, and user. The details of the entities are described as follows:

Food Distribution Agency (FDA). FDA is responsible for the creation and deployment of the contract. After deploying the contract in the Blockchain, FDA is registering the FDU. FDA is also responsible for registering the items with their weight and price to be distributed in the PDS. FDA can also change the details of the item to be distributed.

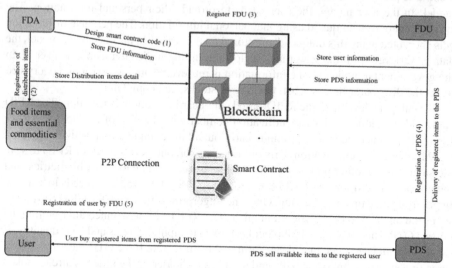

Fig. 1. System overview of the proposed framework

Food Distribution Unit (FDU). The role of the FDU is to register the PDS and individual users. Food Distribution Unit can cancel the registration of the Public Distribution Shop and user. FDU is responsible for the delivery of goods to the PDS.

Public Distribution Shop (PDS). PDS is responsible for the distribution of food items and essential commodities to the user as directed by the FDA and supplied by the FDU.

User. The user can buy food items and essential commodities from any registered PDS. On the first of every month, no PDS will open as the FDA needs to reset the public distribution record. The user has to complete the registration process to buy items from the registered PDS. If an unregistered user tries to buy the item from a registered PDS, the smart contract will reject this transaction. Similarly, an unregistered PDS cannot sell items to the users.

The proposed distribution framework is shown in Fig. 1, which illustrates the complete process of ration distribution in the following steps.

Step (1): FDA will create and deploy the smart contract in the Blockchain network. Once the smart contract is deployed to the network, the FDA cannot change the code.
Step (2): FDA will register the food items and essential commodities required for the distribution process. Only FDA can change the registered item's information.

Step (3): FDA will register the FDU.

Step (4): FDU will register the PDS. FDU will also deliver the items to the PDS. Through this registered PDS, the distribution of goods will be carried out. FDU can cancel the registration of PDS.

Step (5): FDU will register the user. Only registered users can buy items from the registered PDS. FDU can cancel the registration of an individual user.

3.2 Registration Phase

FDU Registration. The FDA can insert FDU data to permit the FDU to carry out the distribution process ahead. The FDA will register the FDU using a unique Ethereum address and with the name of the FDU. If the Ethereum address is not unique, the smart contract will notify a message: *"Already registered with the Ethereum Address"*. So, no two FDUs have the same Ethereum address. If someone other than the FDA tries to register the FDU, the smart contract will notify a message: *"Only the Food Distribution Agency can enroll a Food Distribution Unit"*. So, only FDA can register the FDU.

PDS Registration. The FDU will insert PDS data to allow the shop to sell goods to the user. The FDU will register the PDS using a unique Ethereum address and with the PDS name and address of the owner. If the Ethereum address of the PDS is not unique, the smart contract will notify a message: *"Already registered public distribution shop"*. If other than the FDU tries to register a PDS, the smart contract will notify a message saying *"Only Food Distribution Unit can register public distribution shop"*. So, only registered FDUs can register a PDS.

User Registration. Another important task of the registered FDU is to insert the data of a user so to allow the user to buy goods from the registered PDS. The FDU will register the user using a unique Ethereum address with the name of the user, address of the user, poverty details of the user, and identity proof name with the number of the user. Zero (0) is set for below the poverty line, and one (1) is set for the above poverty line. After successful registration of the user, the validity of the user is set to one (1). If the Ethereum address of the user is not unique, the smart contract will notify a message: *"Already registered user"*. If the registration of the user is not done by the FDU, the smart contract will notify a message: *"Only Registered Food Distribution Unit can register Individual User"*.

3.3 Distributed Items Management

Enrollment of Distributed Items. The primary purpose of this framework is to distribute the food items and essential commodities through the PDS registered by the FDU. The FDA will specify the food items and necessary items to be distributed with their weight and price below and above the poverty line. Figure 6 shows the illustration of the enrollment of distributed items.

Distribution Process. After the disbandment of goods to the PDS by the FDU, the registered user can buy items from PDS. This framework will check whether the user and the PDS are registered or not before selling the item to the user. If anyone of them is not registered, this framework will not allow this process to execute. After the successful validation of the user and PDS, this framework will validate the requested item by the user. If this validation is successful, the PDS will sell the item to the user. After the successful registration of the PDS, FDU will deliver the item to the PDS to sell them. Users can buy items from the registered shop.

Renewal of Distribution Record. On the first day of every month, no distribution shop is opened. The FDA can reset the distribution record as per requirements and change the quantity or price of an item that is already registered. The FDA can remove the item from distribution. FDA will change the details of the items.

Distribution Items Changing. The FDA can change the quantity or price of registered items. The FDA can even remove items from distribution.

3.4 Deactivation of User/PDS Account

When a user wants to give up the food subsidy, the FDU will deactivate the account. Once the user's account gets deactivated, he will not be able to buy items from PDS. If the user wants to avail of the food subsidy again, the user needs to register again.

When the owner of the PDS wants to close the shop, the FDU will remove the PDS from the list. The FDU can close the shop using the deactivation of the closing function. After the deactivation of the shop's license, the owner cannot further sell the goods. PDS needs to register again by the FDU for the selling of items.

4 Experimental Results

4.1 Environment Setup

Smart contracts have been implemented for experimental purposes in Visual Studio Code [18] using the Truffle framework [19] of the Blockchain. Smart contracts are written using Solidity language [20]. To interact with the smart contract, web3 [21] is used. The solidity compiler is used to compile contract codes. The pre-defined accounts of the truffle framework are used using web3. All equipped tools for the experiment and their versions are shown in Table 1.

4.2 Smart Contract Deployment

This section mainly shows the outcomes of the developed smart contract. Two smart contracts have been developed to achieve the desired result. One smart contract is for all the functionality of the distribution process. Another smart contract is used to retrieve the date so that the FDA can reset the distribution record on every first day of the month. Both contracts have been deployed successfully and the instance of contracts is created using web3 (Table 2).

Table 1. Tools used for the experiment

Tools	Description	Version
Truffle	Environment for testing and developing blockchain network	5.4.15
Solidity	Language for implementing smart contracts	0.8.0
Web3.js	Libraries for interaction with smart contracts using HTTP	1.5.3
Node	Runtime environment to execute codes in the backend	13.14.0
Visual studio	Code editor for editing and managing codes	1.60.2

```
truffle(develop)> Ration.FDU(0);
Result {
  '0': '0x94dBae9181fD17a7eD690dE3C7cA14599Bd1fD1B',
  '1': 'Kolkata Food Distribution',
  Food_Distribution_Unit: '0x94dBae9181fD17a7eD690dE3C7cA14599Bd1fD1B',
  Food_Distribution_Unit_name: 'Kolkata Food Distribution'
}
truffle(develop)> █
```

Fig. 2. Registration of FDU

Table 2. Experimental blockchain address of various entities

Entity name	Blockchain address
FDA	0xF5537a1B9Bf7672F55cF12ef1abD3B072223e453
FDU	0x94dbae9181fd17a7ed690de3c7ca14599bd1fd1b
PDS	0xddc07fc661b912b15a96b95349f92f55f1a9fa9b
User	0xce85baf9da8641192934b6addc381a22fe757802
Smart contract distribution	0x39Ba17A5B26cdbe7fcEF82d4734f32E4dAE3DeEc
Smart contract date validation	0x3aA6F76Ef56bd7064a657d3fD9f89885E3d1517C

4.3 Registration of Entities

Figure 2 shows the registration of FDU and details of registered FDU. Figure 3 shows the registration process for PDS. Upon successful registration of PDS is set to one. Figure 4 shows the registration of the user and the details of the registered user. Figure 5 shows the details of the item when it is registered. Figure 6 shows the execution cost of various functions used in smart contracts.

```
truffle(develop)> Ration.shop('0xddc07fc661b912b15a96b95349f92f55f1a9fa9b');
Result {
  '0': 'Kolkata Food Distribution',
  '1': '0xdDC07fc661B912b15A96b95349f92F55f1A9Fa9B',
  '2': 'Abhiraj Singh',
  '3': 'Sealdah, Kolkata',
  '4': BN {
    negative: 0,
    words: [ 1, <1 empty item> ],
    length: 1,
    red: null
  },
  register_by_Food_Distribution_Unit: 'Kolkata Food Distribution',
  Ethereum_address_of_Ration_shop: '0xdDC07fc661B912b15A96b95349f92F55f1A9Fa9B',
  ration_dealer_name: 'Abhiraj Singh',
  ration_dealer_address: 'Sealdah, Kolkata',
  valid: BN {
    negative: 0,
    words: [ 1, <1 empty item> ],
    length: 1,
    red: null
  }
}
truffle(develop)> █
```

Fig. 3. Registration of PDS

```
register_by_Food_Distribution_Unit: 'Kolkata Food Distribution',
Ethereum_address_of_individual: '0xcE85bAf9dA8641192934b6Addc381A22FE757802',
individual_name: 'Rajdeep Roy',
address_of_individual: 'Kolkata, 700001',
poverty_line: BN {
  negative: 0,
  words: [ 1, <1 empty item> ],
  length: 1,
  red: null
},
identity_proof_name: 'Adhaar Card',
identity_proof: '15005548621483410',
valid: BN {
  negative: 0,
  words: [ 1, <1 empty item> ],
  length: 1,
  red: null
}
}
```

Fig. 4. User registration

```
truffle(develop)> Ration.GoodsList(0);
Result {
  '0': 'Kolkata Food Distribution',
  '1': '0xdDC07fc661B912b15A96b95349f92F55f1A9Fa9B',
  '2': 'Rice',
  '3': BN {
    negative: 0,
    words: [ 100, <1 empty item> ],
    length: 1,
    red: null
```

Fig. 5. Item list

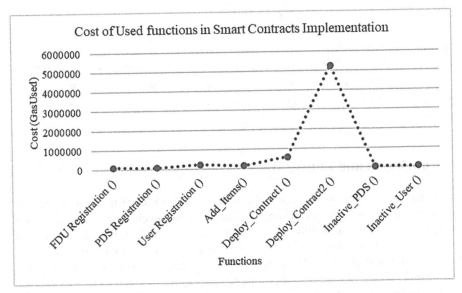

Fig. 6. Execution cost of smart contracts' functions

5 Comparison Analysis of the Proposed System

This section mainly focuses on the comparison of the existing work with the proposed framework in the Blockchain-enabled PDS. Table 1 shows the comparative analysis. Most of the existing PDS systems are designed and developed using centralized infrastructure raising an issue in security and privacy of the data of the user. PDS data in the existing system can be manipulated by the administrator of the system. The proposed framework resolves this issue with the immutable distributed ledger. PDS data in the proposed framework are stored in the Blockchain. The issue of low accessibility in the existing system is resolved using a distributed ledger of the Blockchain. Users can buy the item from any one PDS creating high accessibility in the system (Table 3).

Table 3. Comparison analysis of proposed framework with existing PDSs

Authors	Years	Cyber-attack	Transparency	Data security	Data immutability	Data availability
[3]	2018	✔	✖	✖	✖	✖
[4]	2019	✔	✖	✖	✖	✖
[7]	2018	✔	✖	✖	✖	✖
[8]	2019	✔	✖	✖	✖	✖
[10]	2016	✔	✖	✖	✖	✖

(continued)

Table 3. (*continued*)

Authors	Years	Cyber-attack	Transparency	Data security	Data immutability	Data availability
[11]	2017	✔	✖	✖	✖	✖
Proposed system	2022	✖	✔	✔	✔	✔

6 Conclusion and Future Work

In this paper, A portion of the food and essential commodities distribution framework is designed using blockchain and demonstrated in detail. Blockchain is incorporated to overcome the existing limitation of the centralized system. The proposed framework mainly deals with the distribution of food items and essential commodities from the FDA to FDU and then from FDU to the user via PDS. The automated authentication and verification process of distribution is completed using a smart contract. The proposed framework provides transparency and trust in the system and resolves the issue of low accessibility. The smart contract is designed and deployed on the local blockchain for the experiment. The results show the requirements of a decentralized, reliable, and secure distribution system. In the future, we want to introduce biometric authentication of the beneficiary to provide additional security to the framework. We want to design a notification alert system where it will provide notification to the beneficiary after the successful purchase of items.

References

1. Pinstrup-Andersen, P.: Food security: definition and measurement. Food Sec. **1**, 5–7 (2009). https://doi.org/10.1007/s12571-008-0002-y
2. Kasim, C.M., Kumar, S.H.: Public distribution system (PDS) and food security: a brief survey of literature. Indian J. Econ. Dev. **6**, 1–7 (2018)
3. Shukla, S., Patil, A., Selvin, B.: A step towards smart ration card system using RFID & IoT. In: 2018 International Conference on Smart City and Emerging Technology (ICSCET), pp. 1–5 (2018). https://doi.org/10.1109/ICSCET.2018.8537337
4. Ingale, V.B., Rathavade, A.V., Sankpal, S.B., Sutar, R.B.: Smart ration card system using RFID, Biometric and SMS gateway. Int. J. Eng. Appl. Sci. Technol. **3**(10), 17–19 (2019). https://doi.org/10.33564/ijeast.2019.v03i10.004
5. Banerjee, S., Das, D., Biswas, M., Biswas, U.: Study and survey on blockchain privacy and security issues. In: Williams, I. (ed.) Cross-Industry Use of Blockchain Technology and Opportunities for the Future, pp. 80–102. IGI Global (2020). https://doi.org/10.4018/978-1-7998-3632-2.ch005
6. Wikipedia contributors.: Peer-to-peer. Wikipedia. https://en.wikipedia.org/wiki/Peer-to-peer. Accessed 04 Feb 2022
7. Sonawane, V.: Smart ration card system using RFID and biometrics. Int. J. Res. Appl. Sci. Eng. Technol. **6**(1), 2511–2514 (2018). https://doi.org/10.22214/ijraset.2018.1345

8. Kurkute, S., Chaudhari, P., Deore, B.D., Kavare, K., Musale, P., Bhoye, D.: Advanced automatic ration material distribution system. In: Proceedings 2019: Conference on Technologies for Future Cities (CTFC) (2019). https://doi.org/10.2139/ssrn.3361580

9. Wikipedia contributors: ATmega328, Wikipedia. https://en.wikipedia.org/wiki/ATmega328. Accessed 25 Jan 2022

10. Sengar, S., Chakrawarti, R.K.: Implementation of PDS system with improved security and transparency under cloud environment. In: 2016 Symposium on Colossal Data Analysis and Networking (CDAN), pp. 1–6 (2016). https://doi.org/10.1109/CDAN.2016.7570929

11. Padmavathi, R., Azeezulla, K.M.M., Venkatesh, P., Mahato, K.K., Nithin, G.: Digitalized Aadhar enabled ration distribution using smart card. In: 2017 2nd IEEE International Conference on Recent Trends in Electronics, Information & Communication Technology (RTEICT), pp. 615–618 (2017). https://doi.org/10.1109/RTEICT.2017.8256670

12. Wikipedia contributors: NXP LPC, Wikipedia. https://en.wikipedia.org/wiki/NXP_LPC. Accessed 01 Feb 2022

13. Gaurav, D., Rodriguez, F.O., Tiwari, S., Jabbar, M.A.: Review of machine learning approach for drug development process. In: Deep Learning in Biomedical and Health Informatics, pp. 53–77. CRC Press (2021)

14. Makwana, Y., Iyer, S.S., Tiwari, S.: The food recognition and nutrition assessment from images using artificial intelligence: a survey. ECS Trans. **107**(1), 3547 (2022)

15. Ortiz-Rodriguez, F., Medina-Quintero, J.M., Tiwari, S., Villanueva, V.: EGODO ontology: sharing, retrieving, and exchanging legal documentation across e-government. In: Futuristic Trends for Sustainable Development and Sustainable Ecosystems, pp. 261–276. IGI Global (2022)

16. Ethereum, Introduction to smart contracts, Ethereum.Org. https://ethereum.org/en/developers/docs/smart-contracts/. Accessed 15 Jan 2022

17. Wikipedia contributors, Distributed ledger, Wikipedia. https://en.wikipedia.org/wiki/Distributed_ledger. Accessed 18 Jan 2022

18. Documentation for Visual Studio Code, Visual Studio Code. https://code.visualstudio.com/docs. Accessed 02 Dec 2021

19. Truffle, Overview Truffle Suite (n.d.), Truffle Suite. https://trufflesuite.com/docs/truffle/. Accessed 10 Dec 2021

20. Solidity-Solidity 0.8.0 documentation. (n.d.). Solidity. https://docs.soliditylang.org/en/v0.8.7/. Accessed 30 Nov 2021

21. web3.js-Ethereum JavaScript API - web3.js 1.0.0 documentation. (n.d.). Web3.Js - Ethereum JavaScript API. https://web3js.readthedocs.io/en/v1.7.0/. Accessed 30 Nov 2021

Administration of Vaccine Mechanism for COVID-19 Using Blockchain

Shipra Ravi Kumar and Mukta Goyal[✉]

Jaypee Institute of Information Technology, Noida, UP, India
shipra.chaudhary85@gmail.com, mukta.goyal20@gmail.com

Abstract. Information related to Covid-19 either it is vaccination status of the country or the active Covid-19 cases both are the confidential matters. The privacy is utmost important concern in pandemic situation to secure access of patient vaccine data. Blockchain technique is one of the good techniques that affirm the privacy and data security. The consensus mechanisms in blockchain confirm that data stored in it, is authentic and secured. Proof of Work is one of the consensus algorithms, where miners in the blockchain network solves the puzzle and receive the reward accordingly. The difficulty level of the puzzle decides the security of the data in the network. Hence, this paper proposes blockchain based framework to store the vaccination data of patient by enhancing security using proof of work consensus algorithm. The performance of the proposed framework is measured on different level of difficulties, corresponding to time. The result shows that higher the difficulty level, take more time to solve the puzzle, results in more secure data.

Keywords: Proof of work · Blockchain · Consensus algorithm · Healthcare

1 Introduction

Over the last few decades, preserving privacy in healthcare data become the most important issue. Majorly when the pandemic Covid-19 hits to the world, the data storage and keeping patient's information private among all the healthcare verticals is the most attention drawing issue. To deal with Covid-19 situation, healthcare providers needs to share the vital useful data among all the stakeholders in the healthcare sector. This data sharing among international research community would be very beneficial to deal with powerful data sets of Covid-19 Vaccination. Preserving data for future research and maintaining security and privacy in the patient's information is the most important concern amid data sharing mechanisms. One has to take care, to avoid violating National and International data sharing regulations.

Decentralized and distributed paradigm of blockchain technology uplifts the internet of value, which excels an astounding momentum in the last years. It enables all the distributed participated nodes, which should not necessarily trust each other to manage the shared ledger [4]. With the integration of Medical IoT (MIoT) devices, all the information gathering like, to monitor Blood Sugar Level, SPO2 level, Heart Rate would be convenient to make data sets for Covid-19 research. This also helps to analyze the figures of what type pf people getting easily infection Covid-19 virus and their recovery rate. Moreover, the cost of maintaining the data through mediators between patient and hospital get extremely reduced, due to the decentralized storage of data. In addition, implementation of blockchain could be able to break the conventional silos of medical records and makes the process of data sharing between patients and healthcare sector is much easier even at global level. The decentralized storage of blockchain could surely enhance the privacy and security of healthcare data.

Blockchain consists of two different types of participants, first is the data node which declares the tasks and second is the consensus nodes and miners which work to solve the declared tasks. This can be implemented with a consensus mechanism between all decentralized nodes. Consensus mechanism in a blockchain grants patient's command and agreement to manage their health records. Proof of work consensus algorithm, works on the mathematical computation which makes it tamperproof. In the proposed work, a blockchain is created using the PoW consensus algorithm on Covid-19 vaccination data set. The aim of this work is to provide the maximum security while storing the data, so that it can't be tempered. Section 3, discusses the background study behind this work. Next Sect. 4, discusses the methodology while the next section demonstrates the implementation of proposed algorithm and its results, which shows the enhanced level of security while storing the data on blocks. The paper also suggested, improving the efficiency in the mining process on different performance metrics. Following Research questions has been emerged from the study.

Research Questions:

Q1. What is the use of Blockchain in Healthcare Sector?
Q2. How the data can be protected from tempering and stored securely?
Q3. What is the benefit of consensuses in blockchain?

2 Literature Survey

In healthcare industry, medical data plays a significant role. The expansion of medical data accompanied by the requirement of process in the secure way [7]. As the infrastructure, the healthcare sector needs connected devices and software applications that interact with IT systems, which helps to encourage healthcare market in blockchain. In the recent times, data management systems of healthcare industry facing various key challenges like traceability, data transparency, audit, immutability, trust, flexible access, data provenance, privacy and security. Moreover, the maximum data in healthcare systems leveraged for managing data centrally that poses risk of failures in single point data storage and access due to natural disasters [9, 10, 14]. Blockchain has eminent characteristics which include traceability, immutability, transparency, tamper-proof, and programmability.Blockchain technology administered immutable digital shared ledger that is distributed in nature and peer validated. It can also be used to track the transactions in the system; these transactions can be made actionable by using smart contracts [6]. Blockchain provides us that benefit to store the data in decentralized manner and promises the tamperproof chain of records. In permission-less blockchain environment any unauthenticated participant can join voluntarily and leave it any moment while, it assures the system security as well. Here, in this research work security is completely based upon Proof of Work consensus algorithm, which restricts the proposal rate and preventing the attacks due to complex cryptographic puzzle technique, besides this it permits the unauthenticated nodes to introduce a new block by examining the sufficient computation power [21]. All these advantages of blockchain technology make it an equitable choice to store all patients' healthcare records in it. The recent innovation in healthcare industry has put up the patient's data security on the top most priority. There are many consensus algorithms which are available to provide data consistency among multiple participated distributed nodes, but proof of work is the one which is most commonly used in the healthcare sector [3].

With the advancement in the Blockchain Technology, the efficiency of the blockchain network are drawing the huge attention. The mining process takes huge time to process but besides this it makes the system highly tamper proof. The added difficulty in the mining process increased the time of computation to the double in just one step of it. In today's fast paced world, in this pandemic situation, people needs to move on a regular basis for work as well as personal matters that leads to an environment where a communicable disease can easily get spread from one continent to other and can only be tackled through a well-coordinated, documented full proof mechanism which provides the details about each individual vaccination status and medical history. Information stored in blockchain in reality requires a consensus to process the blocks in its transactions due to its distributed nature which gives the secure and higher data quality [24, 25].

3 Background Material

In this section, the background information related to Covid-19 pandemic is discussed. Indeed, the most probable use cases in blockchain in healthcare sector vary accordingly to appease the distinct requirement, such as security, data access, and data sharing. Utilization of blockchain can be done to gather and investigate the patient's medical record in a constructive way and can also help in screening patient movement history in order to ensure enforcement of requirement for social distancing with complete protection of their identity [21].

3.1 Consensus Algorithms

To obtain the data consistency among multiple distributed nodes consensus algorithms are used. The most common used consensus method is proof of work (PoW) which was proposed in Bitcoin white paper. In PoW algorithm, each node repeatedly generates nonce while "mining" a valid block, until the hash value calculated by the nonce and content of the current and previous blocks less than a target value is worked out, which will be used as the hash value of the current block. Wherein, Nonce (number used once) is a semi-random or random number which is automatically generated for specific use. The blockchain model is effective when it creates the longest chain. When the content of previous block needs to get modified, it requires to re-compute the hash value of all the existing block after that block and create the length of the modified blockchain longer the previous unmodified chain. This process needs the high computational power, which ensures the data consistency and data security in the blockchain systems [22].

Consensus mechanism is the way to ensures the participating nodes in the network to verify the transactions and agree their sequence order on distributed ledger. In some blockchain applications like cryptocurrency, this method is critical to prevent double spending or other corrupt data written on the underlying ledger, which is database of all transactions [4]. With consensus, there are various solutions that fit in different scenarios. The major difference between consensus algorithms is the way in which they delegate and reward the verification of transactions. Proof of stake and Proof of Work are the most commonly used consensus algorithms [18].

3.2 Proof-of Work

There are certain rules to reach out the consensus among the participating nodes in the consensus algorithms, and it can be decided on the basis of required conditions, that what operations should be performed [13]. PoW algorithm works on the rule: a node can only be verified by the whole network if it can calculate the block that confronts the target value [12]. If the target value is greater than the output Hash, it will be accepted as a valid block by the miner and will move on to find the next one after with- drawing all his efforts of solving the block. Credibility of a node increases with number of blocks built upon it. In order to reach the target, miners need to try different nonce values randomly, since this can be done by brute force only it becomes mathematically time consuming and hard [4].

Next Section discusses the methodology of secure transmission of data of Covid-19 patient data.

4 Methodology

This section discusses the methodology of consensus algorithm to develop a secure transmission of data for COVID-19 Patient data. Figure 1 shows the working of Consensus algorithm i.e. PoW with mining difficulty.

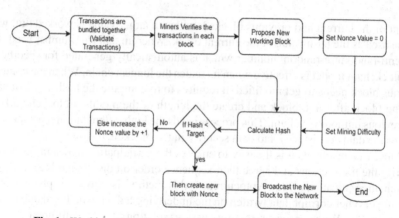

Fig. 1. Working of POW with trade-off mining difficulty computation

In the above Fig. 1, the flow of chart illustrates the working of proof of work. This algorithm is based on complex cryptographic puzzle which searches for a value and then generate a new Hash code. Initially, it compiles all the transactions together and validates them. Then, the participating miners in blockchain verify the transaction in each block. New working block has been proposed by setting nonce value to zero; simultaneously difficulty level has been decided to make the mining process more complex to the miners. Every single zero which appends to the hash, take the double computational effort to find out the required hash. Now, the calculated hash value has been verified with the target value, such as, it had to be unique and start with decided difficulty level. If it matches with the condition, then the new block will be created at that nonce value. Otherwise, it will go back and increase the nonce value by one and check again with the target hash value, this process will keep going on until the desired hash value received. Then, lastly, the new created block has been broadcasted to the network.

In Fig. 2, how the patient's data can be stored in a blockchain has been illustrated. In Covid-19 scenario, data privacy and security is the most important concern. Any information related to Covid-19 either it is vaccination status of the country or the active covid cases both are the confidential matters. Related to this, in the created blockchain, each block consists its hash value and data. This can beelaborated as there is one block header, which contains the information of block hash, nonce value, difficulty of blockchain and previous hash. And another is the transaction counter, which keeps the record of all transaction.

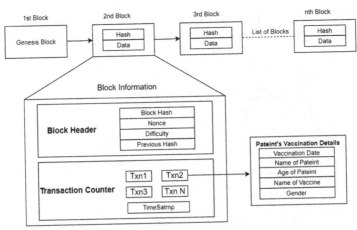

Fig. 2. Use case of patient vaccination detail in a blockchain

Figure 3, shows the complete working of consensus mechanism using proof of work in the healthcare sector. In the pool of miners, all the participating miners have to solve the cryptographic puzzle in the minimal time and win the race. The winner mining node has got the chance to add new block in the existing blockchain. In the above scenario, the miners can add the patient vaccination details in each block and mining difficulties make it more complex, so that it can't be tempered easily.

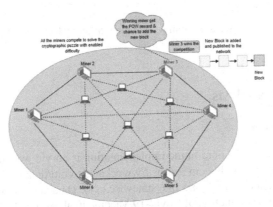

Fig. 3. Working of consensus mechanism for vaccine data in blockchain

Figure 4, shows the proposed algorithm illustrates the mining difficulty in proof of work consensus method. This difficulty is compiled with the Hash value generated with starting zeros. It can be increased by increasing the number of zeroes preceding in the Hash value, like if zeros can be added in starting hash value, then the matching Nonce value to create that particular hash, starting with defined zeros will take time. Hence, tempering is not possible. This makes the proof of work algorithm more secure and temper proof. The Covid-19 Vaccination can be stored in blockchain using PoW, tempering this will demand huge computational power that is feasibly possible

```
Algorithm1:
N ← value of current block
m ← required memory
l ← Hash Function Length
H ← Computed Hash Function
Result: Nonce; hash when success
1 Nonce = Set.difficulty // difficulty = 2
2 for Nonce ← 1 to max − nonce do //randomly
select nonce {0,1}
2      X = str(Nonce) //X←Nonce value
3      p = m/l
4      output begin length
5          for i ← 1 to p do
while not computed_hash.
Startswith('0' * self.difficulty):
7              block.nonce += 1
8                  h = Hash(x) //Compute Hash
8              end
9                  X = X||h // Compute inverse
of Hash {increase target/Difficulty}
10             end
11         output end length
12         S = Hash(N||X)
13         if S>H then
14             output
15         else
16             continue
17         end
18 end
```

Fig. 4. Proposed algorithm with mining difficulty for proof of work.

5   Result and Analysis

5.1   Data Collection

The data set which is used here in the implementation is co-vid_vaccine_statewise.csv collected from www.kaggle.com (https://www.kaggle.com/datasets/sudalairajkumar/covid19-in-india?select=covid_vaccine_statewise.csv). Data set contains all the information regarding the conduction of Covid-19 Vaccine in all over India, state-wise. Data set consists the information regarding the number of booths conducting the Covaxin and Covishield corresponding to the doses given to males, females and transgender.

In the above Fig. 5, the analysis of available Covid-19 Vaccination has been observed based on the data set for the specific duration of time. It is being seen that 29% population has been vaccinated by Covaxin whereas 71% population has been vaccinated by Covishield. In Fig. 6 shows the total vaccination done among the population in the country between the Male, Female and transgender.

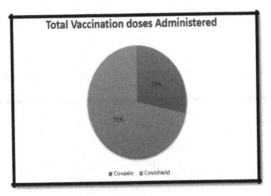

Fig. 5. Total Vaccination administered of Covid-19

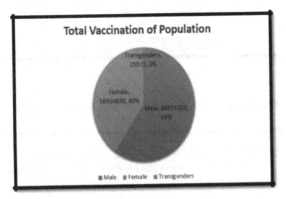

Fig. 6. Total Vaccination done among Population

6   Implementation

The purpose behind the implementation of proof of work, in the Covid-19 scenario, the information privacy is the most important concern. How much vaccine has been given to the entire Indian citizen is the primary agenda these when the new Covid-19 cases started arriving across the country that too with the new variant. The people who are fully vaccinated can be considered to fight against this virus. But still research is going on, and everyone is focusing that only vaccinated people will be given some relaxation to move out, like in other European countries. This implementation basically focuses on mining difficulty of proof of work, which make the computation effort exactly just double only adding one zero in the starting of new hash value. This algorithm is used to validate the transactions and to depict the security while creating the new blockchain with high computational effort and variable difficulty to create the Hash values, the data of vaccination booth conducted per day has been stored in separate JSON data file and date of vaccination is marked as primary key. The implementation has been done in Python 3. The Nonce value at different set of Difficulty level is measured as shown in Table 1 and 2. In the below tables, index number depicts the Block number in the chain and current Hash is Hash value of the data inside the Block. (Current Hash = SHA256 x Nonce).

Table 1. Computation of HASH value and Nonce value at difficulty level 2

Index No.	Curr Nonce	Prev Nonce	CurrHash	PrevHash
1	36	0	0029851eb0f46424c6e10e6c4cffa2ccf5f7 6fa87bbc75e7dd9fd3c482d1e2d1	5f6d1a3abfc257e742a99a4cf2a19a224b8 8b53631f4db2e06b801cf28f30647
2	228	36	00440bbebede39bf308862db32e61ca670 696d7d6a5230b0e10e4d5925682927	0029851eb0f46424c6e10e6c4cffa2ccf5f7 6fa87bbc75e7dd9fd3c482d1e2d1
3	246	228	00462fb5639801c5981e981b974e53db5b eaf8bc322e85c34da2febc870cdc38	00440bbebede39bf308862db32e61ca670 696d7d6a5230b0e10e4d5925682927
121	55	1512	0055cab1ec9a910c5e80913042dc1b3885 19a02000c402b4f3e5583698b0b3f7	0041055bb9123c21dfb6baa88b51497b7d e4217dc3347b8fea0218b816f305f7
122	172	55	003e8d66c734719bd5a8b358d851e90dc2 a52bc26261bafed4a9709cb8ef95ad	0055cab1ec9a910c5e80913042dc1b3885 19a02000c402b4f3e5583698b0b3f7
123	111	172	0061c5b6281a78a5c09799f49e45e951a1 bf0e5fa3f7cf906645a6c57a21b67a	003e8d66c734719bd5a8b358d851e90dc2 a52bc26261bafed4a9709cb8ef95ad

Table 2. Computation of HASH value and Nonce value at difficulty level 3

Index No.	Curr Nonce	Prev Nonce	Curr Hash	PrevHash
1	185	0	000fd396f0bcee5f44590e03a6851bbd7 3616ceeedd827775aca6c9060103cfa	3776d436091ca570e1a3ecf364caff1d35c290 38cfcfab504eaf3a0552eb6807
2	2687	185	0008111adbab09e1571dbb36157d6b92 2cf237ecf34386017952d23a03fb32c3	000fd396f0bcee5f44590e03a6851bbd73616 ceeedd827775aca6c9060103cfa
3	7419	2687	000cdbe49693fb67174c62f99d80c4367 06d7f69bd5836d3eeee0040176fc402	0008111adbab09e1571dbb36157d6b922cf23 7ecf34386017952d23a03fb32c3
121	3954	382	000db1734d832525979b4866e11da145 489046db96a17d0969d29ebc48036c0a	000d62ea070694691f0e9a5c592905792397a 1135b2f58e7fbf5b077caf886ec
122	648	3954	000e6e2e2d8a64f0d1bae13a35ecf39c3 3a0808d4269c4d2b82a132c6d34b8f8	000db1734d832525979b4866e11da1454890 46db96a17d0969d29ebc48036c0a
123	2982	648	00057db7d722a11998dc13035995989e 77131f7fc80a11f6ed664fd065ef6d94	000e6e2e2d8a64f0d1bae13a35ecf39c33a08 08d4269c4d2b82a132c6d34b8f8

It is shown in Table 3 that the nonce value will go drastically varies, when the difficulty level is increased at every single zero. The difficulty level has been set to 2, and the attributes of the table are Index number, current nonce, previous nonce, current hash and previous hash. Wherein, Index number shows the number of the concerned block in the blockchain and current hash is the Hash of the most recent block and current nonce will give the nonce value at which the most recent block has been created. Similarly, previous nonce and previous hash is the value which was received at immediate previous block. Here, in this implementation we have used data set with 123 records. Hence, the Index number ranges from 1 to 123. In the above table we have shown the outcome of initial and last 3 blocks. Similarly, the same attributes and process has been used in Table 3, but with the new mining difficulty which is 3. The results appeared in nonce value in both the table is far way different, which proves mining difficulty provides the high security in the data.

The total time to create the entire blockchain at different difficulty is illustrated in Table 3. The value which appeared in the result is system dependent value. It would be different, if the same data set on varying difficulty level has been executed on some other configuration. But it will give relevant result results on different difficulties.

Table 3. Time consumed to create blockchain on different level of difficulty

Time Taken to Create Blockchain:

Total number of blocks: 123

	On Difficulty Level 1	On Difficulty Level 2	On Difficulty Level 3
Time taken to create Blocks	20 Sec	68 Sec	170 Sec

6.1 Analysis

Based on the above results, there is comparative analysis between nonce value of created blocks at varying difficulty level of 2 & 3. It is seen that, when the difficulty value has been increased to one zero, then it is taking more time to create desired hash value. The mining difficulty in the proof of work algorithm makes it more secure in terms of tampering of data. In the below Fig. 7, there is comparison of randomly generated Nonce value on difficulty level 2 and 3 to create desired Hash using SHA -256. On the x-axis number of blocks has been taken and on y-axis, nonce value has been shown. In this graph, out of 123 blocks of blockchain, 10 blocks have been considered; in which starting five values are index value 1 to 5 and last five values are index number 119 to 123. In the addition of block number 3, it is clearly shown that after increasing the mining difficulty from 2 to 3 the nonce value will go drastically high, and can be achieved after the three times computational effort to reach the desired hash value.

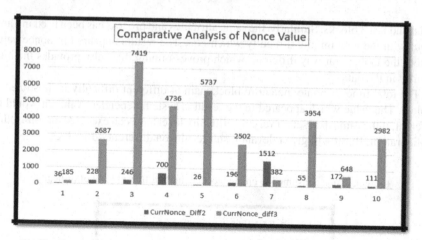

Fig. 7. Comparison based upon Nonce value generated at different difficulty level

7   Conclusion and Future Work

In this Pandemic situation, the major emphasis in the healthcare industry is on to privacy preserving in Covid-19 patient's information. Information can be shared on the consensus based mechanism among the healthcare practitioners. Blockchain provides us facility to store Covid-19 patient information in decentralized manner. Proof of Work consensus algorithm is used to store the Covid-19 patient information either it could be its healthcare vitals, age, vaccination information or other related information. This work presented a proof of work system which shows its implementation and test result on the data set available on Kaggle.com, to depict the authenticity and integrity of the proof of work consensus algorithm on certain restrictions which makes the blockchain temper proof. It is being seen that the computation of hash function on different set of difficulty, gives the sustainable result. The time consumed during the computation of mathematical puzzle, could be used in the data training and testing, which reduces the time to add the block in existing blockchain. However, the challenges arise in the deployment of Blockchain in Healthcare are interoperability, security, and privacy (confidentiality and access control), data storage, and operationally inexpensive.

After the extensive literature survey, it has been found that various consensus algorithms have been applied in various domains. But, still there are many issues with these consensus algorithms. Future work include to design a new approach for hybrid consensus algorithm with reduced delay and combination of supervised machine learning techniques will be focused, which is specific to the healthcare domain only.

References

1. Bonawitz, K., et al.: Practical secure aggregation for privacy-preserving machine learning. In: Proceed ings of the 2017 ACM SIGSAC Conference on Computer and Communications Security, pp. 1175–1191 (2017)

2. Gervais, A., Karame, G.O., Wüst, K., Glykantzis, V., Ritzdorf, H., Capkun, S.: On the security and performance of proof of work blockchains. In: Proceedings of the 2016 ACM SIGSAC Conference on Computer and Communications Security, pp. 3–16 (2016)
3. Anderson, J.P.: Computer security technology planning study. Anderson (James P) and Co Fort Washington Pa Fort Washington (1972)
4. Salimitari, M., Chatterjee, M., Yuksel, M., Pasiliao, E.: Profit maximization for bitcoin pool mining: a prospect theoretic approach. In: 2017 IEEE 3rd International Conference On Collaboration and Internet Computing (CIC), pp. 267–274. IEEE (2017)
5. Christidis, K., Devetsikiotis, M.: Blockchains and smart contracts for the Internet of Things. IEEE Access 4, 2292–2303 (2016)
6. Cachin, C., Vukolic, M.: Blockchain consensus protocols in the wild. In: International Symposium on Distributed Computing (DISC), pp. 1–16 (2017)
7. King, S., Nadal, S.: Ppcoin: Peer-to-peer crypto-currency with proof-of-stake. 19(1) (2012)
8. Gauld, S., Von Ancoina, F., Stadler, R.: The burst dymaxion: an arbitrary scalable, energy efficient and anonymous transaction network based on colored tangles. In: Proceedings of Cryp toGuru PoC SIG (2017)
9. McGhin, T., Choo, K.K.R., Liu, C.Z., He, D.: Blockchain in healthcare applications: research challenges and opportunities. J. Netw. Comput. Appl. 135, 62–75 (2019)
10. Eyal, I., Sirer, E.G.: Majority is not enough: bitcoin mining is vulnerable. In: Christin, N., Safavi-Naini, R. (eds.) Financial Cryptography and Data Security, vol. 8437, pp. 436–454. Springer, Heidelberg (2014). https://doi.org/10.1007/978-3-662-45472-5_28
11. Lin, I.C., Liao, T.C.: A survey of blockchain security issues and challenges. Int. J. Netw. Secur. 19(5), 653–659 (2017)
12. Wu, M., Wang, K., Cai, X., Guo, S., Guo, M., Rong, C.: A comprehensive survey of blockchain: from theory to IoT applications and beyond. IEEE Internet Things J. 6(5), 8114–8154 (2019)
13. Zhang, H., Sakurai, K.: Blockchain for IoT-based digital supply chain: a survey. In: Barolli, L., Okada, Y., Amato, F. (eds.) Advances in Internet, Data and Web Technologies, vol. 47, pp. 564–573. Springer, Cham. (2020). https://doi.org/10.1007/978-3-030-39746-3_57
14. Zheng, Z., Xie, S., Dai, H.N., Chen, X., Wang, H.: Blockchain challenges and opportunities: a survey. Int. J. Web Grid Serv. 14(4), 352–375 (2018)
15. Xie, J., et al.: A survey of blockchain technology applied to smart cities: research issues and challenges. IEEE Commun. Surv. Tutor. 21(3), 2794–2830 (2019)
16. Wang, X., et al.: Survey on block- chain for Internet of Things. Comput. Commun. 136, 10–29 (2019)
17. Sankar, L.S., Sindhu, M., Sethumadhavan, M.: Survey of consensus protocols on block-chain applications. In: 2017 4th International Conference on Advanced Computing and Communication Systems (ICACCS), pp. 1–5. IEEE (2017)
18. Tapscott, D., Euchner, J.: Blockchain and the Internet of Value: An Interview with Don Tapscott Don Tapscott talks with Jim Euchner about blockchain, the Internet of value, and the next Internet revolution. Res. Technol. Manag. 62(1), 12–19 (2019)
19. Dinh, T.T.A., Liu, R., Zhang, M., Chen, G., Ooi, B.C., Wang, J.: Untangling block- chain: a data processing view of blockchain systems. IEEE Trans. Knowl. Data Eng. 30(7), 1366–1385 (2018)
20. Nakamoto, S.: Bitcoin: a peer-to-peer electronic cash system. Decent. Bus. Rev. 21260 (2008)
21. Mitchell. T.M.: Machine Learning, 1st edn. McGraw-Hill, New York (1997)
22. Louridas, P., Ebert, C.: Machine learning. IEEE Softw. 33(5), 110–115 (2016)
23. Tanwar, S., Bhatia, Q., Patel, P., Kumari, A., Singh, P.K., Hong, W.C.: Machine learning adoption in blockchain-based smart applications: the challenges, and a way forward. IEEE Access 8, 474–488 (2019)

24. Ølnes, S., Ubacht, J., Janssen, M.: Blockchain in government: benefits and implications of distributed ledger technology for information sharing. Gov. Inf. Q. **34**(3), 355–364 (2017)
25. Hölbl, M., Kompara, M., Kamišalić, A., Nemec Zlatolas, L.: A systematic review of the use of blockchain in healthcare. Symmetry **10**(10), 470 (2018)

Cyber Security Strategies While Safeguarding Information Systems in Public/Private Sectors

Alya Al Mehairi[1], Rita Zgheib[1(✉)], Tamer Mohamed Abdellatif[1], and Emmanuel Conchon[2]

[1] Department of Computer Engineering, Canadian University Dubai, Dubai, UAE
{alya,rita.zgheib,tamer.mohamed}@cud.ac.ae
[2] University of Limoges, CNRS, XLIM, UMR 7252, 87000 Limoges, France
emmanuel.conchon@unilim.fr

Abstract. Many private and public organizations in the UAE and around the world are facing challenges in protecting their information and systems from external cyber-attacks due to the increase in the usage of computer networks within worldwide businesses. The objective of this research study is to explore the strategies that are implemented by the public and private sectors in the UAE to safeguard their data and information systems from cyber-attacks. The findings of the study indicated that public organizations in the UAE do have effective strategies in place to safeguard their information and systems against any cyber-attacks. These strategies include providing adequate training to their employees to create awareness among them and developing robust cyber security strategies in line with the UAE National Cyber Security strategy framework. Public and some private organizations are vigilant in assessing, identifying, and mitigating cyber security risks and threats through well-designed organizational strategies. The research also concludes that protecting the information system can reduce cyber threats and can lead to improved business practices. The findings of this study will lay the foundations for other private and public sectors to use them in their organizational practices, which will help them to decrease the data breaches, and protect their company and customers' confidential data, thereby reducing the cost and risk of cyber-attacks.

Keywords: Cyber security · Cyber-attacks · IT governance · Information systems · UAE organizations

1 Introduction

Policymakers and business leaders of international relations are facing cyber security challenges in the digital information age.

Cyber security is defined by Reid and Van Niekerk [1] as a collection of multiple variants such as strategic management, security models, risk management

F. Ortiz-Rodríguez et al. (Eds.): EGETC 2022, CCIS 1666, pp. 49–63, 2022.
https://doi.org/10.1007/978-3-031-22950-3_5

policies, preparation, actions, best practices, technology, instruments, user data, and institutes. The authors also state that the term cyber security is interchangeable with the term information security. Some authors such as Paulsen [2], feel that there is no definition of the term cyber security which is widely accepted. Manworren, Letwat, and Daily [3] states that business leaders are more prone to the cyber threat, which often damages the profitability and revenue of the business. According to Prince [4], leaders of business organizations have noted that frequent cyber-related threats are affecting the profitability of their companies and call for the implementation of cyber security programs in policies, software, hardware, and information levels within the organization.

Even though business leaders implement cyber security programs at all levels of their information, infrastructure, hardware, and software policies [5], cyber-crimes are high in the Middle East, and these cyber breaches cost the organizations around $1 billion annually. Since the digital economy era has set in, many traditional organizations have shifted towards an online business presence, and the use of technology and communications has become an important part [6]. These endless possibilities over the internet have led businesses towards online e-data systems, which makes them vulnerable to cybercriminals who attack these private and public networks using various software and hardware tools.

Lallie et al. [7] state that the cyber threat landscape across the UAE is constantly evolving, and 32% of users in the UAE are under threat from malware hiding in their devices. Digital 14 [8], a cyber-security firm, suggests that the reason for such attacks is that UAE organizations have outdated cyber security approaches, and they are ignorant of the expanding risk landscape and the humongous costs that result from such cyber breaches.

In the first address after the formation of the new cabinet, the government stressed the importance of adopting the cyber security standards for the government agencies so that cyberspace is protected from external threats and helps to consolidate their defense [9].

UAE leads the region with the highest digital adoption rates. With the advancing digital phenomenon, organizations in the country are more likely to get vulnerable to such cyber-attacks. The main objective of the study is to investigate the cyber security strategies that are employed by the public and private organizations in the UAE to protect or safeguard their data and systems.

However, Cyber security remains a challenge for organizations and their economic development in the UAE.

The aim of this qualitative study is to study the cyber security strategies that the public and private sectors employ in the UAE to safeguard information systems from cyber-attacks. The sample population in this research comprises IT managers/IT executives from private and public sectors in the UAE. The research questions explore the cyber security strategies implemented by these executives or their organizations successfully to keep their information systems safe from cyber threats. The implications require these executives and their organizations to safeguard the information systems, reduce data breaches of the customers at the same time, and reduce the cost and risk of theft of identity of the customer.

Setting aims and objectives will help with the knowledge and understanding of the cyber security strategies that are employed by the private and public sectors in the UAE, as this will help answer the research questions as well. The following aims will help the research to establish clear links between the research paper and the motivation behind it:

- To determine if the private and public organizations in the UAE have adequate cyber security strategies to protect themselves from cyber threats. This is very important as it will give us information and insights on whether or not enough provisions are put in place.
- To understand if the organizations have implemented any related frameworks
- To understand how do the private and public organizations in the UAE safeguard the data systems from cyber-crimes and threats.
- To study cyber security strategies (if any) implemented by private and public organizations under study in this research.

The rest of the paper is organized as follows. Section 2 provides a state of the art of the Cyber security principles and approaches in the UAE and different countries. In Sect. 3 the methodology adopted in this research is presented. Section 4 presents and discusses the results of conducted research; Some recommendations are also stated. Finally, conclusions are drawn, and future directions are discussed in Sect. 5.

2   Literature Review

2.1   Principles of Cyber Security

The main objective of cyber security is to protect information systems or any sensitive data from cybercriminals. The principle that ensures that data is secure is known as the CIA triad [10] i.e., a triangle of three related principles by the security community. Confidentiality: the first principle of the CIA triad ensures that sensitive data is accessible only to the people who need it. They can access it only as per the organizational policies, and the same data will be blocked for the others. Integrity: the second principle of the CIA triad ensures that information systems are not changed or in any way modified by the actions of external threats or any accidental modification. In case any such event occurs, drastic measures will be taken to recover from the loss of sensitive data. Availability: this ensures that data is useful and available for the end-users without any hindrance, such as cyber-attacks, malfunctions, or any security measures.

2.2   Impact of COVID-19 on Cyber Security

The COVID-19 pandemic brought many new challenges for businesses and individuals as they adapted to a new operating model of working from home, which

has become the new normal. Businesses around the globe are rushing to digital transformation, which has led to increased cyber security concerns. If the
organizations neglect the cyber-security risks, their reputation, legal, and compliance will be impacted sooner or later. The pandemic has made technology a
very important part for businesses and individuals. With the rise in technology
needs, the remote working environment is still not considered safe, according to
a report by Deloitte [11]. In June 2020 National Cyber Security Center reported
about 350 cases of cyber-attacks in Switzerland in April compared to the normal
attacks of 100–150. In light of this pandemic, working from home was cited as the
major cause of the rise of the attacks as people working from home do not have
the same security measures as those working in the organization wherein internet security is provided. Cybercriminals see this pandemic as a very lucrative
opportunity to exploit people working from home with malicious fake COVID-
19 websites. According to the report by Deloitte [11], the City of London Police
reports a loss of GBP 11 million in COVID-19 scams in January 2020. More
than half a million people were affected by the cyber-attacks while video confer-
encing as their vital information such as user names, passwords, and names were
stolen and sold on the dark web. Also, 47% of the individuals were victims of
phishing scams while working from home. Changing nature of the cyber-attacks
points to the fact that before the pandemic, cyber-attacks had risen to 35%, and
the attacks have become sophisticated, and can adapt to the environment and
go undetected. One common way was the news of the vaccine developments, a
major phishing campaign.

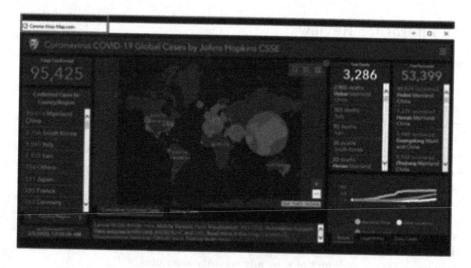

Fig. 1. Fake map with breakout information

Figure 1 shows a map wherein websites were being masked as official communication channels such as the Center for Disease Control (CDC) or WHO and

asking the public to download the information and documents containing safety tips against the virus.

Amid the pandemic, cyber security needs extra attention to put in place stringent methods to protect their information/systems. Organizations should proactively plan to prevent cyber-attacks successfully. They should be ready to respond to the attacks before they occur rather than after. The ability of the organizations to prevent the attack before it occurs can reduce the risks of exposure and this will also help them to secure themselves against the continuous increase in cyber threats.

2.3   Impact of COVID-19 on Cyber Security in UAE

UAE in 2020 saw an increase in cyber-attacks by 250% and suffered an annual loss of USD 1.4 billion. In 2018, UAE was the most targeted nation globally for cyber-attacks. In 2020, amidst the pandemic, UAE experienced over 1.1 million phishing attacks which were the result of working from home as people were restricted to their homes and had to depend on the internet platforms for their work, according to the Cyber Resilience Report [12]. According to a report by global cyber security company Kaspersky [13], the increase in the remote working shifts due to the current COVID-19 to curb the spread of the coronavirus led to an increase in cyber-attacks by over 190% in the UAE. The report further revealed that the cyber-attacks against the remote access protocols in the UAE in 2020 alone touched 15.8 million. Work from home is not going away anytime soon; even with the organizations opening up to their full capacity, they will continue to work remotely. The decrease in cash transactions has led both individuals and businesses to use online transactions, which will further increase cyber threats. Hence there is a need to understand what strategies private and public organizations in the UAE are employing to safeguard their information and systems from such threats. In the light of the above, there is a need for such as study.

The Telecommunication and Regulatory Authority [14] of UAE proposed a National Cyber Security Plan [15]. The structure of NCSP, shown in Fig. 2, was proposed in 2016 by the Dubai Electronic Security Center. The aim of this proposed strategy was to:

1. Establish a society that is cyber smart.
2. Support R&D in the area of cyber security.
3. Implement controls to monitor cyber security
4. Liaison with the international entities to keep in line with the latest developments.
5. Adopt new and emerging technologies in cyber security.

The National Security aims to provide a path to achieve the national vision to secure the state information and advice.

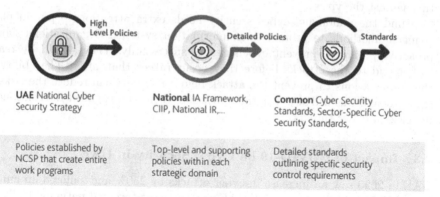

Fig. 2. Structure of National Cyber Security Plan NCSP (https://dict.gov.ph/national-cybersecurity-plan-2022/).

As an example case study in UAE In 2014, Etisalat was a victim of a cyber-attack when its main home page and the corporate website were replaced with a very basic portal-style Chinese website (National, 2014). The big question that arose from this was whether the user information was compromised or not. The origin of the cyber-attack was not disclosed by Etisalat, although it did claim its competitor Du's website was not affected. In response to the above, Etisalat came up with network security solutions in order to protect itself against complex Distributed Denial of Service (DDoS) attacks by employing a Cloud Access Security Broker (CASB) to improve the security of all types of cloud services, such as private, public or hybrid. The company has put in place resilient and robust platform to protect against data breaches or cyber-attacks [12].

2.4   Cybersecurity in Other Countries

The UK takes their cyber security development every serious [16]. UK has founded a Center for Protection of National Infrastructure, which works to reduce any weakness in the cyber security infrastructure on a national level. The second country on the list is the USA which is known for its level of cyber security level in the world, according to the GCI 2018. The USA has a dedicated department of Homeland Security that monitors its cyber security with its dedicated and comprehensive strategies. In addition, they also focus on providing training on local, state, and tribal levels, and they also provide training to their workforce on critical infrastructure security [17]. France is third in the world with its strategic objective for cyber security in the country[1]. France bases its cybersecurity strategies on the international level rather than the national level for its regulatory framework for cyber security critical infrastructure protection.

---

[1] ITU. (2019). Global Cybersecurity Index (GCI) 2018. Geneva: ITU.

France places serious effort on the protection of its CI and makes it a priority. In terms of good governance in the cyber security framework, the country is still developing an adequate framework. Fourth in place is Estonia; although the country is deeply invested in the cyber security cause, it lacks an understanding of the cyber threats impacts and the insufficient cyber security infrastructure. Fifth and last on the list is Lithuania; the country launched its own National Cyber Security Center, which was a result of a security incident concerning the protection of cyberspace [18].

3   Research Methodology

This paper uses a qualitative study method to explore the cyber security strategies employed by private and public sectors to safeguard information and systems from attacks or threats. The data gathered from this study is collected from the private and public sectors by using semi-structured interviews with open-ended questions. Pope and Mays [19] state that a qualitative research study gives voice to the participants in the study. Gibson et al. [20] state that qualitative research enhances the involvement of all members involved in the study. In such a study, the relationship between the researcher and the participants is informal as opposed to what is seen in quantitative research studies.

Table 1. Participants roles

Organization	Designation
Etisalat	Senior IT manager
Nawah energy company	IT
Ministry of health	Head of IT department
Dubai machines	CEO
Adra events	IT manager
TechAccess Asia distribution	IT/marketing manager

3.1   Sample and Population

The selected sample in this research study is comprised of IT executives in various positions who have successfully implemented the strategies, or their organizations have a successful framework for cyber security to protect themselves from cyber threats. The study implicates a social change that organizations can use to protect confidential customer information and reduce data breaches or customer identity theft. The sample included six participants as a proper sample size to investigate the research questions. The participants selected for the study were IT executives who knew the cyber security strategies and had experience in implementing them within their organization. The interview questions were sent through their email, and it took a day or two for the participants to reply. These interviews were followed up by telephonic calls to clarify details if left vague and also to check the precision of the interpretation of the data collected. The participants in the research were given full freedom to choose to have their names mentioned or to be kept confidential. Three public and three private organizations were approached that have implemented cyber security strategies successfully to safeguard their information systems in the UAE. Only those organizations were interviewed who have implemented cyber security strategies within their organizations. The interviewed persons were from the following organizations: Etisalat, Nawah Energy Company, Ministry of Health, Dubai Machines, Asiatech Distribution Services, and Adra Events. More details regarding the participants from these organizations are shown in Table 1. The interviewed organizations covered divert of verticals, including Telecommunications, Healthcare, Energy, Events Management, IT Retailer, and IT distribution services. The interviews were conducted under a non-disclosure agreement; therefore, the names are kept confidential. Thus, to conceal the identity of the participants' pseudonym such as P1 to P6 is used in the analysis. The profile of the interviewed organizations is tabulated in Table 2. These interviews were the primary source of data collection and helped in getting the answers to the research questions.

3.2   Research Questions

The main objective of this research study was to explore the cyber security strategies that are used to protect the information/system from cyber-attacks or threats. Therefore, we sought an answer to the following research questions:

- RQ1: What are the cyber security strategies employed by the private and public organizations in the UAE to safeguard the data information systems from cyber threats?
- RQ2: Are there any relevant frameworks for cyber security strategies in the UAE?
- RQ3: What cyber security strategies are employed by the organizations in the UAE that are effective in minimizing cyber risks?

4   Discussion

4.1   Analysis

For the data analysis, the data were analyzed using the five-step data analysis process of Yin (2018), which involves compilation, disassembly, reassembly, interpretation, and conclusion of the data. This is illustrated in Fig. 3. Regarding RQ1, the survey results showed that P1, P3, P4, and P6 all agree that the UAE National Cyber security strategy will promote cyber security innovation, cultivate an entrepreneurial culture in cyber security, and enable SMEs to defend

Table 2. Participant organizations description

Organization	Sector	Description
Etisalat	Telecommunication	A Multinational based telecommunication service provider in the UAE and operates in 15 countries in the MENA region
Nawah energy company	Energy	A subsidiary of the Emirates Nuclear Corporation (ENEC) and Korea Electric Power Corporation (KEPCO), that looks after operations and maintenance of Units 1–4 of Barakah Nuclear Energy Plant in the UAE and the Arab World
Ministry of health	Healthcare	Ministry of Government of Dubai who looks into the implementation of healthcare policies in the UAE
Dubai machines	IT retailer	Leading retailer of Niche Technology Products in the UAE with 90,000 SKUs on their website and ships worldwide
Adra events	Events management	Events Management company in the UAE working with private and public organizations for the past 14 years
TechAccess Asia distribution	IT solutions	Leading IT value-added distributor in the UAE and MENA region

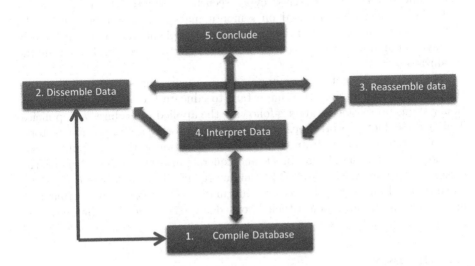

Fig. 3. Five step data analysis process [21]

themselves against the most prevalent cyber assaults, protect the UAE's vital information infrastructure assets, and develop a world-class cyber security workforce. For RQ2, Another cyber security strategy employed by the private and public organizations also aligned with Lucas [22] study, wherein organizations implemented information systems effectively by identifying the risks and threats and keeping their hardware and software updated and implementing cyber security policies, and monitoring their information networks continuously such as the organization of P3 employed CCTV monitoring for the sensitive IT areas in IDF and MDF. They have also enabled their data center protection in the IDF and MDF rooms with an authentication and password change policy. The organization of P2 outsources the job to the experts. The organization of P5 ensures controlled perimeters such as firewalls and WAN connections. Encryption of network form management access and monitoring the firewall rules, and ensuring the network is maintained.

Regarding RQ3, P1, P2, P3, P4, and P5, all agree that it is important to communicate strategies to their employees by training them and making creating awareness through orientations, emails, workshops, and audits. All participants agree that risk assessment is very important to secure the systems and protect customer information. In addition, all participants agree that it is important to educate the staff on the information systems protection strategies following the applied procedures and policies. Training, conducting workshops, audits, and monitoring are important factors.

In addition, the interviews revealed that the UAE National Cyber security strategy would promote cyber security innovation, cultivate an entrepreneurial culture in cyber security, and enable SMEs to defend themselves against the most prevalent cyber assaults, protect the UAE's vital information infrastructure assets, and develop a world-class cyber security workforce. P4 further states that "the strategies are focused on senior management understanding of the Cyber Security challenges and the importance of implementing and continuously improving the Information Security Management Systems (ISMS) set in the organizations."

The risk assessment is very important to secure the systems and protect the customer information. It is important to educate the staff on the information systems protection strategies following the applied procedures and policies. Training, conducting workshops, audits, and monitoring are important factors.

An overall conclusion from the interview execution is that the public organizations had more hands-on, direct, and concrete answers to the cyber security topics than the private sectors. The public organizations interviewed here provided detailed and in-depth accurate information; one reason can be that they have direct information hence their knowledge of the topic that they have discussed at length.

4.2 Discussion

The UAE National Strategy's concept of cyber security strategy is based on a known reality that the strategy will positively impact the various segments of society by improving and securing the confidence of the citizens in the digital world. The strategy also encourages the innovation in the field of cyber security as this will foster a culture of entrepreneurship in the cyber security which will help the small and medium enterprises to protect themselves against the common cyber threats which will help to protect the important and critical information thereby building a dynamic workforce to combat cyber security threats in the UAE. P1 from the Telecommunication sector (public sector) further elaborated in his response that the strategy will enable the ecosystem to capture the huge cyber security opportunity and tap into the AED 1.8bn UAE cyber security market and effectively contribute to the AED 18bn MENA cyber security market. The strategy will help develop the abilities of 40,000+ cyber security specialists by encouraging them to follow a career in cyber security. Also, the strategy will help them learn necessary cyber security skills to meet the country's goals and promote a vibrant network of cyber security training providers. Agreeing with him, P3 from the Healthcare (public sector) stresses the need for this national cyber security strategy as a key component to manage and prevent risks and to have a readiness plan for cyberspace security. Furthermore, P3 agrees that the new plan will help promote cyber security innovation, cultivate an entrepreneurial culture in cyber security, and enable SMEs to defend themselves against the most prevalent cyber assaults. P3 states also that the plan will help protecting the UAE's vital information infrastructure assets, and develop a world-class cyber security workforce. Another important cyber security strategy is to provide awareness education for cyber security as an effective method to keep organizations safe from cyber threats and attacks. P4 from the Energy public sector completely agrees with Iverson and Terry [23] that apart from the general awareness messages, they have an onboarding cybersecurity-related session, which educates new employees on the cyber security strategy and controls. Furthermore, when some cyber security controls are implemented, especially the controls that may require staff involvement or attention, such as DLP, awareness messages are sent out to the employees on different occasions. P3 also agrees that educating staff on information systems protection strategies is the key to preventing security breaches and incidents such as data leaks and data breaches. Training sessions are also regularly provided to staff. P2 from a private IT organization in the UAE also agrees with P3 and& P4, and their organization hires cyber security companies to train their employees. The company also provides periodic training for the employees to internally revise their understanding of data protection and ethical usage within the organization. P1, from the public telecom sector, believes in building an educated workforce with knowledge of cyber security; they support their workforce with training, workshops, and conferences. Another cyber security strategy that was highlighted in the study encourages tailoring the strategies to protect their information system, which was agreed on by all participants. This is aligned with the findings of Gordon et al. [24] research which showed that small businesses were willing to increase their resources, such as investing in the infrastructure to protect the systems from external threats, and in addition, these systems should be updated periodically, and they should also ensure that the cyber security strategies are backed by the government motivation and guidelines.

The participants part of this research study was of a similar opinion that cyber security policy, risk management, organizational strategy, and information security management help to safeguard information systems from cyber threats.

The strategies used by the organizations of the participants in the study are aligned with the CIA triad principle, which ensures confidentiality, integrity, and availability of the organization's data information, such as customer information, financial information, internal communication, etc. The results of the interview highlighted the fact that the public sectors are more involved in cyber security strategies, especially the healthcare sector has clear and detailed strategies to protect customer information from any threats. The public sector also highlighted some of the frameworks that they used, such as ISO and NIST. One of the reasons can be that the public sectors have more resources in terms of money and manpower as opposed to the private sector, wherein they may not have huge budgets to spend on acquiring strong security measures.

The results of the study will help other similar organizations to identify potential risks, threats, and vulnerabilities. All participants in this study agree that UAE National Cyber Security Strategy will be helpful to the organizations in the UAE to protect their information systems from threats. We agree with this as the world is moving towards a massive change, especially in the light of the current pandemic, which has forced organizations to conduct their business online in major industries such as Healthcare, telecommunication, and energy, which makes these industries more vulnerable to cyber-attacks. An effective framework such as UAE National Cyber Security Strategy is needed so that organizations in the private and public sectors can protect their valuable information and data from cyber threats. The results of the study could lead to positive social change by reducing the number of data breach incidents, protecting the data of the customers, and reducing the risk of the customers' information leakage.

4.3   Recommendations

In this section, we present some of the key recommendations based on the study. These recommendations could act as guidelines to any public/private organization while planning the cyber security strategy. These recommendations could be summarized as follows:

- Organizations in the UAE should have a robust training program for their employee, which is a key to protecting the information system. This was also emphasized by the participants in the study as this will instill hand on application, communication, and flexibility in the critical infrastructure of the organization. The participants felt the factors important to the compliance of cyber security programs.
- A flexible infrastructure that emphasizes the urgency of organization environment adjustment should be made a priority as it can be adjusted as per the needs and requirements of the organization to protect itself from cyber threats.

- Creating security awareness at all levels within the organization.
- Organizations need to create and customize their collaborative cyber security and compliance strategies and related programs.
- A crucial need for cyber security education among the employees.
- IT professionals should stress the importance of security awareness to curb cyber threats.
- The leaders of the organizations need to support the cyber security programs and provide investment for the critical infrastructure as resource investment plays a key role in establishing a secure system to protect the information/system from cyber threats.
- The leaders of the organizations should have cyber knowledge to face challenges through their decision process.

4.4   Future Directions

In addition to the overall recommendations provided in the previous section, we thought that sharing some future research directions will be beneficial. These research directions could be considered by practitioners in planning for future comprehensive research studies. The proposed research directions include the following:

- The effectiveness of employing more robust and recent protection mechanisms such as Artificial Intelligence-based (AI) and Nature-inspired Cyber Security (NICS) [25] could be studied. This could be achieved through real case studies in collaboration with our current research partners involved in our survey.
- To study in more depth the impact of the cyber security training in addition to organizations cyber security initiatives on the organizations data security maturity level, robust models could be developed such as the System Dynamics Modelling (SDM) introduced in [26].
- Additional empirical studies could be employed to test the effectiveness of the existing cyber security protection mechanisms within the organization. Accordingly, benchmarks and test-beds from the literature could be employed including the test-bed provided by [27].

5   Conclusion

In this paper, a qualitative study was presented. This qualitative research study helped to study and explores the cyber security strategies by the private and public organizations in the UAE to protect the information systems. This was achieved by answering three main research questions. The results answered the main research questions and led to the positive findings, which highlighted that the selected organizations are implementing successful cyber security strategies in protecting their systems and have left the study open for further research and investigation. Also, the results emphasized that the UAE National Cyber Security Strategy will be helpful to the organizations in the UAE to protect their information systems from threats.

In overall observation, the public organizations had more hands-on, direct, and concrete answers to the cyber security topics than the private sectors. The public organizations interviewed here provided detailed and in-depth accurate information for one reason. The results and findings of this research study will pave the way for the knowledge and best practices to protect the information systems in private and public organizations. Thus, we provided high-level recommendations from the public sector in UAE. These recommendations could act as a guideline to public/private organizations while planning their cyber security strategies. This research study may help other organizations to improve their cyber security practices, thereby reducing cyber threats.

Although one area that was not mentioned by the participants of this research was proper cyber security laws in the country, this is an area that has to be further investigated and could be considered for future research work.

References

1. Reid, R., Van Niekerk, J.: From information security to cyber security cultures. In: 2014 Information Security for South Africa, pp. 1–7. IEEE (2014)
2. Paulsen, C.: Cybersecuring small businesses. Computer **49**(8), 92–97 (2016)
3. Manworren, N., Letwat, J., Daily, O.: Why you should care about the target data breach. Bus. Horiz. **59**(3), 257–266 (2016)
4. Prince, D.: Cybersecurity: the security and protection challenges of our digital world. Computer **51**(4), 16–19 (2018)
5. Udroiu, A.M., et al.: Implementing the cybersecurity awareness program using e-learning platform. In: Conference Proceedings of» eLearning and Software for Education «(eLSE), vol. 4, pp. 101–104. "Carol I" National Defence University Publishing House (2018)
6. Bernik, I.: Cybercrime: the cost of investments into protection. Varstvoslovje: J. Crim. Justice Secur. **16**(2), 105–116 (2014)
7. Lallie, H.S., et al.: Cyber security in the age of COVID-19: a timeline and analysis of cyber-crime and cyber-attacks during the pandemic. Comput. Secur. **105**, 102248 (2021)
8. https://www.digital14.com/docs/default-source/reports/digital-14-cyber-threat-report-may. 2021.pdf. Digital 14 (2021). Accessed 26 Apr 2022
9. https://www.wam.ae/ar/details/1395302980024. Wam (2021). Accessed 26 Apr 2022
10. Fenrich, K.: Securing your control system. Power Eng. **112**, 44–49 (2008)
11. https://www2.deloitte.com/ch/en/pages/risk/articles/impact-covidcybersecurity.html. Deloitte, 2021. impact of COVID-19 on cybersecurity. Accessed 26 Apr 2022
12. https://www.metricstream.com/blog/cyber-resilience-in. 2021.html. Cyber resilience report (2021). Accessed 26 Apr 2022
13. https://www.kaspersky.com/blog/secure-futures-magazine/2020-cybersecuritypredictions/32068/. Kaspersky (2020). what cybersecurity trends should you look out for in 2020? Accessed 26 Apr 2022
14. https://www.tra.gov.ae/userfiles/assets/vzjmlB3CM34.pdf. tra, 2021. Accessed 26 Apr 2022
15. https://cybercenter.org/. National cybersecurity center. 2020. home - national cybersecurity center. Accessed 26 Apr 2022

16. Tvaronaviienė, M., Plėta, T., Della Casa, S., Latvys, J.: Cyber security management of critical energy infrastructure in national cybersecurity strategies: cases of USA, UK, France, Estonia and Lithuania. Insights Reg. Dev. **2**, 802–813 (2020)
17. https://www.cisa.gov/nationalinfrastructure-protection. plan. Cisa. (2018). national infrastructure protection. tratto il giorno may 8, 2020 da. Accessed 26 Apr 2022
18. Government of the republic of lithuania: Resolution on the Approval of the National Cyber Security Strategy. Government of the Republic of Lithuania, Vilnius (2018)
19. Pope, C., Mays, N., et al.: Qualitative research in health care (2006)
20. Gibson, G., Timlin, A., Curran, S., Wattis, J.: The scope for qualitative methods in research and clinical trials in dementia. Age Ageing **33**(4), 422–426 (2004)
21. Yin, R.K.: Case Study Research and Applications. Sage, New York (2018)
22. Lucas, M.L.: Exploring the strategies cybersecurity managers recommend for implementing or transitioning to the cloud. PhD thesis, Colorado Technical University (2018)
23. Iverson, A., Terry, P.: Cybersecurity hot topics for closely held businesses. J. Pension Benefits: Issues Adm. **25**, 60–62 (2018)
24. Gordon, L.A., Loeb, M.P., Lucyshyn, W., Zhou, L.: Increasing cybersecurity investments in private sector firms. J. Cybersecur. **1**(1), 3–17 (2015)
25. Shandilya, S.K.: Paradigm shift in adaptive cyber defense for securing the web data: the future ahead. J. Web Eng. **21**(4), 1371–1376 (2022)
26. Medoh, C., Telukdarie, A.: The future of cybersecurity: a system dynamics approach. In: Conference Proceedings of» 3rd International Conference on Industry 4.0 and Smart Manufacturing «(eLSE), vol. 200, pp. 318–326. "Procedia Computer Science" (2022)
27. Shandilya, S.K., Upadhyay, S., Kumar, A., Nagar, A.K.: Ai-assisted computer network operations testbed for nature-inspired cyber security based adaptive defense simulation and analysis. Future Gener. Comput. Syst. **127**, 297–308 (2022)

The Spatial Relationships of Meteorological Data for Unmanned Aerial System Decision-Making Support

Yuliya Averyanova$^{(\boxtimes)}$ (ID) and Yevheniia Znakovska (ID)

National Aviation University, Kyiv 03058, Ukraine
zea@nau.edu.ua

Abstract. This paper analyses the variation of atmospheric parameters in an urban environment. The examples of measurements and calculations are done for temperature variations as they can be relatively easily measured in many different places of the city. The general structure of the meteorological decision-making support system for UAS operators or autonomous vehicles is developed. The recommendations on decision making are proposed to make according to weather hazards risk analysis and assessment. The presented structure of the meteorological decision-making support system can be used to design and develop applications for UAS operators and other relevant users to make operational access to current spatial meteorological data within the area of UAS flights.

Keywords: UAS · Meteorology · Decision-making · Weather hazards

1 Introduction

Nowadays small Unmanned Aerial Systems (UAS) are considered for use in many civilian applications including agriculture [1], filmmaking and photography [2], cargo transportation [3], urban planning [4], search and rescue [5], meteorology [6] and many others. All these operations require harmonized regulations to create a basis for successful UAS integration into Single European Sky airspace, together with manned aircraft [7].

Many UAS operations are time-based and planned to be realized in an urban environment. At the same time UAS flights, especially small UAS, are dependent on weather significantly. According to [8] the seven UAS mission classes are distinguished to understand the requirements in meteorological services. The classification is made on the altitude, duration, and range of the mission. According to the classification given in [8], the flight altitude of mission classes from 1 to 4 are from 0 to 500 feet. This altitude corresponds to the so-called boundary layer of the atmosphere. The weather and atmospheric characteristics in the boundary layer are marked with diversity, they are dependent on topography significantly and can be abrupt and unexpected. In turn, the weather service products, that are commonly used for air navigation provision, usually represent the state of the atmosphere of the restricted area. For example, current weather information in METAR format or aerodrome forecasts in TAF format are prepared as aerodrome information. This can be insufficient for many UAS missions, especially in an urban environment. Moreover, the UAS navigation in the urban and populated areas should take into account additional risks for the property and people. The operation of the equipment can be under the influence of relief on radio waves propagation [9] as well. The flight routes of commercial navigation as well as navigation aids should be taken into account [10–12] to plan the UAS flights. The safety of UAS operations also requires precise positioning [13]. So, the different risks to the safety of UAS flights and mission realization exists. Thus, the pilots of remotely-piloted UASs should be prepared to make risk-aware decisions. For this task the meteorological data in the entire area of flight that can influence flight operation is one of the crucial needs for success in mission realization. Taking into account the potentials of autonomous vehicles for different missions made in urban environments the decision support system for urban UAS flight operations are also should be considered and designed.

This paper analyses the variation of atmospheric parameters in an urban environment. The more precise examples of measurements are devoted to temperature variations as they can be relatively easily measured in many different places of the city. The atmospheric parameters' precision for a particular area is based on spatial interpolation. The spatial relationship between temperature is calculated using inverse distance weighting. The general structure of the meteorological decision-making sup-port system for UAS operators or autonomous vehicles is developed. The decision-making is made according to weather hazards risk analysis and assessment and recommendations of [14, 15].

The paper is organized as follows: Sect. 2 gives a brief overview of the literature, and Sect. 3 presents the analysis of temperature variations in different areas of Kyiv city to show the difference between the aviation weather service products and the current situation in different urban areas, Sect. 4 presents and explain the general architecture of meteorological decision support system, and conclusions, remarks as well as suggestions on future research are presented in Sect. 5.

2 Brief Literature Review

Development of a decision support system requires understanding restrictions, hazards, and risks for UAS of different types and their missions. Papers [16–19] consider the wide range of UAS vulnerabilities and threats connected with UAS equipment and supporting systems as computer software. Paper [16] focuses on understanding and outlining UAVs threats and vulnerabilities based on statistical data analysis and developing the general taxonomy that gives a classification of vulnerabilities depending on the phase of the UAS life cycle. Paper [17] gives an analysis and qualitative assessment of threats connected with communication, navigation, control and surveillance equipment of modern UASs. In [18] the functional safety methodology for drone operation was proposed using qualitative and quantitative risk analyses. One more risk analysis method for UAVs is discussed in [19] and different scenarios of risks for drones are presented there. Papers [20–23] focuses on the understanding of weather-related risks and try to analyze the adverse weather impact on drone operations. Paper [20] is devoted to the quantification of risk to small UAS caused by adverse weather and presents Weather Risk Model that considers small UAS properties, population density, structure density, and weather forecast data. In paper [21] the software framework for analyzing weather data is developed. The framework can provide analysis of weather reports to the UAS operators or autonomous decision-making software. The presented framework operated with historical meteorological data. In [22] the comparison of the small UAS measurements of temperature, humidity and wind speed with real-time implementation of a numerical weather prediction model that additionally takes into account local scale wind field. And the analysis of the range of weather hazards in the boundary layer of the atmosphere that can influence the safety of UAS operations, mostly small UAS, is given in [23].

3 Temperature Variation in Urban Environment Analysis

A meteorological decision-making support system can be useful for UAS flight planning and executing flight path correction. This is of crucial importance for flight in urban areas where buildings, different urban constructions as well as the presence of a large number of concrete surfaces, cars, and operating equipment can cause significant variations in atmospheric parameters and cause the unpredictable formation of weather phenomena. Meteorological hazards analysis presented in [21, 23–25] designates the next weather-related hazards to UAS flights: Strong wind, High-density altitude, Precipitation, Icing, Windshear, Updraft or downdraft, Temperature extreme, Wind aloft, Convective weather, Turbulence, Phenomena that reduce visibility, Humidity.

The urban environment is usually characterized by increased day temperature connected with concrete surfaces and the operation of different equipment including heating and conditioning. This in turn can lead to local instability and an increased number of turbulent areas. Tall buildings can be the origin of increased wind with poorly predictable directions, creating the "wind tunnel effect" and wind shears. Automobiles, boiler rooms as well as industrial enterprises can serve as an additional source of water vapor in the atmosphere, thus increasing air humidity. The analysis of the influence of mentioned phenomena on UAS operation as well as risks connected with them is given in [23, 24].

To demonstrate the diversity of basic atmospheric parameters in Kyiv city the statistical data was collected during short periods of autumn and winter at four points. These data are presented in Table 1, 2, 3, 4, 5 and 6. Two sources of data are meteorological information for Boryspil and Kyiv airports. The other two sources are official information for Podilsky and Solomensky districts of Kyiv city is located at about 20 m height. In Fig. 1 Map of Kyiv city with indicated areas of observation. The map of Kyiv city is shown as well as areas of mentioned districts.

In Fig. 1 Map of Kyiv city with indicated areas of observation., area 1 corresponds to the position of the Kyiv airport, 2 is the area of the Boryspil airport, 3 is Podilsky district and 4 is Solomensky district.

In Fig. 2 and Table 1 the data of observed temperature during the period between 17, October 2021 and 20, October 2021 is shown. In Fig. 3 and Table 2 the data of observed temperature during the period from 17 of January 2022 to 21, January 2022. The temperature measurements were fixed 4 times a day – 9 a.m, 3 p.m, 6 p.m, and 9 p.m. In Fig. 2 and Fig. 3 the vertical axis shows the temperature measurements in Celsius degrees and the horizontal axis shows the time and dates of measurements.

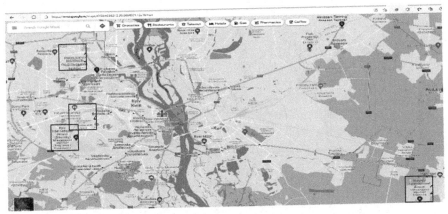

Fig. 1. Map of Kyiv city with indicated areas of observation.

Tables 1, 2, 3, 4, 5 and 6 show the measurement of temperature in different areas of Kyiv city.

Table 1. Temperature variations at 4 points in Kyiv city between 17, October 2021 and 20, October 2021.

Date	Time	Kyiv airport	Boryspil airport	Podilsky	Solomensky
17.10.2021	15:00	11	12	13	12
17.10.2021	18:00	9	9	9	9
17.10.2021	21:00	8	8	8	8
18.10.2021	09:00	7	7	7	7
18.10.2021	15:00	10	11	9	10
18.10.2021	18:00	10	10	10	10
18.10.2021	21:00	7	7	7	7
19.10.2021	09:00	4	4	4	4
19.10.2021	15:00	10	11	9	10
19.10.2021	18:00	7	7	7	7
19.10.2021	21:00	2	−1	4	2
20.10.2021	09:00	5	3	4	5
20.10.2021	15:00	15	14	14	14
20.10.2021	18:00	14	14	14	14
20.10.2021	21:00	14	13	14	14

In Fig. 2 and Fig. 3, the solid line shows the temperature at the Kyiv airport; dotted line shows the temperature at the Boryspil airport; the dashed line shows the readings

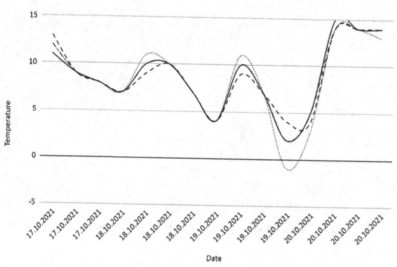

Fig. 2. Temperature variations at 4 points in Kyiv city between 17, October 2021 and 20, October 2021.

Table 2. Temperature variations at 4 points in Kyiv city between 17, January 2022 and 21, January 2022.

Date	Time	Kyiv airport	Boryspil airport	Podilsky	Solomensky
17.01.2022	21:00	−1	0	−1	−1
18.01.2022	09:00	−4	−3	−4	−4
18.01.2022	15:00	−3	−2	−4	−3
18.01.2022	18:00	−3	−3	−3	−3
18.01.2022	21:00	−4	−3	−3	−3
19.01.2022	09:00	−6	−5	−6	−6
19.01.2022	15:00	−1	−1	−1	−1
19.01.2022	18:00	−1	−1	−2	−1
19.01.2022	21:00	−2	−1	−2	−2
20.01.2022	11:00	−1	−1	−3	−1
20.01.2022	15:00	2	2	2	2
20.01.2022	18:00	1	1	1	1
20.01.2022	21:00	0	0	0	0
21.01.2022	11:00	−2	−1	−2	−2
21.01.2022	15:00	−1	0	−1	−1

of temperature in the Podilsky district of Kyiv city; dash point line in the readings of temperature at the flights in Solomensky district of Kyiv city.

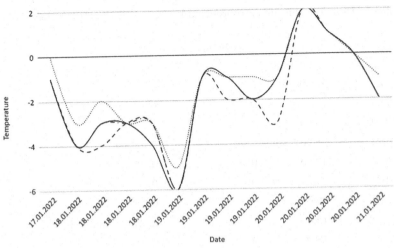

Fig. 3. Temperature variations at 4 points in Kyiv city between 17, January 2022 and 21, January 2022.

It is possible to see from Fig. 2 that the temperature in the Solomensky district coincides with the temperature readings at the Kyiv airport. It is ordinarily as these two areas are located close to each other. Then the temperature of the Solomensky district almost coincides with the dashed line that indicates temperature measurements in the Podilsky district. But at this time the temperatures of all places of measurement are similar. The maximum difference in measurements can be found between Podilsky district and Boryspil airport as the distance between these areas is the largest. Therefore, it seems that the temperature information given for Kyiv airport can be used for the Podilsky district of Kyiv.

In Fig. 3 much higher variations between temperature measurements can be seen. It should be mentioned that these days the sky was almost clear, so the influence of the underlying surface on temperature could be prevailing.

Figure 4 and Table 3 and Fig. 5 and Table 4 show the calculation of the difference between the temperature at Boryspil airport and temperatures at Kyiv airport and districts of Kyiv city for the periods from 17, October 2021 and 20, October 2021 and from 17 of January 2022 to 21, January 2022. In Fig. 4, 5, 6 and 7 the vertical axis shows the temperature difference (delta of temperature) in Celsius degrees and the horizontal axis shows the time and dates of the measurements.

In Fig. 4 and Fig. 5 solid line indicates the difference between the temperature at Boryspil airport and temperature at Kyiv airport; dashed line indicates the calculated difference between the temperature at Boryspil airport and temperature at Podilsky district of Kyiv city; dash point line is the calculation of the difference between the temperature at Boryspil airport and temperature at Solomensky district of Kyiv city.

From Fig. 4 it is possible to see again and more evidently that the maximum difference can be found between Boryspil airport and temperature at Podilsky district of Kyiv city. These two areas have the largest distance between each other. This tendency is true for the period of observation in January, which is shown in Fig. 5.

Table 3. The temperature difference between 17, October 2021 and 20, October 2021.

Date	Time	Kyiv airport	Podilsky	Solomensky
17.10.2021	15:00	1	−1	0
17.10.2021	18:00	0	0	0
17.10.2021	21:00	0	0	0
18.10.2021	09:00	0	0	0
18.10.2021	15:00	1	2	1
18.10.2021	18:00	0	0	0
18.10.2021	21:00	0	0	0
19.10.2021	09:00	0	0	0
19.10.2021	15:00	1	2	1
19.10.2021	18:00	0	0	0
19.10.2021	21:00	−3	−5	−3
20.10.2021	09:00	−2	−1	−2
20.10.2021	15:00	−1	0	0
20.10.2021	18:00	0	0	0
20.10.2021	21:00	−1	−1	−1

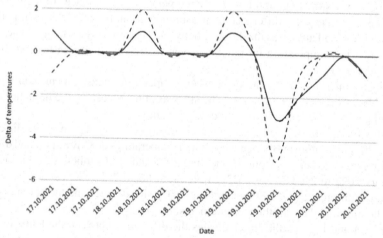

Fig. 4. The temperature difference between 17, October 2021 and 20, October 2021.

Table 4. The temperature difference between 17, January 2022 and 21, January 2022.

Date	Time	Kyiv airport	Podilsky	Solomensky
17.01.2022	21:00	1	1	1
18.01.2022	09:00	1	1	1
18.01.2022	15:00	1	2	1
18.01.2022	18:00	0	0	0
18.01.2022	21:00	1	0	0
19.01.2022	09:00	1	1	1
19.01.2022	15:00	0	0	0
19.01.2022	18:00	0	1	0
19.01.2022	21:00	1	1	1
20.01.2022	11:00	0	2	0
20.01.2022	15:00	0	0	0
20.01.2022	18:00	0	0	0
20.01.2022	21:00	0	0	0
21.01.2022	11:00	1	1	1
21.01.2022	15:00	0	0	0

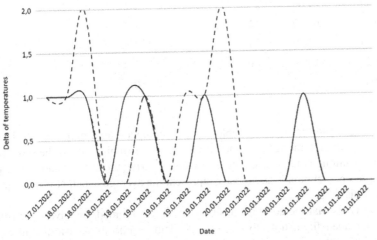

Fig. 5. The temperature difference between 17, January 2022 and 21, January 2022.

Figure 6 and Table 5 and Fig. 7 and Table 6 indicate differences between other points of measurement. In these figures dotted line indicates the difference between the temperature at Kyiv airport and temperature at Boryspil airport; dashed line indicates the difference between the temperature at Kyiv airport and temperature at Podilsky district of Kyiv city; dash point line is the calculation of the difference between the temperature at Kyiv airport and temperature at Solomensky district of Kyiv city.

Table 5. The temperature difference between 17, October 2021 and 20, October 2021.

Date	Time	Boryspil airport	Podilsky	Solomensky
17.10.2021	15:00	−1	−2	−1
17.10.2021	18:00	0	0	0
17.10.2021	21:00	0	0	0
18.10.2021	09:00	0	0	0
18.10.2021	15:00	−1	1	0
18.10.2021	18:00	0	0	0
18.10.2021	21:00	0	0	0
19.10.2021	09:00	0	0	0
19.10.2021	15:00	−1	1	0
19.10.2021	18:00	0	0	0
19.10.2021	21:00	3	−2	0
20.10.2021	09:00	2	1	0
20.10.2021	15:00	1	1	1
20.10.2021	18:00	0	0	0
20.10.2021	21:00	1	0	0

From Fig. 6 and Fig. 7 it is possible to see the temperature difference at Kyiv airport and Podilsky district, the value of the difference is not significant. At the same time, it should be mentioned that measurements are taken during the autumn and winter period with the presence of clouds and mostly represent the average data that is averaged over the area of districts.

It is obvious that meteorological observation can be made relatively far from the place of intended flight trajectory. Let us to demonstrate the possibility to estimate unknown atmospheric parameters using interpolation and inverse distance weighting (IDW). For this purpose, we calculate the spatial weights and show the spatial relations of the atmospheric parameters. The results are presented in Fig. 8 and Fig. 9 and Table 7 and Table 8.

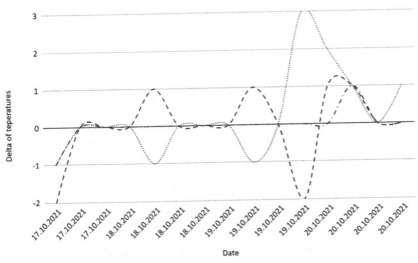

Fig. 6. The temperature difference between 17, October 2021 and 20, October 2021.

Table 6. The temperature difference between 17, January 2022 and 21, January 2022.

Date	Time	Boryspil airport	Podilsky	Solomensky
17.01.2022	21:00	−1	0	0
18.01.2022	09:00	−1	0	0
18.01.2022	15:00	−1	1	0
18.01.2022	18:00	0	0	0
18.01.2022	21:00	−1	−1	−1
19.01.2022	09:00	−1	0	0
19.01.2022	15:00	0	0	0
19.01.2022	18:00	0	1	0
19.01.2022	21:00	−1	0	0
20.01.2022	11:00	0	2	0
20.01.2022	15:00	0	0	0
20.01.2022	18:00	0	0	0
20.01.2022	21:00	0	0	0
21.01.2022	11:00	−1	0	0
21.01.2022	15:00	0	0	0

In Fig. 8 and Fig. 9 the spatial weights of the atmospheric parameters measured at different weather stations is shown. The calculations are made using inverse distance weighting and a formula taken from [26]. Table 7 and Table 8 give numerical values of

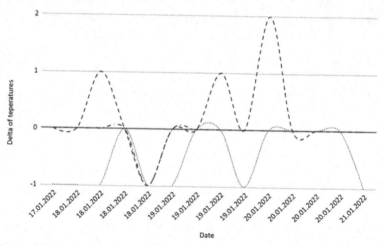

Fig. 7. The temperature difference between 17, January 2022 and 21, January 2022.

spatial weights that were used for calculations presented in Fig. 8, Fig. 9 correspondingly. In Table 7, Table 8 r is the radial distance from a target point, α is the shape parameter.

Table 7. The spatial weights of the atmospheric parameters measured for the Kyiv airport.

r \ α	3	6,25
1,8	0,8766658672	0,8509379071
4	0,6359612473	0,4537669572
8,6	0,1250653143	0,02450777765
9,1	0,09213508168	0,015186949
32,9	0	0

Along vertical plane in the Fig. 8 and Fig. 9 the weights of the atmospheric parameters are taken. The distances are taken along the horizontal plane.

From the comparison of the Fig. 8 and Fig. 9 it is seen that the larger distance from this place is measurement is, the less weight of the measured parameters. It is true for the both figures. The weather sensors of Fig. 9 are located farer from the place of intended flight, so the weight of the atmospheric parameters taken from these sensors is less than the weight of the parameters measured on the sensors on the Fig. 8.

The shape of the curves of Fig. 8 and Fig. 9 is different as well. This is because the number of position of measurements is higher for the case of Fig. 8.

The spatial weights of the atmospheric parameters are taken into account in the "weather precision" block of the diagram that represents the general architecture of the meteorological decision support system and are presented in Sect. 4 of this study.

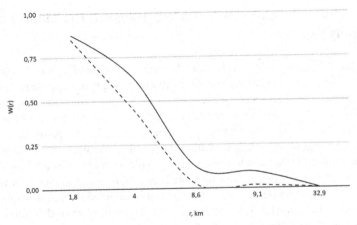

Fig. 8. The spatial weights of the atmospheric parameters measured for the Kyiv airport.

Table 8. The spatial weights of the atmospheric parameters measured for the Boryspil airport

r ╲ α	3	6,25
32,8	0,01374639067	0,001277699884
32,9	0,01268596729	0,001167152527
34,3	0	0
34,9	0	0
36,2	0	0

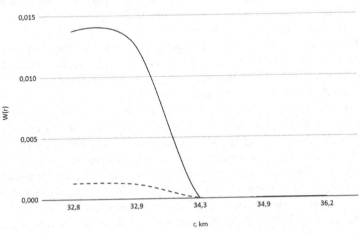

Fig. 9. The spatial weights of the atmospheric parameters measured for the Boryspil airport.

4　The General Architecture of Meteorological Decision-Making Support System

The decision-making when flight planning depends on a range of factors. One of the key elements in this process is weather conditions and weather phenomena that can influence flight operation. The analysis of the weather on UAS flight safety and mission success [21, 23, 24, 27] allows exploring the weather-related limitations for UAS operation to support decision making. These limitations depend on the UAV type (model), mission, area of the planned operation, and weather information. Weather information, in turn, includes general climatic information including typical seasonal variation, general and aviation present weather information and forecasts, and revised weather information for a particular area. The revised weather information is intended to minimize or eliminate weather-related risks for UAS operations. The decision diagram to determine weather conditions suitable for flight in a particular area is shown in Fig. 10.

The first two components of the diagram show the connection between UAV type and the planned mission. Then, information on planned flight areas is analyzed as well as general meteorological information. If there is no restriction on current weather and short-term forecasts, the weather information is specified for a particular area of flight and UAS type. The narrow arrows from corresponding blocks to "weather precision block" indicate the necessity of this information for final decision-making on weather constraints for UAS mission realization. The bold arrows indicate the general sequence of information required for decision-making. After these steps, the recommendation can be done.

The decision-making process according to the diagram of Fig. 10 can be realized by the next steps:

1. Defining the mission for UAV flight. During this stage the factors that include expected time of mission realization, payload in the frame of mission, the urgency of mission should be taken into account.

   This will help to define UAV type (its required characteristics), and necessity to perform tasks under relatively complex flight conditions. Further, this will help as well to correlate expanses with potential benefits of the mission.
2. After definition of mission and required UAV characteristics the corrections can be done taking into account the planned area of mission realization. For example, in Urban area there are more risks for people and property can be caused in case of emergency situations including those connected with dangerous weather conditions.
3. Next step is analysis of weather situation and weather precision for particular area, UAV characteristics and primary mission. The weather precision for particular area can be based on spatial interpolation of basic atmospheric parameters as it is considered in the paper. Also, the data from the stations or sensors that are located too far from the planned flight area can be taken with smaller weights according to Fig. 8, Fig. 9 or omitted.
4. The next stage is the report given by the system on possible limitations and final recommendation for flight and mission realization.

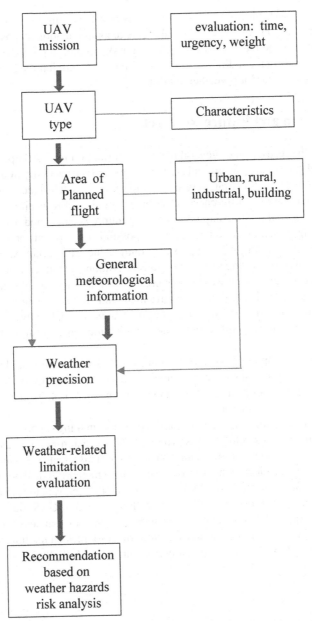

Fig. 10. The general architecture of meteorological decision support system.

It is reasonable to use a risk-oriented approach and for final recommendation use the indicators of severity and probability of appearance of weather-related hazards for UAV flight operation in a particular area of operation. According to [14, 28] the recommendation can be performed as an acceptable risk, tolerable risk, and intolerable risk. Acceptable risk means low-risk conditions and UAS mission realization can be done under the current conditions. Tolerable risk recommendation means moderate risk conditions and it is better to consider additional risk mitigation procedures. Intolerable risk indicates high-risk conditions. In this case, the UAS mission realization should be postponed due to hazardous weather conditions.

5 Conclusion and Future Research

In this paper, the restriction of general aviation information for UAS operation, as well as weather-related hazards, were analyzed to understand the necessity of meteorological decision support of UAS operators or autonomous vehicles. The calculation of general and averaged temperature differences between two districts of Kyiv city and two airports was done. The spatial relationship between temperature is calculated using inverse distance weighting to demonstrate necessity and possibility of spatial forecast of weather situation along the UAS flight in complex environment including urban environment. The averaged data observed during the short periods in autumn and winter have demonstrated a rather small difference, so it would be interesting to make additional measurements in particular places with different urban environment and compare them with general and aviation information. Also, it would be interesting to watch and analyze the local wind conditions as they can vary sufficiently due to high buildings and can be hazardous for UAS flights.

Taking into account the growth of the number of UAS flights it would be reasonable to use them as an additional source of meteorological information for weather observing systems. UAS can be used as well to obtain current meteorological information for operative trajectories correction [29].

The general structure of the meteorological decision-making support system for UAS operators or autonomous vehicles was proposed. The decision-making and support are proposed to realize on the basis of weather hazards risk analysis and assessment. In future studies, we plan to develop on the base of the presented meteorological decision-making support system the application for UAS operators and other relevant users for operational access to current spatial meteorological data within the area of UAS flights when flight planning. It is expected that the application in the final version can demonstrate the data for different cities taking information from authorized sources on the Internet, and from the data set formed on the base of previous and current UAS flights.

References

1. Yinka-Banjo, C., Ajayi, O.: Sky-farmers: applications of unmanned aerial vehicles (UAV) in agriculture. In: Autonomous Vehicles. IntechOpen, London (2019). https://www.intechopen.com/chapters/70496
2. Adams, C.: Dual control: investigating the role of drone (UAV) operators in TV and online journalism. Media and Commun. 8(3), 93–100 (2020)
3. Gupta, A., Afrin, T., Scully, E., Yodo, N.: Advances of UAVs toward future transportation: the state-of-the-art, challenges, and opportunities. In: Future Transportation, vol. 1, no. 2, pp. 326–350 (2021)

4. Vanderhorst, R., Suresh, S., Renukappa, S., Heesom, D.: UAS application for urban planning development. In: European Conference on Computing in Construction, pp. 189–196 (2021)
5. Waharte S., Trigoni N.: Supporting search and rescue operations with UAVs. In: 2010 International Conference on Emerging Security Technologies, pp. 142–147 (2010)
6. Elston, J.: Overview of small fixed-wing unmanned aircraft for meteorological sampling. J. Atmos. Oceanic Tech. **32**(1), 97–115 (2015)
7. Easy Access Rules for Unmanned Aircraft Systems, EASA (2021). https://www.easa.europa.eu/document-library/easy-access-rules/online-publications/easy-access-rules-unmanned-aircraft-systems
8. Campbell, S., Clark, D., Evans, J.: Preliminary weather information gap analysis for UAS operations. In: Project Report ATC-437, p. 99 (2017)
9. Ostroumov, I., Kuzmenko, N., Sushchenko, O., Pavlikov, V., Zhyla, S., Solomentsev O., et al.: Modelling and simulation of DME navigation global service volume. In: Advances in Space Research, vol. 68, issue 8, pp. 3495–3507 (2021)
10. Ivashchuk, O., et al.: A configuration analysis of Ukrainian flight routes network. In: 16th International Conference on the Experience of Designing and Application of CAD Systems (CADSM), Lviv, Ukraine, pp. 6–10 (2021)
11. Ostroumov, I., et al.: Ukrainian navigational aids network configuration estimation. In: 16th International Conference on the Experience of Designing and Application of CAD Systems (CADSM), Lviv, Ukraine, pp. 5–9 (2021)
12. Ostroumov, I., et al.: A probability estimation of aircraft departures and arrivals delays. In: Gervasi, O., et al. (eds.) ICCSA 2021. LNCS, vol. 12950, pp. 363–377. Springer, Cham (2021). https://doi.org/10.1007/978-3-030-86960-1_26
13. Ilnytska, S., Kondratiuk, V., Kutsenko, O., Konin, V.: Potential possibilities of highly accurate satellite navigation use for landing operations of unmanned aerial systems. In: 5th International Conference on Actual Problems of Unmanned Aerial Vehicles Developments (APUAVD) Proceedings, pp. 174–177. IEEE, Ukraine (2019)
14. Safety Management Manual, the 4th edition, ICAO Doc 9859 (2017)
15. Annex 19 to the Convention on International Civil Aviation - Safety Management. ICAO, Second Edition (2016)
16. Averyanova, Yu., Blahaja, L.: A study on unmanned aerial system vulnerabilities for durability enhancement. In: 5th International Conference on Actual Problems of Unmanned Aerial Vehicles Development (APUAVD-2019) Proceedings, pp.40–43. IEEE, Ukraine (2019)
17. Averyanova, Y., et al.: UAS cyber security hazards analysis and approach to qualitative assessment. In: Shukla, S., Unal, A., Varghese Kureethara, J., Mishra, D.K., Han, D.S. (eds.) Data Science and Security. LNNS, vol. 290, pp. 258–265. Springer, Singapore (2021). https://doi.org/10.1007/978-981-16-4486-3_28
18. Allouch, A., Koubaa, A., Khalgui, M., Abbes, T.: Qualitative and quantitative risk analysis and safety assessment of unmanned aerial vehicles missions over the internet. IEEE Access **7**, 53392–53410 (2019)
19. Janik, P., Zawistowski, M., Fellner, R., Zawistowski, G.: Unmanned aircraft systems risk assessment based on SORA for first responders and disaster management. Appl. Sci. **11**, 53–64 (2021)
20. Roseman, C.A., Argrow, B.M.: Weather hazard risk quantification for sUAS safety risk management. J. Atmos. Oceanic Tech. **37**(7), 1251–1268 (2020)
21. Lundby, T., Christiansen, M.P., Jensen, K.: Towards a weather analysis software framework to improve UAS operational safety. In: 2019 International Conference on Unmanned Aircraft Systems (ICUAS) Proceedings, pp. 1372–1380. IEEE, United States (2019)
22. Glasheen, K., Pinto, J., Steiner, M., Frew, E.W.: Experimental assessment of local weather forecasts for small unmanned aircraft flight. In: AIAA SCITECH 2019 forum, pp. 11–93 (2019)

23. Averyanova, Yu., Znakovskaja, E.: Weather hazards analysis for small UASs durability enhancement. In: 6-th International Conference on Actual Problems of Unmanned Air Vehicles Developments (APUAVD) Proceedings, pp. 41–44. IEEE, Ukraine (2021)
24. Ranquist, E., Steiner, M., Argrow, B.: Exploring the range of weather impacts on UAS operations. In: 18th Conference on Aviation, Range and Aerospace Meteorology Proceedings, pp. 1–11. AMS, United States (2018)
25. Gao, M., Hugenholtz, C.H., Fox, T.A., Kucharczyk, M., Barchyn, T.E., Nesbit, P.R.: Weather constraints on global drone flyability. Sci. Rep. **11**, 12092 (2021)
26. Caceres, M., et al.: Estimating daily meteorological data and downscaling climate models over landscapes. Environ. Model. Softw. **108**, 186–196 (2018)
27. Remote Pilot – Small Unmanned Aircraft Systems (sUAS) Study Guide, The Federal Aviation Administration, FAA-G-8082-22, 2016, faa.gov
28. Manual on Remotely Piloted Aircraft Systems, ICAO Doc 10019, ICAO (2015)
29. Averyanova, Yu.A., Rudiakova, A.N., Yanovsky, F.J.: Aircraft trajectories correction using operative meteorological radar information. In: International Radar symposium Proceedings, pp. 256–259. IEEE, Poland (2020)

HIAS: Hybrid Intelligence Approach for Soil Classification and Recommendation of Crops

S. Palvannan[1] and Gerard Deepak[2,3]([✉])

[1] Department of Metallurgical and Materials Engineering, National Institute of Technology, Tiruchirappalli, India

[2] Department of Computer Science and Engineering, National Institute of Technology, Tiruchirappalli, India
gerard.deepak.cse.nitt@gmail.com

[3] Manipal Institute of Technology Bengaluru, Manipal Academy of Higher Education, Bengaluru, India

Abstract. Agriculture is the largest industry in the world, and it is vital to any country's economic development. Farmers' failure to select the appropriate crop for cultivation is a significant and severe mistake that results in poor agricultural output. For the surplus of crop production, a soil classification and crop recommendation system were developed, which used a semantically driven hybrid intelligence method. In this paper, the Hybrid Intelligence Approach for Soil (HIAS) model was presented and tested with several baseline models using southern South Australian Soil datasets to evaluate the proper prediction. Besides, ontology is generated from the summarised content of agricultural and geological eBooks. Textbooks and then the query and Soil dataset are pre-processed. The semantic similarity is calculated using Jaccard similarity, Cosine similarity, and SemantoSim measure under the Squirrel search algorithm to ensure that the relevant result is optimised and set entities formed from a set of recommendations are optimised. The term enrichment is done using MediaWiki and WikiData, and then the LSTM classifier is used for classification. Finally, the precision, accuracy, recall, F-measure, and FNR for the soil classification and crop recommendation system are evaluated. The precision percentage of 99.78% and the lowest FNR of 0.01 is obtained from the HIAS model.

Keywords: Crop recommendation · LSTM · Soil classification · Semantic intelligence · Squirrel search algorithm

1 Introduction

The soil tends to be a solid body covering most of the earth's land surface, where plants grow, and humans reside. Soil is also essential to humans and other living creatures on the planet since it serves as the source of food, medicine, and agriculture. Soils come in various textures, and the texture of the soil influences its capacity to hold water and fertility. Therefore, the categorization of soil texture is essential for agricultural applications and the tracking of environmental activities to know which crops grow

F. Ortiz-Rodríguez et al. (Eds.): EGETC 2022, CCIS 1666, pp. 81–94, 2022.
https://doi.org/10.1007/978-3-031-22950-3_7

better on what soil types and what fertilizers/ insecticides to make the crop flourish healthily.

There is also a need for soil classification to determine the soil in a particular regional geographical location and understand the diverse types of crops over the types of soil. Geographical location tremendously impacts differences in crop yield from place to place. Several crop parameters will also influence food or other raw material production. So, the classification based on the geographical and the crop parameter will ensure that crop rotation and a surplus of crop production can be obtained.

The existing soil approaches are driven by machine learning or deep learning; traditional data mining and clustering have been used. However, in the era of the semantics web, where the data density has been exceptionally high recently, Semantic intelligence can be used as an alternative in all recommendation systems. This classification mechanism yields better results, and better efficiency is obtained. Therefore, in this paper, we used a semantically driven approach using semantic similarity, which is used for future intrusion. The classification approach has been incorporated to classify the soil and recommend the crop based on the other geographical parameter for the surplus of crop production.

Motivation: IN the era of Web 3.0, there is a need for semantically driven crop recommendations based on categorised soil, which would undoubtedly have an impact on surplus crop output. Therefore, there is always a need for an expert who can semantically enhance the categorisation of soil entities based on various parameters. As a result, the suggested technique may be used for both soil classification and crop recommendation. The suggested Hybrid Intelligence Approach for Soil Classification and Crop Recommendation System model offers the user information about the soil and crop while enhancing semantic intelligence expertise, among other recommendation systems.

Contribution: The proposed model had a process of Ontologies generation for the agriculture domain, which is done by generating ontology from summarised contents of geographical, crop information and agriculture eBooks/textbooks. Apart from that, the query is subjected to pre-processing then the semantic similarity is computed using Jaccard similarity, Cosine similarity and SemantoSim measure under the Squirrel search algorithm to ensure that the relevant result is maximised, and optimised set entities formed from the set of recommendations. The term enrichment is done using MediaWiki and WikiData. The classification uses LSTM as a classifier. Experiments were conducted on the data crawled from southern South Australian Soil datasets. Combining several algorithms and concepts into one allowed to achieve greater accuracy, precision, recall, F-Measure, and a shallow False Negative Rate (FNR).

Organization The following is how the rest of the article is organised. A summary of related work is provided in Sect. 2. The Proposed Architecture is depicted in Sect. 3. The Implementation is extensively discussed in Sect. 4. Section 5 discusses the Performance Analysis and Results. Section 6 deals with the paper's Conclusion, followed by the last Section, which is the Reference to the paper.

2 Related Work

Many researchers have expressed interest in using machine learning approaches in soil classification and crop recommendation. The work on a few innovative soil classification and crop recommendation-related techniques is discussed in the following paragraphs. Selvi et al. [1] used the Recurrent Convolutional Neural Network's mapping and classification tasks to assess soil properties. The model is then compared to geostatistical spatial interpolation methods used in the old days. Mythili et al. [2] created a DLT (Deep Learning Technique) crop recommender system, which generates recommendations based on previous crop and climatic data. In a study by Rahman et al. [3], several machine learning techniques were compared. They used data from Bangladesh to carry out the classification. Utilized the geographical features for classification while considering the six district soil data. They finally compared the outcomes of the three algorithms—k Nearest Neighbor, Bagged Tree, and SVM—and developed a model for classifying the various soil types and the suitable crops that can be grown in each. SVM has gotten the average accuracy out of the three algorithms used. Kulkarni et al. [3] & Pudumalar et al. [7] used a majority vote approach to combine the classifiers of various base learners to construct a method that incorporates the predictions of several machine learning models to accurately suggest the right crop depending on soil type and features. Masare et al. [4] have built a Naive Bayes machine learning method for agricultural yield prediction utilizing a variety of characteristics such as temperature, rainfall, pesticides, and fertilizer prediction using user input such as crop name, location or district name, and season to maximize crop yield rates. Varsha et al. [5] have developed a project using IoT devices to gather data and machine learning algorithms to forecast the best crop suited for the soil. For optical picture segmentation and incomplete data recovery due to clouds and shadows, Kussul et al. [8] proposed architecture with one unsupervised neural network (NN) pillar and an ensemble of supervised NNs. Murali et al. [9] developed a novel hybrid model that uses whale optimization techniques to enhance the recurrent neural network's weights and thresholds to increase the neural network's efficiency and produce accurate results. Doshi et al. [10] built AgroConsultant. This intelligent tool combines Big Data Analytics and Machine Learning to aid Indian farmers in making intelligent crop selections based on the season of sowing, their farm's location, soil characteristics, and climatic elements such as temperature and rainfall. The Squirrel search algorithm was created by Jain et al. [11] to mimic the dynamic searching behaviours of southern flying squirrels and their efficient moving method termed gliding. In [12–16], several machine learning-based approaches for modelling recommendation system in support of the proposed approach has been discussed. The primary goal of their article is to identify the farmer's requirements and expectations and suggest the best crop for excess crop production.

3 Proposed Work

The suggested architecture for recommending soil and crop properties using soil classification and artificial intelligence semantic techniques is depicted in Fig. 1. The first step comprises utilising LSTM to classify the Soil classification dataset.

LSTM networks are a form of recurrent neural network (RNN) created to solve problems that RNNs could not solve. The vanishing gradient problem is avoided, but the training model remains unaltered. In certain situations, LSTMs are used to bridge lengthy time delays, and they can also deal with noise, dispersed representations, and continuous data. With LSTMs, keeping a finite number of states from the outset is no necessity. LSTMs give a variety of parameters, including learning rates, input, and output biases, and learning rates.

The LSTM approach is used to categorise the dataset, which combines domain knowledge with query themes. This way, the LSTM algorithm was used to capture data across arbitrary periods, and the gates were employed to control the flow of data entering and departing the unit. The memory unit in LSTM cells is better than in traditional recurrent unit cells. Because of the benefits described above, LSTM has been used to categorise the soil classification dataset instead of RNN. We are free to utilise as many LSTM cells as we like for this procedure, but we will utilise a group of LSTM cells to save time. The output layer receives from the outcome of the final LSTM cell.

Since the dataset is already categorised, it will be subjected to pre-processing. Tokenisation, lemmatisation, stop word removal, NER (Name Entity Recognition), and WSD (Word Sense Disambiguation) processing are all part of the pre-processing. After preprocessing the dataset, we acquire the unique terms or categories from the soil classification dataset. Term enrichment is done by obtaining information from WikiData and MediaWiki based on the dataset's unique term/word retrieved. WikiData and MediaWiki are semantic wikis where the WikiData uses the WikiData API to gather auxiliary knowledge, background knowledge, relevant entities, and keywords from the real-world semantic knowledge store.

Similarly, to MediaWiki, it is also utilised as a semantic knowledge repository, including content provided by many users and collaborative community knowledge. Then MediaWiki is accessed using the framework's interface. WikiData and MediaWiki increase the quantity of background knowledge and the number of entities which may supply into the proposed framework, making it easier to enhance in the future.

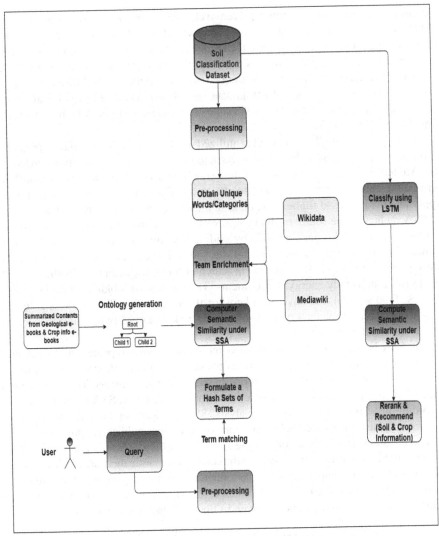

Fig. 1. Proposed architecture for HIAS model

Another essential aspect of the suggested technique is that it incorporates material from geology textbooks on soil, soil mechanics, and soil properties, as well as technical textbooks and e-books. The standard summarising method is used to summarise soil-related material, which is then utilized to generate ontologies. Aside from that, crop information e-books, crop rotation, and agricultural books based on crops are summarised, and the summarised content is utilized to build ontologies using the Onto-Collab tool. The ontology and its axiomatized work are created in OWL format for future usage. The Jaccard similarity, SemantoSim measure and Cosine similarity are used as objective functions for the multi-metaheuristic optimization using the Squirrel search algorithm (SSA). Since the dataset is already categorized, it will be subjected to pre-processing.

Tokenisation, lemmatization, stop word removal, NER (Name Entity Recognition), and WSD (Word Sense Disambiguation) processing are all part of the pre-processing. After pre-processing the dataset, we acquire the unique terms or categories from the soil classification dataset. Term enrichment is done by obtaining information from WikiData and MediaWiki based on the dataset's unique term/word retrieved. WikiData and MediaWiki are semantic wikis where the WikiData uses the WikiData API to gather auxiliary knowledge, background knowledge, relevant entities, and keywords from the real-world semantic knowledge store.

Similarly, to MediaWiki, it is also utilized as a semantic knowledge repository, including content provided by many users and collaborative community knowledge. Then MediaWiki is accessed using the framework's interface. WikiData and MediaWiki increase the quantity of background knowledge and the number of entities which may supply into the proposed framework, making it easier to enhance in the future.

SSA replicates the southern flying squirrels with the dynamic foraging activity in deciduous woods of Europe and Asia by gliding, an efficient method adopted by tiny animals for long distance travel. During the summer, the squirrels move around the forest, gliding from one tree to the next in search of food. They can readily obtain acorn nuts to fulfil their daily energy requirements. They then start looking for hickory nuts (the best food source) that have been kept for the winter. They become less active in the winter and meet their energy needs by storing hickory nuts. Flying squirrels become busy as the weather warms up.

The SSA is built based on the process mentioned above, repeated, and continues throughout the squirrels' life span. Various phases theoretically describe the optimization of SSA, and the method is developed based on flying squirrels. Then, utilizing a range of unconstrained benchmark functions, both old and new, SSA is put to the test. According to comparative statistical analysis, SSA produces optimal global solutions with remarkable convergence behaviour compared to other published optimisers.

The threshold for Jaccard and Cosine similarity is 0.75, whereas the threshold for the SemantoSim measure is 0.5. Because the standard semantic measures of Jaccard and Cosine similarity are simple and effective semantic similarity algorithms, they are not as stringent as the SematoSim. The mathematical Equation for Jaccard similarity, Cosine similarity and SemantoSim measure given in Eqs. 1, 2 and 3, respectively.

$$J(A, B) = A \cap B \vee \overline{A \cup B\vee} = A \cap B \vee \overline{|A| + |B| - A \cap B\vee} \tag{1}$$

$$cos(A, B) = \frac{AB}{|A| * B\vee} \tag{2}$$

$$SemantoSim(A, B) = pmi(A, B) + p(A, B)log \tag{3}$$

If two terms exist in the query, they are paired as (A, B). The Jaccard similarity is calculated by dividing the intersection of the two data set items by the union of the data set items. Cosine similarity is a measure that may be used to determine how similar data items are regardless of their size. Cosine Similarity can be used to compare two phrases. The data objects in a dataset are represented as a vector in cosine similarity. Compared to Cosine or Jaccard similarity, SemantoSim incorporates Pointwise Mutual Information measure and the probabilistic or statistics.

Then the classified entity using the LSTM is further used for the final recommendation. The user is allowed to submit the Query and the user query input is subject to pre-processing. As it is pre-processed, the term from which a hash set is initially formulated for all the matching terms application of SSA. The Query pre-process from the user is matched with the hash set of terms. Further semantic similarity is again computed using the SSA metaheuristic algorithm between the set of user queries matched with the set of terms in the hash sets and the instances classified from the LSTM. Finally, the soil and crop information are ranked and recommended. Reranking is done by increasing the order of semantic similarity, which is recommended to the user.

4 Implementation and Performance Evaluation

The proposed hybrid intelligence approach for soil classification crop recommendation approach was developed in Python with Google Collaborator as the IDE. The ontology is manually modelled in Protege 5.3 and generated automatically from several blogs and textbooks using the Onto Collab tool. MediaWiki and WikiData have been accessed through the framework's interface and API libraries, respectively, and the auxiliary knowledge is also included in the framework. The data was obtained from the Department for Environment and Water on the official website of the Government of South Australia. Based on an interpretation of Soil Landscape Map Units, sixty-one soils have been identified as representative of the range across southern South Australia. In each Soil Landscape Map Unit, the soil is classified using a total of 64 attribute classes, with the value of area extent percentage of each soil type. Algorithm 1 depicts the proposed model algorithm.

Algorithm 1: Algorithm of the proposed HIAS model

Input: User queries, Soil Classification Dataset **Output:** Recommendation of crop based on user inputs.

Start
Step 1: The input queries are formalized to yield pre-processed query terms.
Step 2: Based on the summarized content derived from geological eBooks and crop information eBooks ontologies are generated.
Step 3: Pre-processing is done for the soil classification data
Step 4: Unique words or categories from the pre-processed soil classification datasets are obtained.
Step 5: Term enrichment is employed using WikiData and MediaWiki.
Step 6: The semantic similarity for the entities of the generated ontology is computed using SSA semantic similarity measure.
      Step 7: The semantic similarity is also computed for the modified soil classification dataset upon term enrichment using SSA semantic similarity measure.
Step 8: Terms are formulated into a hash based on term matching from the pre-processed user input query and based on the ontology generated from the summarized content from geological books and crop books and the modified soil classification dataset.
Step 9: Finally, classification is performed on the modified soil classification dataset using LSTM (Long Short-Term Memory).
            Initialize the algorithm for classification
            RNN is operated for updating weights
            Error percentage is calculated
            Causing some disturbance to the weights
            RNN is used again to update weights
            Error percentage is calculated after the disturbance caused
            Final weights are updated
Step 10: Upon classification semantic similarity is again computed using SSA.
Step 11: Terms are ranked and recommended for the soil and crop information based on the semantic similarity measure computed upon classification.
End

The input to the algorithm is the user queries and the soil classification dataset, and the algorithm yields the most relevant crop recommendation that captures the user's requirement based on user queries as the output. The input query obtained undergoes pre-processing steps such as Tokenization, lemmatization, stop word removal, NER (Name Entity Recognition), and WSD. Upon pre-processing based on the summarized content derived from the geological eBooks and crop information eBooks, ontologies are formulated. The soil classification data is also pre-processed, and a unique word or category is obtained from it. Upon obtaining the unique word, term enrichment is performed using WikiData and MediaWiki. The proposed architecture incorporates the MHA semantic similarity method to compute the semantic similarity among the entities of the generated ontology. The ontology is generated from the summarised content from geological books and crop books, as well as the modified soil classification dataset, and terms are formulated into hashes based on term matching from the pre-processed user input query. Finally, LSTM (Long Short-Term Memory) is employed to classify the modified soil datasets. Upon classification, one second, the semantic similarity among the entities in the classified dataset is computed using MHA semantic measure. Based on the semantic similarity value obtained in the previous step, the terms are ranked and suggested to the user.

5 Results and Performance Evaluation

Any recommendation system focuses on offering users the most helpful and practical recommendations. The effectiveness of this content-based recommendation system is predicted to achieve this goal. Potential metrics include recall, precision, accuracy, F-measure, and False-Negative Rate (FNR). The ratio of what our model accurately predicted to what our model predicted is known as precision. Accuracy is how effective our model is at guessing the correct category. The ratio of what our model accurately predicted to what the actual labels are is called recall (classes or labels). F-measure calculates the results' relevance, or the harmonic mean of recall & precision.

In contrast, the false negative rate (FNR) quantifies the number of false negatives classified by the approach, resulting in an error rate. As a result, the lower the FNR, the better the approach is. Equations 4, 5, 6, and 7 depict recall, precision, accuracy, and F-measure, respectively, and FNR is depicted as Eq. 8.

$$Recall\% = \frac{TrueNumberofpositive}{TrueNumberofpositives + FalseNumberOfNegatives} \tag{4}$$

$$Precision\% = \frac{TrueNumberofpositive}{TrueNumberofpositives + FalseNumberOfPositives} \tag{5}$$

$$Accuracy\% = \frac{(Precision + Recall)}{2} \tag{6}$$

$$F - measure = \frac{2 * Precision * Recall}{Precision + Recall} \tag{7}$$

$$FNR = \frac{FalseNumberOfPositives}{TrueNumberofpositives + FalseNumberOfNegatives} \tag{8}$$

Table 1 shows comments on the proposed HIAS approach for soil classification and crop recommendation. The suggested HIAS method is compared to the performance of

Table 1. Performance evaluation of the proposed HIAS for soil classification

Search technique	Average precision %	Average recall %	Average accuracy %	Average F-measure %	FNR
ANN	87.46	91.36	89.43	89.36	0.09
RNN	88.23	92.56	91.28	90.34	0.08
CNN	91.18	95.67	93.81	93.37	0.05
RCNN [1]	94.36	98.33	96.12	96.31	0.02
Proposed HIAS	**97.18**	**99.36**	**98.43**	**98.25**	**0.01**

four models: adaptive neural network, recurrent neural network, convolutional neural network, and recurrent convolutional neural network (RCNN) [1].

Table 1 shows that the proposed HIAS has a precision of 97.18%, a recall of 99.36%, an accuracy of 98.43%, a F-measure of 98.25%, and an exceptionally low FNR of 0.01. Similarly, it shows that ANN produces a precision of 87.46%, a recall of 91.36%, an accuracy of 89.43%, a F-measure of 89.36%, and a FNR of 0.09. RNN, on the other hand, has a precision of 88.23%, a recall of 92.56%, an accuracy of 91.28%, with a F-measure of 90.34%, and a FNR of 0.08. Similarly, when the CNN is used as a standalone model in the framework, it achieves a precision of 91.18%, recall of 95.67%, accuracy of 93.81%, with a F-measure of 93.37%, and a FNR of 0.05. The precision of RCNN [1] is 94.36%, with a recall of 98.33%, an accuracy of 96.12%, a F-measure of 96.31%, and a FNR of 0.02%.

The reason is that with ANN, the adaptive neural network is used; it is one of the standalone deep learning models used. In ANN, the train data, if noisy, you get many complex data that the ANN interprets. Also, the attributed instances, which are attribute-value pairs, are highly correlated. As a result, the adaptive neural network does not work. It is severe, and the computation is demanding. Even though the computation complexity is exceptionally high, it does not yield the best classification result when ANN alone is used.

In the case of CNN, the convolutional neural network also does not function flawlessly. It is computationally expensive, and the feature extraction is automatic. The kind of features going to the approach is uncontrollable. As a result, CNN also does not function well.

For the RCNN [1] model, the problem is that the training network ring time is extensively ample, and the selective search algorithm in RCNN [1] is fixed where the candidate generation is going wrong in the RCNN [1]. Then in the RNN, it is computationally expensive. Still, it is not worth it when a standalone like RNN model is used as a classification accuracy is much lower than what could be expected, and the training time is significant. Since the entire data is quite large since the entire data must be used, it becomes extensive.

HIAS is coupled with LSTM; LSTM, even though it is a deep learning model, the feature or data going to the LSTM the training is not concerning dataset itself. Still, it is based on the relationship and the auxiliary knowledge set into the system. The term enrichment is done using the WikiData and MediaWiki, where a high density of auxiliary knowledge is fed into the model. The LSTM is the deep learning approach. Long short-term memory acts as a very vivid classifier though it is computationally complex. When semantics is combined with the LSTM, an extremely high precision percentage, high recall percentage, high accuracy percentage, high F-measure percentage and exceptionally low FNR are achieved. The semantic similarity computation using the semantic similarity model under the squirrel search algorithm ensures that the solution set is optimised, and the best fit solution set is yielded from the initial set of solutions which the SSA furnishes. Also, the ontology generation from the summarised content geological e-books and the crop information ensures that a good amount of verified vivid auxiliary and background knowledge is incorporated into the approach. These are further used for inferencing or feature for learning. It accelerates precision, recall, and accuracy and decreases the error rate.

We did not use a recent classifier because recent classifier is because LSTM is by itself a robust classifier; beyond this, using up to date classifier would be a good solution; however, it may not be relevant here. A robust classifier is required only for coarse level classification, and classification is not a finalized model; when the current method is used sometimes, it leads to overclassification. However, whatever the outcome of the LSTM classifier is further seasoned, chosen, and optimized using optimization algorithm and relevance computation semantic similarity with various indices with the differential threshold at every instance in the framework. So that is why LSTM is the best fit factor compared to the previous or recent model. However, LSTM is the best deep learning model, which is the best fit for textual data when the data concentration is very high.

The RNN, CNN, ANN and RCNN [1] are chosen as vase-lined models. They are incorporated in the HIAS approach in the same environment, and experimentation is conducted to record the precision, recall, accuracy, F-measure and FNR values.

Figure 2 depicts the precision versus the number of instances of the proposed approach. It is noticeably clear that despite the number of instances, the proposed HIAS approach has the highest precision percentage. The RNN, CNN, ANN and RCNN [1] have much lower precision than the number of instances.

HIAS performs better mainly because term-enrichment uses WikiData and MediaWiki, where auxiliary knowledge and verified instances are incorporated into the approach. LSTM, which is a deep learning classifier, is used, but it is not framed directly to the data but with the relation and generating ontologies. The metaheuristic algorithm under the semantic search ensures that the solution sets are yielded. The yielded solution sets are the best solutions used for further classification. The ontology generated ensures the knowledge density is exceptionally high and as a result proposed HIAS is much better than other approaches. As previously said, ANN was not chosen for this project since it is severe, and the calculations are high.

Similarly, while CNN is computationally expensive and feature extraction is automatic, the types of features that go into the approach are uncontrollable. While RNN is computationally expensive, it is not worth it when used as a standalone model because the standard accuracy is significantly lower. Finally, the difficulty with the RCNN [1]

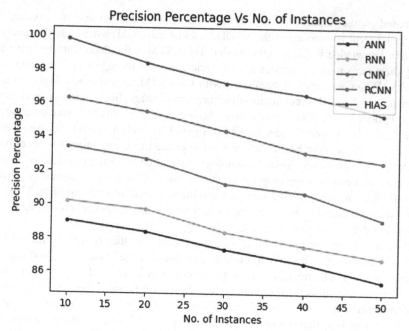

Fig. 2. Precision percentage Vs No. of instances

model is that the training network ring time is quite long. As a result, HIAS is picked as the ultimate method.

6 Conclusions

For soil classification and crop suggestion, the suggested model uses the Hybrid Intelligence Approach. The suggestions are based on the input queries of the user and the southern South Australian dataset, which are precisely linked to provide further accuracy and F-Measure than other baseline models. The input user query and Soil Dataset are pre-processed in the proposed model. Term enrichment is done in a dataset using WikiData and MediaWiki. Categorisation using LSTM with Similarity Measures using Jaccard, Cosine, and SemantoSim under Squirrel search algorithm as Optimisation algorithm yields better precision, recall, accuracy, and F-Measure percentages with a low FNR when ensembled. Experiments have shown that utilising Ontology creation, Term enrichment, LSTM Classification, and Similarity Measures using Jaccard, Cosine, and SemantoSim under the Squirrel search algorithm as an optimiser improves recommendation quality. The HIAS model has a 99.78% overall accuracy and a low FNR of 0.01, making it the best class system for crop recommendation. As part of future work, by changing optimization algorithm with upcoming meta-heuristic algorithms will be made to improve the model's efficacy.

References

1. Selvi, S., Saravanan, V.: Mapping and classification of soil properties from text dataset using recurrent convolutional neural network. ICTACT Journal on Soft Computing **11**(4), 2438–2443 (2021)
2. Mythili, K., Rangaraj, R.: Crop recommendation for better crop yield for precision agriculture using ant colony optimization with deep learning method. Annals of the Romanian Society for Cell Biology, 4783–4794 (2021)
3. Rahman, S.A.Z., Mitra, K.C., Islam, S.M.: Soil classification using machine learning methods and crop suggestion based on soil series. In: 2018 21st International Conference of Computer and Information Technology (ICCIT), pp. 1–4. IEEE (2018 December)
4. Kulkarni, N.H., Srinivasan, G.N., Sagar, B.M., Cauvery, N.K.: Improving crop productivity through a crop recommendation system using ensembling technique. In: 2018 3rd International Conference on Computational Systems and Information Technology for Sustainable Solutions (CSITSS), pp. 114–119. IEEE (2018 December)
5. Masare, Y., Mahale, S., Kele, M., Upadhyay, A., Nandwalkar, B.: Maximize the yielding rate of crops using machine learning algorithm. In: International Journal of Research and Technology, ISSN, 2278–0181 (2020)
6. Varsha, A., Midhuna, V.M., Rilty, A.P., Divya, R.: Soil Classification and Crop recommendation using IoT and Machine Learning (2020)
7. Pudumalar, S., Ramanujam, E., Rajashree, R.H., Kavya, C., Kiruthika, T., Nisha, J.: Crop recommendation system for precision agriculture. In: 2016 Eighth International Conference on Advanced Computing (ICoAC), pp. 32–36. IEEE (2017 January)
8. Kussul, N., Lavreniuk, M., Skakun, S., Shelestov, A.: Deep learning classification of land cover and crop types using remote sensing data. IEEE Geosci. Remote Sens. Lett. **14**(5), 778–782 (2017)
9. Murali, P., Revathy, R., Balamurali, S., Tayade, A.S.: Integration of RNN with GARCH refined by whale optimization algorithm for yield forecasting: a hybrid machine learning approach. Journal of Ambient Intelligence and Humanized Computing, 1-13 (2020)
10. Doshi, Z., Nadkarni, S., Agrawal, R., Shah, N.: Agroconsultant: Intelligent crop recommendation system using machine learning algorithms. In: 2018 Fourth International Conference on Computing Communication Control and Automation (ICCUBEA), pp. 1–6. IEEE (2018 August)
11. Jain, M., Singh, V., Rani, A.: A novel nature-inspired algorithm for optimization: Squirrel search algorithm. Swarm Evol. Comput. **44**, 148–175 (2019)
12. Lacasta, J., Lopez-Pellicer, F.J., Espejo-García, B., Nogueras-Iso, J., Zarazaga-Soria, F.J.: Agricultural recommendation system for crop protection. Comput. Electron. Agric. **152**, 82–89 (2018)
13. Kumar, V., Dave, V., Bhadauriya, R., Chaudhary, S.: Krishimantra: agricultural recommendation system. In: Proceedings of the 3rd ACM Symposium on Computing for Development, pp. 1–2 (2013 January)
14. Rajak, R.K., Pawar, A., Pendke, M., Shinde, P., Rathod, S., Devare, A.: Crop recommendation system to maximize crop yield using machine learning technique. Int. Res. J. Eng. Technol. **4**(12), 950–953 (2017)
15. Banavlikar, T., Mahir, A., Budukh, M., Dhodapkar, S.: Crop recommendation system using neural networks. Int. Res. J. Eng. Technol. (IRJET) **5**(5), 1475–1480 (2018)
16. Priyadharshini, A., Chakraborty, S., Kumar, A., Pooniwala, O.R.: Intelligent crop recommendation system using machine learning. In: 2021 5th International Conference on Computing Methodologies and Communication (ICCMC), pp. 843–848. IEEE (2021 April)

17. Arulmozhivarman, M., Deepak, G.: OWLW: ontology focused user centric architecture for web service recommendation based on LSTM and whale optimization. In: European, Asian, Middle Eastern, North African Conference on Management & Information Systems, pp. 334–344. Springer, Cham (2021 March)
18. Ortiz-Rodriguez, F., Medina-Quintero, J.M., Tiwari, S., Villanueva, V.: EGODO Ontology: Sharing, Retrieving, and Exchanging Legal Documentation Across E-Government. In: Futuristic Trends for Sustainable Development and Sustainable Ecosystems, pp. 261–276. IGI Global (2022)
19. Villazón-Terrazas, B., Ortiz-Rodríguez, F., Tiwari, S.M., Shandilya, S.K.: Knowledge graphs and semantic web. Springer International Publishing (2021)
20. Tiwari, S., Al-Aswadi, F.N., Gaurav, D.: Recent trends in knowledge graphs: theory and practice. Soft. Comput. **25**(13), 8337–8355 (2021). https://doi.org/10.1007/s00500-021-057 56-8
21. Palvannan, S., Deepak, G.: TriboOnto: a strategic domain ontology model for conceptualization of tribology as a principal domain. In: International Conference on Electrical and Electronics Engineering, pp. 215–223. Springer, Singapore (2022)
22. Deepak, G.: Conceptualization, Modeling, Visualization, and Evaluation of Specialized Domain Ontologies for Nano-energy as a Domain. In: Data Science and Security, pp. 199–208. Springer, Singapore (2022)

Education 5.0 Maturity Index: Concept and Prospects for Development

Volodymyr Skitsko⬤ and Olha Osypova(✉)⬤

Kyiv National Economic University Named After Vadym Hetman, 54/1 Peremoga Avenue, Kyiv 03057, Ukraine
{skitsko,osypova}@kneu.edu.ua

Abstract. E-governance covers all areas of society where the state regulates activities, manages processes, and so on. Education is no exception. In the context of digital transformations and challenges of recent years, the state's managerial capabilities in the field of education have become even more relevant. Therefore, there is a need for a comprehensive understanding of changes in the field of education and identification of future directions for its development in order to take into account the development of digital technologies and future possible crises.

This paper further developed the ideas of Education 4.0, as well as describes the author's vision of the new trend Education 5.0. The result of the research is a conceptual vision of the Education 5.0 Maturity Index, which is a comprehensive indicator consisting of the following components: Participants in the learning process; Knowledge acquisition; Location; Technical Learning tools and Learning outcomes.

Participants in the learning process are the teacher and the learner. The "Knowledge acquisition" covers the sources of knowledge; the curriculum; methods and techniques of the learning process. The "Location" describes the location of the learner and teacher during the learning process. The "Technical learning tools" describes technical tools and learning technologies (EdTech) are used in the learning process. The "Learning outcomes" characterizes the type of education document and the obtained digital competencies proficiency level.

The concept of the Education 5.0 Maturity Index presented in this paper requires further development towards providing its components with qualitative and quantitative characteristics.

Keywords: Education 5.0 · Digital transformation · Education 5.0 maturity index

1 Introduction

Over the past decade, we have had the opportunity to observe the rapid digital transformation and spread of new technologies in our daily lives. Today we are dealing with such technologies as Artificial Intelligence (AI), Internet of Things (IoT), Virtual and Augmented reality (VR/AR) at home, at work and anywhere. The Covid-19 pandemic and the resulting quarantine restrictions have made our lives more digital, and educational institutions have also undergone significant transformations under the influence of accelerated digitalization. Virtual classrooms and online learning quickly became commonplace, and everyone had to quickly adapt to this way of learning [1].

Before COVID-19, it was customary to talk about the new concept of Education 4.0, which was formed in response to the requirements of Industry 4.0. In turn, Industry 4.0 relies on the creation of cyber-physical systems, the widespread use of digital technologies and automation. Education has been directly affected as digital technologies have become widely used in the learning process, and new skills have emerged that help humans and machines interact and that both learners and teachers should master.

The use of technology in education has huge potential. Today, using technology, we can organize the educational process in a way that was almost impossible to organize a few years ago. Learning using technology has many advantages, such as cost-effectiveness, the ability to reach a wider audience, the possibility of personalized learning, flexibility, etc. Without a doubt, digital technologies are an excellent tool for education. However, it is worth remembering that while digital technologies are an important tool for education, they cannot fully replace other tools for education. Moreover, improper and inappropriate use of technology can harm the learning process. For example, digitizing outdated content and inefficient learning methods does not improve the efficiency and quality of learning. In addition, some of the non-digital approaches that are currently relevant and effective may lose their effectiveness in digitized form [2, 3].

Also, distance learning during the pandemic highlighted such problems that both learners and teachers faced[1]: difficulties in adapting the latest technologies, reduced motivation, reduced student performance, deterioration of physical and emotional state, rapid fatigue. And most importantly, quarantine restrictions in educational institutions have clearly shown that live communication is extremely important in the learning process, especially for elementary school students, first-year students, as well as when students begin to study a new discipline with a new teacher [2].

Thus, distance learning in the full sense of the term has both its advantages and disadvantages. More and more experts suggest move towards the concepts of Industry 5.0 and Society 5.0, which provide for the "humanization" of all spheres of life, focusing on a human and his needs, and deepening effective and efficient cooperation between people and machines. Therefore, the concept of education should be rethought in two dimensions – the "humanization" of education and the transformation of the learning process itself and the acquisition of new knowledge. The "humanization" of education involves assigning a key role in education to the person, and not to technology. With this human-centered approach, technologies take into account human needs and are designed to make the learning process more comfortable, exciting and efficient. As for the adaptation of the learning process to the realities of today, the main changes should relate to changing the role of the teacher and his functions. Since now a huge amount of information is freely available, the teacher is no longer the main source of knowledge.

---

[1] In the paper, the term "learnen" refers to a person who studies at any educational institution or is engaged in self-education (school students, college and university students, PhD students, course participants, etc.). By the term "teacher" we mean a person who teaches (school teachers, university teachers, coaches, tutors, etc.).

In addition, AI is endowed with the ability to collect, analyze and transmit information to a person, which makes it a potential substitute for teachers in the process of providing knowledge to learners. Thus, today teachers are not those who only transmit information to learners, but those who help learners to develop certain skills, motivate learners to learn, stimulate their cognitive activity and guide them in the right direction in the learning process [4]. These approaches to learning are embodied in the new concept of Education 5.0.

The organisation of the paper is designed in the following way. In Sect. 2 we briefly describe the concepts of Industry 5.0, Society 5.0, and discuss why the above concepts require further transformation of education and the transition to Education 5.0. In Sect. 3 we briefly outline the path of transformation from Education 1.0 to Education 4.0. In Sect. 4, we reveal in more detail the main idea of the concept Education 5.0 and describe the main educational trends that will prevail during Education 5.0. In Sect. 5, we describe our own vision for the Education 5.0 Maturity Index.

2 Industry 5.0, Society 5.0 and Their Impact on Future Education

A Brief Description of Industry 5.0 and Society 5.0. The concept of Industry 5.0 complements the main features of the concept of Industry 4.0, which was formed in Germany and described in detail by Klaus Schwab in his book "The fourth industrial revolution" [5]. According to Schwab, a characteristic features of Industry 4.0 is "the fusion of technologies that blurs the boundaries between the physical, digital and biological spheres, collectively called cyberphysical systems" [5]. Over recent years, the concept of Industry 4.0 has focused less on the initial principles of social justice and sustainable development, and more on digitalization and the implementation of new technologies to improve the efficiency and flexibility of production.

The concept of Industry 5.0 suggests shifting the focus of attention and emphasizes the importance of innovation and the introduction of new technologies for the development of industry based on the principles of social justice and sustainable development. It is important to emphasize that Industry 5.0 should not be characterized as a chronological continuation or replacement of the existing Industry 4.0 paradigm. Industry 5.0 complements and extends the main features of Industry 4.0 [6]. The combination of knowledge, experience, competencies of specialists (people) and technology capabilities has a synergy effect in the context of digital transformations for both production and employees. Therefore, Industry 5.0 provides safer, more comfortable and ergonomic working conditions that provide employees with various opportunities to use a creative approach to solve various work tasks, master new professional roles and constantly improve their skills. The main idea of Industry 5.0 is that the use of technologies are based on an ethical explanation of how technologies take into account human values and needs, and not just what technologies can achieve from a purely technical or economic point of view. Technologies such as human-machine interfaces, combining the capabilities of the human intelligence with artificial intelligence, or collaborating with robots and machines are used to create products and services. A special feature of such products and services is that they can be further adapted to the needs of customers, reduce the impact on the environment and allow you to implement concepts such as energy self-sufficiency, emission neutrality or a closed-loop economy [7]. That is, in Industry 5.0, instead of putting new technologies at the center of the production process and using their potential to improve efficiency, a human-centered approach is used, when in industrial enterprises the main human needs and interests are taken into account in the production process [6].

The Society 5.0 concept was formed in 2016 by Japan's most important business federation, Keidanren. Subsequently, the Japanese government supported this concept and took a course towards Society 5.0. Society 5.0 is described as "a super-smart society" in which physical space and cyberspace are closely integrated [8]. The concept of Society 5.0 is designed to harmoniously combine economic development with the solution of social and environmental problems. Society 5.0 is a society in which advanced IT technologies, the Internet of things, robots, artificial intelligence and augmented reality are actively used in everyday life, industry, healthcare and other areas of activity, primarily not for economic benefits, but for the benefit and convenience of each person [6]. The goal of Society 5.0 is to create a human-centered society in which both economic development and social problem solving are achieved, and people can enjoy a high quality of life that is fully active and comfortable. It is a society that will take care of different needs of people, regardless of place of residence, age, gender, language, etc., providing the necessary goods and services. The key to its implementation is the fusion of cyberspace and the real world, which will create new values and solutions for solving social problems [9].

Impact of Industry 5.0 and Society 5.0 on Education. The key difference between the two new concepts of Society 5.0 and Industry 5.0 and their previous generations is that Society/Industry 5.0 implements the principles of personalization and a human-centered approach much more widely than Society 4.0 and Industry 4.0 [10]. The concepts of Society 5.0 and Industry 5.0 emphasize the need to rethink existing methods and approaches to innovation and focus them on developing human-centered solutions and on social innovations. Society 5.0 and Industry 5.0 reflect a fundamental shift in societies and economies towards a new concept that allows us to harmoniously combine economic development with solving social, environmental and problems related to human-machine interaction. In this new concept, the importance of knowledge is determined not only by competitiveness and productivity, but also by taking into account the creation of social well-being, the impact on quality of life and the joint creation of knowledge within the framework of public-private partnerships. The new concepts also emphasize that even the most advanced technologies should not be superior to humanity [11, 12]. It is clear that along with the development of new concepts of Industry 5.0 and Society 5.0, there is also a change in the way we learn using e-learning technologies and tools [13]. A number of researchers note that educational institutions can play an important role in building a super-intelligent society and are mainly tasked with preparing people to live and work in such a society. But to do this, teachers at all levels need to be prepared for the challenges they face when moving to the concepts of Industry 5.0 and Society 5.0 [10, 11, 14].

And here the question arises: how will the concept of education change in order to meet the requirements of Industry 5.0 and Society 5.0, and how can education help shift the focus from technologies to humans in all spheres of our lives.

As we noted above, the concept of education should be rethought in two dimensions: assigning a key role in education to a human, not technology, humanizing education; rethinking the very approach to the learning process and obtaining new knowledge. If we describe the necessary transformations in education in more detail, then in order to meet the requirements of Industry 5.0 and Society 5.0, educational systems must follow such prospective directions [3, 11, 15]:

- Education and training should ensure the mobility of skilled workers between professions and sectors.
- Promote intelligent learning and create new flexible, inclusive, accessible and adaptive learning systems for all generations.
- Learners have the opportunity to participate in the development of curricula.
- Promote cross-sectoral and multilateral cooperation, especially by strengthening cooperation between industry, academia and education.
- In the process of digitalization of education, systematically take into account social and sustainable development priorities.
- Finding the right combination of traditional learning and using technology.
- Support initiatives aimed at improving teacher skills and encouraging innovation in teaching.
- Encourage the use of artificial intelligence wherever it can be useful in the learning process. At the same time, adhere to a responsible approach to training and research in order to prevent the negative impact of AI.
- Promote new learning programs focused on the eco-friendly, digital, quantitative and ethical skills needed to ensure efficient and proper use of AI and comfortable human-machine interaction.
- Pay more attention to the social, emotional and physical well-being of students.
- Learning provides development of not only professional and digital skills, but also soft skills (collaboration, empathy, tolerance for diversity, creativity, conflict management, etc.).

The implementation of these principles and approaches in education will make learning using the new technologies more efficient and convenient and provide young people with the knowledge and skills necessary for a full life and comfortable coexistence with machines and AI in the new realities of Industry 5.0 and Society 5.0. These principles and approaches underlie the concept of Education 5.0, which will be described in detail in the following sections.

3   Evolution of Education

The internet, smartphones, smart watches, smart-anything have changed and continue to change the life of every person and the way people interact with each other, with business, with the service sector, and so on. The sphere of education is also undergoing changes. For the first time, a detailed description of various educational concepts was made by Jacques Gerstein. He described the concepts of Education 1.0, 2.0, 3.0, which were based on the origin and development of the concepts of Web 1.0, 2.0, 3.0 [16]. The next significant changes in education are associated with the emergence of Industry 4.0. The Education 4.0 concept focuses mainly on the widespread use of digital technologies and the development of new skills in accordance with the requirements of Industry 4.0. Today, the concept of Education 5.0 is being worked as a response to the emergence of Industry 5.0 and Society 5.0 and the spread of the idea of humanizing society. Based on [16, 17], we will briefly describe Education 1.0–4.0. The main ideas of the Education 5.0 concept are presented in the next section.

Education 1.0. Is based on a traditional approach to learning. In this concept of education, a teacher is the main source of knowledge, a learner is mainly assigned a passive role, the learning process involves simply transferring knowledge from teacher to learners. The learning process can take place using technologies (video lectures, e-books, websites), but it is not Interactive, since learners can only passively receive information and cannot interact with learning content (for example, comment or share content). A personalized approach to learning is not used.

Education 2.0. The learning process itself does not differ significantly from the previous concept, but the concept of Education 2.0 has a number of characteristic features. The learner's role in the learning process becomes more active. The development of social networks allows learners to interact with learning content (comment, share or even supplement learning content), actively communicate with each other and with the teacher in both synchronous and asynchronous modes. The use of technology allows you to conduct learning both in the classroom and online.

Education 3.0. Involves the use of personalized and interest-based approaches in learning. The roles of teacher and learner have changed. The learner is an active participant in the learning process, he can be the creator of knowledge that he shares with the teacher and other learners in social networks. The role of the teacher is to organize a learning environment (in the classroom or online) in which learners can develop their knowledge together. Another feature of Education 3.0 is the change of learning content, which should be available via the Internet with the ability to view and modify this content.

Education 4.0. Is based on the active use of technology, involves the active use of gadgets and interaction between humans and machines in the learning process. Online learning platforms and mobile applications are an excellent tool for personalized learning, allowing a learner to independently choose the pace of learning and form the curriculum. Technologies also allow teachers to monitor individual learning and development processes for each learner. The approach to learning has also changed significantly. Learning has a practical direction and involves not just gaining knowledge by learners, but working on real projects and acquiring skills that will be necessary for them in future work.

4 The Concept of Education 5.0

Despite the fact that the concept of Education 5.0 is currently being formed, there are already a small number of works that reveal the essence and describe the main features of the new concept of education. At the moment, there can be considerable uncertainty about what the new concept of education will bring and how it will affect society, business and our lives in detail, as well as the potential of Education 5.0 to blur the boundaries between the real and virtual worlds in the sphere of education. Education 5.0 involves the use of new technologies to provide more humane teaching, with a focus on learner's social and emotional development and solutions that improve life in society [1]. Education 5.0 can be defined as "an educational model of the future based on personalized education, learning flexibility, continuous improvement, critical thinking and problem solving, data interpretation, a student-led curriculum, project-based learning and, most importantly, the dynamics of partnership in technology and education that form the basis for creating the Society of the future" [18].

Although both Education 4.0 and Education 5.0 provides for the widespread use of technologies in the educational process, welcomes automation and human-machine interaction, but they are still somewhat different. In Education 4.0 the role of technology in education is to increase speed, accuracy, and efficiency in learning. The main idea is to introduce Industry 4.0 technologies into the learning process. It means that the goal of Education 4.0 is to bring education closer to the technological achievements of Industry 4.0, already used by society and companies, and to create a closer connection with new generations who can no longer live without technology.

Education 5.0 is a continuation of this idea. This concept does not negate Education 4.0 offerings, but adds a more humane approach to learning that focuses on developing learner's social and emotional skills. In addition, Education 5.0, as well as Industry 5.0 and Society 5.0, harmonizes the interaction between people and technology, putting people and their needs first, not technology.

Key Trends in Education 5.0. Based on works [3, 18, 19] we can indicate the following key trends in Education 5.0:

Trend 1. Personalized education. Since Education 5.0 is based on the principles of humanity and social inclusion, it is necessary to guarantee a full-fledged and high-quality education for everyone, regardless of their abilities and capabilities. Each person's learning ability, speed, curiosity, and developmental stages differ from each other. Therefore, the learning process should be flexible and adapted to the needs and capabilities of each learner. Also, personalized education allows learners to independently form their own learning trajectory, depending on their interests and the need to acquire new knowledge or develop new skills.

Trend 2. Lifelong learning. Today, technologies are changing at an incredible rate, radically changing all areas of our lives. The need for new skills is developing as fast as technologies. Employers are increasingly facing a shortage of qualified manpower and educational institutions do not have time to train in-demand qualified employees. As for employees, young people who are just starting their career path do not feel sufficiently equipped with the skills necessary for the future labor market [6]. According to a Deloitte study, 70% of young people realize that they only have some of the skills that will be required to build a successful career in the Future [20]. Therefore, employees who want to remain competitive will need to constantly improve their skills. Therefore, after completing the official part of education (for example, college or university), continuous learning and professional development should follow. This requires educational institutions to form an understanding of the need for self-education among their learners, as well as among their teachers. The Education 5.0 concept welcomes students' acquisition of the skills necessary for self-education in the learning process.

Trend 3. Reduced concentration of learners' attention. Simultaneously with the spread of technology in education and everyday life, learners' concentration time is decreasing. The tendency to reduce learners' concentration is caused by the very nature of technology [21]. First, constant distraction from gadgets and pocket-size devices reduces learners' ability to focus on work for a long time. Secondly, new technologies make it possible to add visualizations, audio and video effects to learning content which allows you to make learning content more interesting and exciting. Learners expect that the learning content will be exactly like this, otherwise they lose interest in it and start to be distracted by the smartphone, etc. Teachers should take into account the tendency to reduce concentration of learners' attention while they develop their classes and involve students in the learning process. And here you can use the latest technologies such as VR, AR, the use of 3-d images and digital twins.

Trend 4. Focus on acquiring soft skills. This trend may sound a little unexpected, but digital and professional skills aren't the only skills that will be relevant to employees of the future. So, the world manufacturing forum has identified the top 10 skills that will be needed in the future to work in factories and factories. Only four of them relate to digital skills: "digital literacy, artificial intelligence and data analysis", "working with new technologies", "cybersecurity" and "data mindfulness". Other skills are soft skills related to creative, entrepreneurial, flexible and unbiased thinking [22]. In addition, the ability of AI and machines to replace humans in certain types of work makes such purely "human" skills as emotional intelligence, empathy, critical thinking, and problem-solving skills particularly valuable. Therefore, in an effort to prepare students for their future careers, educational institutions should conduct training that helps students develop their soft skills. However, the widespread use of online learning does not contribute to the development of soft skills. Therefore, teachers will need to organize the learning process so that there is room for live communication in order to promote the development of soft skills.

Trend 5. Technologies. Although the concept of Education 5.0 gives a central place to a human, new technologies are still an extremely important part of this concept. It is technology that provides the opportunity to learn anytime, anywhere. Also, as noted above, creating interactive content and vivid visual effects using the latest technologies will allow teachers to better keep learners' attention and contribute to greater learner interest in the learning process. It is new technologies that make it possible to offer learners flexible and personalized learning. Finally, the active use of the latest technologies allows learners to acquire digital skills and improve their level of digital literacy, which is a prerequisite for a future successful career. Within the framework of the concept of Education 5.0, educational institutions should focus on providing learners with comprehensive information about their interaction with technology, and in particular about safety and ergonomics when using technology, as well as the possible consequences of excessive or improper exposure to technology. Also, the learning process should be organized in such a way that learners can develop the necessary skills that will allow them to use the latest technologies to solve social problems, ensure human well-being and comfortable living and working conditions.

5   Education 5.0 Maturity Index

Today, it is a common practice to construct Maturity Indices for various areas that are actively changing in the context of digital transformations, and therefore require constant monitoring of the progress of their development, tracking various changes, and so on. Examples of such well-known indices are the GovTech Maturity Index (GTMI) [23], Industrie 4.0 Maturity Index [24]. Inspired by the approach to constructing these indices and works on the evolution of education [16, 25–27], in this paper we describe our own vision regarding the Education 5.0 Maturity index. Namely, we chose the most informative and interesting, in our opinion, indicators that can be used to assess the educational Maturity Index 5.0, added some new indicators, clarified existing indicators, grouped indicators by areas of analysis of changes in education and based on these indicators characterized the concepts of education 1.0–5.0. The results are presented in Table 1.

Table 1. Education 5.0 maturity index: structural components.

Indicator	Education 1.0	Education 2.0	Education 3.0	Education 4.0	Education 5.0
Participants in the learning process					
Primary roles of student	Passive	Passive/active	Active, enthusiastic, string and confidence	Independent, active, innovative	SAP (students as partners), active, research
Primary roles of teachers	Source of knowledge	Guide and source of knowledge	Facilitator of collaborative knowledge creation	Monitor and observe of learning	Motivate in the learning process and stimulate the learner's cognitive activity
Knowledge acquisition					
Source of content	Traditional copyright materials	Copyright and free/open educational resources for students	E-books and educational websites	User-generated content, technology-based dynamic and 3D materials	AI, Big Data analysis
Curriculum structure	Rigid and fixed	Fixed/flexible	Just-in-time, Just-for-me, Just-enough	Flexible and organic	Are developed with the participation of learners
Methods & techniques	Traditional, transfer and reproduction of information, some group work within classroom	Cooperative learning, online learning	Blended and flipped learning, interactive learning	Problem-based learning and practice-based learning	Project-based learning, personalized learning
Location					
Location of institution	Specific building	Specific building, online	Everywhere in a creative society (cafes, libraries, workplaces, etc.)	Anytime, anywhere, any device, any platform, replacing the classroom	Anytime, anywhere, any device, any platform, replacing the classroom

(*continued*)

Table 1. (*continued*)

Indicator	Education 1.0	Education 2.0	Education 3.0	Education 4.0	Education 5.0
Academic mobility	Not common, as learners/usually need to change the place of residence	Increasing cooperation between universities, including through online learning	Entry of new institutions that provide higher education services, regional and institutional boundaries breakdown	Emergence of massive open online courses, informal and non-formal education becomes common-used learning activity	Boundaryless education
Technical learning tools					
Hardware & Software	Are purchased at great cost and ignored	Are open source and available at lower cost	Are available at low cost and are used purposively	Software-as-a-Service (SaaS), Platform-as-a-service (PaaS):	Software-as-a-Service (SaaS), Platform-as-a-service (PaaS):
				prevailing approach is Machine 2 Human (M2H)	prevailing approach is Human 2 Machine (H2M)
EdTech	PreEdTech: Video lectures, Internet (often lack any type of capabilities for the learner to comment, share or interact with the content)	PreEdTech: Video lectures, Internet, blogs, podcasts (the learner has a possibility to comment, share or interact with the content)	Collaborative web tools, mobile apps, social media	IoT, AI, VR, AR, MR, Simulations, Robotics:	IoT, AI, VR, AR, MR, Simulations, Robotics:
				prevailing approach is M2H	prevailing approach is H2M
Gadgets	Are forbidden at a classroom	Cautiously adopted	Bring Your Own Device (BYOD)	BYOD, Cloud-based, Gadgets on body:	BYOD, Cloud-based, Gadgets on body:
				prevailing approach is M2H	prevailing approach is H2M
Learning outcomes					
Education documents/verification of education documents	Paper, handwritten, plastic, printed on a printer or in a printing house/seal, ink signature, serial number	Paper, handwritten, plastic, printed on a printer or in a printing house/seal, ink signature, serial number	Paper, plastic, electronic document with electronic or digital signature/public and private keys	Paper, plastic, electronic document with electronic or digital signature, online registers of education (diplomas, certificates)/public and private keys	Paper, plastic, electronic document with electronic or digital signature, online registers of education (diplomas, certificates)/public and private keys
Digital competence according to DigComp 2.2 [28]	Digital competence proficiency level is foundation	Digital competence proficiency level is foundation/intermediate	Digital competence proficiency level is intermediate	Digital competence proficiency level is advanced	Digital competence proficiency level is highly specialised

Source: formed on the basis of [16, 25–28] and further developed by the authors

Further, we will briefly describe some of the index components. The curriculum structure defines the set of topics that the learner has to study and the list of skills and abilities that the learner has to master in order to successfully complete a certain stage of learning. Since the concept of Education 1.0 was based on the traditional approach to learning, the structure of the curriculum was rigid, the learner could not adjust or supplement the curriculum. Along with the spread of personalized education and interest-based learning, the curriculum is becoming more flexible and takes into account the wishes and capabilities of the learner.

Education documents/verification of education documents. This component describes what an education document is and how you can confirm or verify the originality of this document.

Digital competence according to DigComp 2.2. Digital literacy (or digital competence) is recognized by the EU as one of the 8 key competencies for a full life and activity. According to DigComp2.2, digital competence consists of such blocks of competencies as information and data literacy, communication and collaboration, digital content creation, safety, problem solving [28]. For each competence, DigComp2.2 describes 8 proficiency levels, which are grouped into the following levels: foundation, intermediate, and advanced highly specialized. Obviously, the required level of digital competencies for a particular person depends on the chosen profession (let's compare an IT specialist and a surgeon). However, in general, the level of digital competencies is growing along with the requirements of all professions for digital technology proficiency. Therefore, digital competence levels can also be applied to Education from 1.0 to 5.0.

To better understand that Education 5.0 and Education 4.0 are mostly similar, but there are some differences, we will provide a more detailed description of some indicators for the concept of Education 5.0:

- Primary roles of learner. Education 5.0 like Education 4.0 also assigns the learner an active, independent and innovative role. In addition, the concept of "student as a partner" is becoming widespread: all participants in the educational process have the opportunity to make an equal contribution. Teachers and learners can work together to improve teaching, learning, develop a curriculum, and participate in practical research [29]. So far, this approach is being implemented mainly in higher education institutions. However, the more significant the role of AI as a transmitter of knowledge and controller of acquired knowledge and skills becomes, the more promising this way of interaction between teachers and learners looks.
- Primary roles of teacher are: to motivate a learner in the learning process, to stimulate his cognitive activity; teach learners to effectively engage in self-study, find the necessary material for learning in compliance with the criteria of its reliability and relevance; teach to perform high-quality and objective self-testing, etc. in order to prepare the learners for further life in the context of the concept of lifelong learning.
- Hardware & Software, Technology, and Gadgets are similar to those used in Education 4.0. But when using technology, there is a shift in the focus of attention from technology to a human. Technologies are used primarily to meet the physical, mental and emotional needs of learners, and only then to improve the efficiency and speed of learning.

6 Conclusions

Education is the sphere of life that should work ahead of time, train specialists who are in demand now and in the near future. To do this, you need to clearly understand the needs of business, the needs of society and public authorities, in particular, in the context of e-governance. Therefore, it is necessary to constantly monitor the current situation and make a forecast for the development of society and business. This issue is becoming particularly relevant in the context of digital transformations, which have become a driver of accelerating changes in various areas. Such changes have led to a reduction in the period of relevance of a significant part of the knowledge that students receive in different educational institutions (schools, universities, academies online platforms, courses, etc.) in various ways (in classroom learning, online learning, blended learning). This does not apply to a greater extent to the fundamental sciences, in particular, mathematics, physics, chemistry, etc., but this problem is extremely relevant in the preparation of specialists in economics, IT, law, public administration (e-governance), etc. Accelerating change requires corresponding accelerated changes in the field of Education. At the same time, these changes should be balanced, economically justified, contribute to improving the level of education in general, meet the needs of learners and teachers. This question is no longer so much about education as a learning process, but about the management of education, education's development strategy and the fact that education should analyze its own situation, determine its advantages and disadvantages, and formulate guidelines for development.

In this paper, we formulated the author's vision of the "Education 5.0" trend, developed the ideas of other authors on digital transformations from Education 1.0 to Education 4.0, and described our own vision of the Education 5.0 Maturity Index. Education 5.0 Maturity Index consists of the following key components of the educational process: Participants in the learning process; Knowledge acquisition; Location; Technical learning tools, Learning outcomes. Participants in the learning process are teachers and learners, and their role changes during the transition from Education 1.0 to Education 5.0. The "Knowledge acquisition" component includes sources of knowledge (where participants in the educational process have the opportunity to receive information); the curriculum (a set of disciplines that are studied by the learner, during his learning); methods and techniques of the learning process (how the teacher and learners interact). The next component of "Location" explains the question of the location of the learner and teacher during the learner process, the need for premises. The fourth component of "Technical learning tools" combines hardware and software of the learning process, learning technologies (EdTech), gadgets (primarily technical devices that participants in the learning process can use in everyday life). The last component is called "Learning outcomes" and includes educational documents (what can be an educational document - a paper, plastic or electronic document, etc.) and the obtained digital competence proficiency level. This index comprehensively allows you to assess the processes of education development and will be useful for heads of educational institutions, representatives of public authorities who deal with education issues, politicians who determine trends in the development of society and the economy, and everyone else who deals with education issues.

In following research, we will focus on the further development of Education 5.0 Maturity Index, which will consist in providing its components not only with qualitative characteristics (description in words), but also with quantitative characteristics (design of rating scales, limit values of indicators, degree of influence of an individual component on the Education 5.0 Maturity Index), etc.

References

1. Education 5.0: What Does It Mean? How Does It Work? SYDLE. https://www.sydle.com/blog/education-5-0-61e71a99edf3b9259714e25a/ (2022). Retrieved 18 May 2022
2. Dervojeda, K.: Education 5.0: Rehumanising Education in the Age of Machines. Linkedin. https://www.linkedin.com/pulse/education-50-rehumanising-age-machines-kristina-dervojeda/ (2021). Retrieved 18 May 2022
3. Digital Education Action Plan (2021–2027): European Education Area (2020). https://education.ec.europa.eu/focus-topics/digital-education/about/digital-education-action-plan. Retrieved 18 May 2022
4. Rahim, M.N.: Post-pandemic of Covid-19 and the need for transforming education 5.0 in Afghanistan Higher Education. Utamax: J. Ultimate Res. Trends Educ. 3(1), 29–39 (2021). https://doi.org/10.31849/utamax.v3i1.6166
5. Schwab, K.: The fourth industrial revolution. Portfolio Penguin (2017)
6. European Commission: Directorate-general for research and innovation. In: Breque, M., De Nul, L., Petridis, A. (eds.) Industry 5.0: towards a sustainable, human-centric and resilient European industry. https://doi.org/10.2777/308407 (2021)
7. European Commission: Directorate-general for research and innovation. In: Müller, J. (eds.) Enabling Technologies for Industry 5.0: results of a workshop with Europe's technology leaders (2020). https://doi.org/10.2777/082634
8. Salgues, B.: Society 5.0: Industry of the Future, Technologies, Methods and Tools. Wiley-Iste (2018)
9. Fukuyama, M.: Society 5.0: aiming for a new human-centered society. Japan Spotlight 2, 47–50 (2018)
10. Mitchell, J., Guile, D.: Fusion skills and industry 5.0: conceptions and challenges. In: Bouezzeddine, M. (ed.) Insights into Global Engineering Education After the Birth of Industry 5.0. IntechOpen (2022). https://doi.org/10.5772/intechopen.100096
11. Carayannis, E. G., Morawska-Jancelewicz, J.: The Futures of Europe: Society 5.0 and Industry 5.0 as Driving Forces of Future Universities. J. Knowl. Econ. 13, 3445–3471 (2022). https://doi.org/10.1007/s13132-021-00854-2
12. European Commission: Directorate-general for research and innovation. In: Breque, M., De Nul, L., Petridis, A. (eds.) Industry 5.0: towards a sustainable, human-centric and resilient European industry (2021). https://doi.org/10.2777/308407
13. Sułkowski, Ł, Kolasińska-Morawska, K., Seliga, R., Morawski, P.: Smart learning technologization in the economy 5.0—the polish perspective. Appl. Sci. 11(11), 5261 (2021). https://doi.org/10.3390/app11115261
14. Grau, F. X., Goddard, J., Hall, B. L., Hazelkorn, E., Tandon, R.: Higher education in the world 6. Towards a socially responsible university: Balancing the global with the local. Global University Network for Innovation, Girona (2017)
15. Banholzer, V.M.: From "Industry 4.0" to "Society 5.0" and "Industry 5.0": Value- and Mission-Oriented Policies: Technological and Social Innovations – Aspects of Systemic Transformation. IKOM WP vol. 3, No. 2/2022. Technische Hochschule Nürnberg Georg Simon Ohm, Nürnberg (2022)
16. Gerstein, J.: Moving from education 1.0 through education 2.0 towards education 3.0. In: Blaschke, L.-M., et al. (eds.) Experience in Self-Determined Learning. Create Space Independent Publishing Platform, pp. 83–99 (2014).
17. Huk, T.: From education 1.0 to education 4.0 - challenges for the contemporary school. The New Educ. Rev. 66(4), 36–46 (2021). https://doi.org/10.15804/tner.21.66.4.03
18. Uysal, L.: EDUCATION 5.0. Levent Uysal. https://www.leventuysal.com/2021/03/28/education-5-0/ (2021). Retrieved 22 May 2022

19. 5 Trends in Education that continue in 2022. Hospitality news. https://hospitalityinsights.ehl. edu/education-trends-2022 (2021). Retrieved 22 May 2022
20. Global, D.: Deloitte research reveals a "generation disrupted": Growing up in a world of accelerated transformation leaves Millennials and Gen Zs feeling unsettled about the future www.prnewswire.com.   https://www.prnewswire.com/news-releases/deloitte-research-rev eals-a-generation-disrupted-growing-up-in-a-world-of-accelerated-transformation-leaves-millennials-and-gen-zs-feeling-unsettled-about-the-future-300851008.html (n.d.). Retrieved 20 May 2022
21. McSpadden, K.: You Now Have a Shorter Attention Span Than a Goldfish. Time. https:// time.com/3858309/attention-spans-goldfish/ (2015). Retrieved 19 May 2022
22. World Manufacturing Forum Report: Skills for the Future of Manufacturing. https://wor ldmanufacturing.org/wp-content/uploads/WorldManufacturingFoundation2019-Report.pdf (2019)
23. Dener, C., et al.: GovTech Maturity Index. World Bank, Washington, DC (2021). https://doi. org/10.1596/978-1-4648-1765-6
24. Schuh, G., Anderl, R., Gausemeier, J., ten Hompel, M., Wahlster, W. (eds.) Industrie 4.0 Maturity Index: Managing the Digital Transformation of Companies. Utz, München (2017). ISBN: 978-3-8316-4613-5
25. Mokhtar, S., Alshboul, J.A.Q., Shahin, G.O.A.: Towards data-driven education with learning analytics for educator 4.0. J. Phys.: Conf. Ser. **1339**(1), 012079 (2019). https://doi.org/10. 1088/1742-6596/1339/1/012079
26. Bongomin, O., et al.: Industry 4.0 disruption and its neologisms in major industrial sectors: a state of the art. J. Eng. **2020**, 1–45 (2020). https://doi.org/10.1155/2020/8090521
27. Keats, D., Schmidt, P.: The genesis and emergence of education 3.0 in higher education and its potential for Africa. First Monday, **12**(3) (2007). https://doi.org/10.5210/fm.v12i3.1625
28. Vuorikari, R., Kluzer, S., Punie, Y.: DigComp 2.2: The Digital Competence Framework for Citizens –With new examples of knowledge, skills and attitudes. Publications Office of the European Union (2022). https://doi.org/10.2760/115376
29. Healey, M., Flint, A., Harrington, K.: Students as Partners: Reflections on a Conceptual Model. Teach. Learn. Inq.: The ISSOTL J. **4**(2), 8–20 (2016). https://doi.org/10.20343/teachl earninqu.4.2.3

Interpretability of AI Systems in Electronic Governance

Antonella Carbonaro[✉]

Department of Computer Science and Engineering – DISI, Alma Mater Studiorum, University of
Bologna, Bologna, Italy
antonella.carbonaro@unibo.it

Abstract. Modern electronic governance systems require cutting-edge analytical techniques to manage available ever-larger and distributes data, with a known spread of unstructured and unlabeled text documents. Many organizations are turning to data governance to exercise control over the quality of their data and their processes in order to guarantee the delivery of trustworthy decisions. In this context, modern AI breakthroughs give new opportunities to impact many application scenarios, like knowledge extraction and exploration in electronic governance. In this paper we introduce the need to build interpretable AI systems for electronic governance in order to improve trust and consequently user acceptance, highlighting some emergent topics and open challenges, mainly linked to integrating quantitative and qualitative techniques, such as deep learning and knowledge graphs for semantic-aware models.

Keywords: E-governance · Computational intelligence · Semantic web · Neural-symbolic learning · Knowledge graphs

1 Introduction

The progress of the digital economy is continuously accelerated by the dynamic relationship between the advancement of information and communication technologies and the development of real-world problems. Data has become an increasingly valuable driver for the transition of societies towards data-driven economies characterized by rapid innovation. Today, data is an economic resource; those who can collect, store, transform and utilize data are in power. Therefore, the intelligence gathered from the process of analyzing and learning data enhances our knowledge through modern artificial intelligence breakthroughs (AI) and computational intelligence (CI). CI systems constitute a set of information processing methodologies that have been developed to address complex real-world problems based on big data that can no longer be solved and optimized with traditional techniques. Modern electronic governance systems require cutting-edge analytical techniques to manage these ever-larger datasets, with a known spread of unstructured and unlabeled text documents. CI systems process enormous amounts of data to answer specific tasks and make customized intelligent analyses, potentially improving the productivity of the public administration and the quality of user's response.

© The Author(s), under exclusive license to Springer Nature Switzerland AG 2022
F. Ortiz-Rodríguez et al. (Eds.): EGETC 2022, CCIS 1666, pp. 109–116, 2022.
https://doi.org/10.1007/978-3-031-22950-3_9

In previous paper [1], we reported on our experiences in using linked data and semantic technologies to model context information in policy-making. We described three case studies: the first one modeled concepts related to the statistical domain of graduate surveys; the second experience modeled data on a student's entire school career from primary to secondary school and the third framework modeled the Great and General Council of the Single Chamber Parliament of the Republic of San Marino, the body responsible for the country's legislative power, within which laws, decrees and regulations are presented, discussed, amended, approved or rejected. The objective of this paper is twofold. First, to define and conceptualize data governance for AI-based data governance systems. Second, to examine the challenges and approaches of such governance by proposing the concept of interpretable and thus trustworthy AI-based governance systems.

The use of AI for improving and opening government is met with a lot of enthusiasm. However, electronic governance relies heavily on the use of data combined from various sources, some controlled by the public organization, others controlled by partner organizations, yet others controlled by users. Without control over such data to ensure quality and compliance, AI systems would be too risky to be entrusted with consequential decisions. Therefore, many organizations are turning to data governance to exercise control over the quality of their data and their processes in order to guarantee the delivery of trustworthy decisions. The concept of trustworthiness refers to properties through which a trusted entity is serving the interests of the trustor [2].

Lately, the field of trustworthy AI has been gaining attention from the government and different scientific communities. The International Organization for Standardization, The European Union, The National Institute of Standards and Technology and The U.S. Government Accountability Office have presented different approaches, ethical guidelines, and frameworks to establish trust in AI systems using the properties of fairness, transparency, accountability, and controllability and for trustworthy AI to govern and facilitate the development AI systems [3–6]. The EU also passed a law called General Data Protection Regulation (GDPR), which gives individuals the "right to explanations" for AI decisions [7]. The Defense Advanced Research Project Agency [8] also launched a program known as Explainable Artificial Intelligence, whose motive was to make these AI systems explainable and trustworthy. Gartner estimates that 30% of all AI-based digital products will require the use of a trustworthy AI framework by 2025 [9], and 86% of users will trust and remain loyal to companies that use ethical AI principles [10].

These examples demonstrate the current necessity to develop AI systems using a trustworthy framework and how vital trustworthiness is for both the success of AI systems and the safety of users and society.

2 Data Governance for Trusted AI Systems

While most government organizations today recognize that data are crucial, creating a culture that treats data as a resource and uses it for decision support is challenging [11]. While data governance should help to reduce the cost management of data and create value from data, it is often fragmented across many organizations implementing different data policies. This can lead to distributed and unclear responsibilities and unknown data quality, which may compromise the suitability of the use of such data within electronic governance systems [12–14]. A common challenge with data governance is that the flow and data logic may not follow the structure of an organization. The mismatch between organizational structure and data usage can easily lead to data silos, duplication, unclear responsibilities and lack of control of the of the data during their entire life cycle. This is particularly the case with data governance approaches, which generally cross departmental boundaries, are not bound to any function or process, and have to manage data from several multiple departmental silos [15, 16]. The main requirements that need to be taken into account when modelling context information for electronic governance are:

- Heterogeneity: Context information models have to deal with a large variety of context information sources that differ in their update rate and their semantic level [17]. A context model should be able to express different types of context information and the context management system should provide management of the information depending on its type. For example, in open government data, different organizations, institutions and agencies published their data on the community's net, i.e., social work, industry, tourism, education, climate change, transport, health, etc. USA government began the federal government's open data site (www.data.gov) to make government more transparent and accountable in its policies. Open government data increased citizen participation in government, created economic development opportunities, and constituted informed decision-making in private and public sectors [18]. In [19], the authors present a usability study of 41 different unique open government data portals, highlighting the most commonly occurring usability issues associated with open government data portals. Dati.gov.it is the national catalogue of open data of Italian public administrations. It was created with the aim of aggregating in a single portal most of the open data displayed by the various administrations, both local and national in order to promote transparency and re-use.

- Relationships and dependencies: one of the most important characteristics of context modelling systems is relationships between context information entities. For example, we want to express logical constraints and detailed relationships such as disjoint, inverse, part-of, and so on. Even if data is pooled and linked at the conceptual level, physical storage and responsibility for data should be distributed to reduce vulnerability. Pooling and linking should ensure that data is interrelated and can easily be combined, if needed. The concepts of LOD data sharing and reuse are at the core of the FAIR data principles, that is, findable, accessible, interoperable and reusable data. However, governance mechanisms should ensure that data can only be shared if the right authorization or approval by the data protection officer, are met [20]. All the work involved in relationship and dependencies representation can directly benefit users by helping them to visualize and comprehend the relationships between concepts in the different domains. This can trigger associative ways of processing, reflecting and analyzing information.

- Imperfection: Due to its dynamic and heterogeneous nature, data governance information may be of variable quality [21]. For example, the context information may be incomplete or conflicting with other context information. Thus, a good context modelling approach must include modelling of context information quality to support reasoning about context. Reasoning can also be used for automatically detecting inconsistency of the knowledge base [17, 22].

- Reasoning: It is important that the context modelling techniques are able to support both consistency verification of the model and context reasoning techniques. The later can be used to derive new context facts from existing context facts and/or reason about high-level context abstractions that model real world situations [23, 24]. The intrinsic potential of context representation can be exploited using sophisticated data analysis techniques such as automatic reasoning to find patterns and extract information and knowledge in order to enhance decision-making and deliver better governance resources and feedback to users.

In this framework, we believe that linked data, ontologies and reasoning technologies can be considered a natural extension to context modelling approaches to meet the needs of heterogeneity, imperfection and need for reasoning. Using these approaches can improve transparency, foster innovation by exploiting the social and economic value of published data and foster the active participation of citizens in governance processes. The above motivations, while not being the sole ones, are the foundations for most open government data initiatives.

3 Emergent Topics in Interpretable AI Systems

So far, AI techniques have been distinguished according to two main paradigms with complementary strengths. The subsymbolic paradigm, linked to the theories of connectionism driven by neuroscience, and the symbolic paradigm, focused on transforming perceptual stimuli in symbols and rules. The first one comprises Machine Learning and Deep Learning, while the second incorporates Semantic Web, Ontologies, and Knowledge Graphs (KGs). However, the growing complexity of applications has led many experts to believe that the future demands a fusion of these approaches, mixing performance and flexibility with structure, reasoning, and transparency to cover the gap in interpretable AI systems when dealing with complex cognitive processes, as presented below [25].

Learning, that is the process for synthesizing new knowledge and connecting new information with existing knowledge. In highly complex contexts such as electronic governance, it is crucial to set up a dynamic, non-linear knowledge representation to link abstract concepts to concrete representations, and to accelerate the learning process of next-generation systems [26, 27]. The representation must also facilitate learning under conditions of uncertainty, typical of machine learning approaches, where uncertainty may arise from both the data (e.g., noisy data, incorrect measurements, missing data) and the model (e.g. model structure and parameters). In addition, further sources of uncertainty may be those arising from human error, system malfunctioning or lack of information.

Language, that is the process for understanding and communicating through natural and meaning-based language. The recent focus on Natural Language Under-standing (NLU) and Natural Language Generation–related research can help to reduce the gap of understanding user interaction, solving ambiguity, and dealing with uncertainty. Advances in these areas can help in developing systems capable of interfacing with different users and their specificities (e.g., an organizations, citizens and businesses, and society at large), including choosing the level of detail for context-aware interaction [28]. Moreover, learning users' preferences explicitly and implicitly from their interaction with the system can also lead to more user-friendly systems. Advanced techniques for understanding communication and generating accurate and personalized dialogue should be integrated for more realistic, context-aware and accurate interaction.

Reasoning, that is the process for drawing conclusions, making predictions or building models with the help of existing knowledge. Exposing the decision-making process that led the AI system to suggest a decision in the different stages of the systems can prove to be of great help in increasing users' confidence and consequently their acceptance of the system [29]. For instance, the adoption of AI-based support systems among governance professionals could be increased and support everyday practices if its interpretability were increased. In this case, emerging uses of technology can generate four forms of intelligence (data intelligence, Artificial Intelligence, collective intelligence and embodied intelligence) that have the potential to improve development decisions and accelerate progress [30].

Current state-of-the-art contributions belong to the subsymbolic category but still have several problems concerning explainability, small data, and computational needs. In fact, labeling costs and small task-specific datasets can prevent the application of sophisticated deep learning methods, which instead demand large quantities of high-quality annotations, expensive and slow to produce in the medical domain [6]. On the other hand, developing interpretable and trustable models is crucial in areas where bad decisions can compromise usage, frequently preventing the adoption of opaque solutions. Mixed AI, together with topics like Explainable Artificial Intelligence (XAI) and Neural-Symbolic Learning, are promising research directions for the next future [31]. Furthermore, we argue that greater attention should be paid to the exploitation of existing domain resources, as described in previous Section. Injecting such knowledge into neural networks may provide the latter with a form of commonsense capable of significantly increasing downstream performance, better generalizing to unseen sub-specialties, taking advantage of implicit information, encouraging zero/few-shot settings, and exercising superior control over what is truly enclosed in learned parameters. Moreover, governance cognitive computing systems need be trained with knowledge of populations, guidelines, or workflows represented by these existing domain resources, for context-aware and personalized interventions, as proposed in [32].

Natural Language Processing (NLP) is remarkably rising because of its recognized potential for automatically searching, analyzing, reviewing, and interpreting giant (and ever-growing) quantities of unstructured text documents. Particularly, NLU is on the cusp of a revolution, mainly made possible by recent achievements in deep learning, like large pre-trained language models (also specialized in clinical literature, e.g., SciBERT, BioBERT, PubMedBERT, ClinicalBERT) and retrieval-based ones. NLP makes it fast, easy, and efficient for citizens to access proper in-formation exactly when they need it, avoiding reading large corpora and opening the doors to unique opportunities. In this field, information extraction (IE) effectively digests knowledge into expressive forms for management and comprehension. On the trails of sub-symbolic progress and end-to-end architectures, IE is notably shifting from entities and binary relations to events, a more expressive method for capturing the complex, structured, and semantically rich relational graphs buried in text spans. Moreover, event graphs are quantifiable and interpretable, being a potentially effective way to interpret the black-box answers given by neural models and overcome opaqueness. Conceptual graph structures could be good candidates for a general explanation representation in XAI. Beyond semantic parsing, the rapid development of vector modeling techniques for event graphs and the growing popularity of Graph Neural Networks (GNNs) suggest that event-centered NLU will have a wide-ranging impact on knowledge-based AI challenges [33–35]. Following this path, the combination of language models and structured knowledge – like events and knowledge graphs – can bolster factuality, interpretability, reduce toxicity, and hallucinations [36, 37].

4 Conclusion

There are many situations where it would be useful to be able to ensure the quality and proper use of data, meeting compliance requirements, and helping utilize data to create public value. Electronic governance is one of the most important sources of information, relevant to large numbers of domains from government to business and education. We believe that context information data analysis and representation are a foundation for policy prediction, planning and adjustments, and underpin many of the mashups and visualizations we see on the Web. Although the benefits of AI-based computational intelligence systems are undeniable, one aspect that still deserves much attention is public participation and acceptance in electronic governance initiatives, which needs to be improved. In this paper we introduced the need to build interpretable AI systems in order to improve trust and consequently user acceptance, highlighting some emergent topics and open challenges, mainly linked to integrating quantitative and qualitative techniques, such as deep learning and knowledge graphs for semantic-aware models.

References

1. Carbonaro, A.: Linked data and semantic web technologies to model context information for policy-making. J. Ambient. Intell. Humaniz. Comput. **12**(4), 4395–4406 (2019). https://doi.org/10.1007/s12652-019-01341-y
2. Levi, M., Stoker, L.: Political trust and trustworthiness. Annu. Rev. Polit. Sci. **3**(1), 475–507 (2000)
3. ISO 24028:2020: Information Technology–Artificial Intelligence–Overview of Trustworthiness in Artificial Intelligence, Standard. International Organization for Standardization, European Commission (2020)
4. European Commission: Ethics guidelines for trustworthy AI (2018). Retrieved 2 Nov 2021 from https://ec.europa.eu/digital-single-market/en/news/ethics-guidelines-trustworthy-ai
5. National Institute of Standards and Technology: NIST proposes method for evaluating user trust in artificial intelligence systems (2021). https://www.nist.gov/news-events/news/2021/05/nistproposes-method-evaluating-user-trust-artificial-intelligence-systems

6. U.S. Government Accountability Office: Artificial intelligence: an accountability framework for federal agencies and other entities (2021). https://www.gao.gov/products/gao-21-519sp.

7. Wachter, S., Mittelstadt, B., Russell, C.: Counterfactual explanations without opening the black box: automated decisions and the GDPR. Harvard J. Law Technol. **31**(2017), 841 (2017)

8. Gunning, D.: Explainable Artificial Intelligence (XAI). Defense Advanced Research Projects Agency (2017)

9. Burke, B., et al.: Gartner top 10 strategic technology trends for 2020-smarter with Gartner (2019). https://www.gartner.com/smarterwithgartner/gartner-top-10-strategic-technology-trends-for-2020/

10. Edelman Trust Barometer: Edelman Trust Barometer Global Report (2019). https://www.edelman.com/sites/g/files/aatuss191/files/2019-02/2019_Edelman_Trust_Barometer_Global_Report.pdf

11. Benfeldt, O., Persson, J.S., Madsen, S.: Data governance as a collective action problem. Inf. Syst. Front. **22**(2), 299–313 (2020)

12. Saleh, A.A., Alyaseen, I.F.T.: E-governance system key successful implementation factors. Int. J. Percept. Cogn. Comput. **8**(1), 40–46 (2022)

13. Dias, R.C., Gomes, M.A.S.: From Electronic Government to Digital Governance: Transformation Governance Models and Strategies. Public Sci. Pol. **VII**, 119–143

14. Burton, S.: Data governance: the path to a data-driven culture. Appl. Mark. Anal. **6**(4), 298–308 (2021)

15. Cory, N., Dascoli, L.: How Barriers to Cross-Border Data Flows Are Spreading Globally, What They Cost, and How to Address Them. Information Technology and Innovation Foundation (2021)

16. Hazineh, S.A., Eleyan, D., Alkhateeb, M.: E-Government: limitations and challenges: a general framework for to consider in both developed and developing countries. Int J. Sci. Technol. Res. **11**(1), 97–103

17. Tzagkarakis, E., Kondylakis, H., Vardakis, G., Papadakis, N.: Ontology based governance for employee services. Algorithms **14**(4), 104 (2021)

18. Gao, Y., Janssen, M., Zhang, C.: Understanding the evolution of open government data research: towards open data sustainability and smartness. Int. Rev. Admin. Sci. 00208523211009955 (2021)

19. Nikiforova, A., McBride, K.: Open government data portal usability: a user-centred usability analysis of 41 open government data portals. Telematics Inform. **58**, 101539 (2021)

20. Hwang, M.S., Li, C.T., Shen, J.J., Chu, Y.P.: Challenges in e-government and security of information. Inf. Security **15**(1), 9–20 (2004)

21. Çaldağ, M.T., Gökalp, M.O., Gökalp, E.: Open government data: analysing benefits and challenges. In: 1st International Informatics and Software Engineering Conference (UBMYK), pp. 1–6, Nov 2019, IEEE

22. Awad, M.G.: An investigation into ontology based enhancement of search technologies for e-government. Doctoral dissertation, University of Huddersfield (2021)

23. Duberry, J.: Artificial intelligence and democracy: risks and promises of AI-mediated citizen–government relations. In: Artificial Intelligence and Democracy. Edward Elgar Publishing (2022)

24. Ren, Z., Shi, J., Imran, M.: Data evolution governance for ontology-based digital twin product lifecycle management. IEEE Trans. Industrial Inform. (2022). doi: https://doi.org/10.1109/TII.2022.3187715

25. Ebrahimi, M., Eberhart, A., Bianchi, F., Hitzler, P.: Towards bridging the neuro-symbolic gap: deep deductive reasoners. Appl. Intell. **51**(9), 6326–6348 (2021)

26. Charles, V., Rana, N.P., Carter, L.: Artificial Intelligence for data-driven decision-making and governance in public affairs. Gov. Inf. Quart. 101742 (2022)

27. Hasan, I., Rizvi, S.: Knowledge management framework for sustainability and resilience in next-Gen e-governance. In: Nanda, P., Verma, V.K., Srivastava, S., Gupta, R.K., Mazumdar, A.P. (eds.) Data Engineering for Smart Systems. LNNS, vol. 238, pp. 191–203. Springer, Singapore (2022). https://doi.org/10.1007/978-981-16-2641-8_18
28. Carter, L., Yoon, V., Liu, D.: Analyzing e-government design science artifacts: a systematic literature review. Int. J. Inf. Manage. **62**, 102430 (2022)
29. Harrison, T.M., Luna-Reyes, L.F.: Cultivating trustworthy artificial intelligence in digital government. Soc. Sci. Comput. Rev. **40**(2), 494–511 (2022)
30. Verhulst, S., Addo, P.M., Young, A., Zahuranec, A.J., Baumann, D., McMurren, J.: Emerging uses of technology for development: a new intelligence paradigm. Available at SSRN 3937649 (2021)
31. Zuiderwijk, A., Chen, Y.C., Salem, F.: Implications of the use of artificial intelligence in public governance: a systematic literature review and a research agenda. Gov. Inf. Q. **38**(3), 101577 (2021)
32. Andronico, A., Carbonaro, A., Colazzo, L., Molinari, A.: Personalisation services for learning management systems in mobile settings. Int. J. Contin. Eng. Educ. Life Long Learn. **14**(4–5), 353–369 (2004)
33. Frisoni, G., Moro, G., Carlassare, G., Carbonaro, A.: Unsupervised event graph representation and similarity learning on biomedical literature. Sensors **22**, 3 (2022) https://doi.org/10.3390/s22010003
34. Frisoni, G., Moro, G., Carbonaro, A.: Learning interpretable and statistically significant knowledge from unlabeled corpora of social text messages: a novel methodology of descriptive text mining. In: Proceedings of the 9th International Conference on Data Science, Technologies and Applications (DATA), Online, 7–9 July 2020, pp. 121–134
35. Frisoni, G., Moro, G., Carbonaro, A.: A Survey on Event Extraction for Natural Language Understanding: Riding the Biomedical Literature Wave. IEEE Access (2021)
36. Frisoni, G., Moro, G., Carbonaro, A.: Unsupervised descriptive text mining for knowledge graph learning. In: Proceedings of the 12th International Conference on Knowledge Discovery and Information Retrieval KDIR, Budapest, Hungary, 2–4 Nov 2020, vol. 1, pp. 316–324
37. Frisoni, G., Moro, G., Carbonaro, A.: Towards Rare Disease Knowledge Graph Learning from Social Posts of Patients. In: Proceedings of the International Research & Innovation Forum, Athens, Greece, 15–17 Apr 2020. Springer, Berlin/Heidelberg, Germany (2020). https://doi.org/10.1007/978-3-030-62066-0_44

An Automated Stress Recognition for Digital Healthcare: Towards E-Governance

Orchid Chetia Phukan[1]($\boxtimes$), Ghanapriya Singh[2]($\boxtimes$), Sanju Tiwari[3]($\boxtimes$), and Saad Butt[4]($\boxtimes$)

[1] PES University, Bangalore, India
orchidchetiaphukan1@gmail.com
[2] National Institute of Technology, Uttarakhand, India
ghanapriya@nituk.ac.in
[3] Universidad Autonoma de Tamaulipas, Ciudad Victoria, Mexico
tiwarisanju18@ieee.org
[4] James Cook University, Townsville, Australia
drsaadbutt@aol.com

Abstract. Mental health is of utmost importance in present times as mental health problems can have a negative impact on an individual. Stress recognition is an important part of the digital healthcare system as stress may act as a catalyst and lead to mental health problems or further amplify them. With the advancement of technology, the presence of smart wearable devices is seen and it can be used to automate stress recognition for digital healthcare. These smart wearable devices have physiological sensors embedded into them. The data collected from these physiological sensors have paved an efficient way for stress recognition in the user. Most of the previous work related to stress recognition was done using classical machine learning approaches. One of the major drawbacks related to these approaches is that they require manually extracting important features that will be helpful in stress recognition. Extracting these features requires human domain expertise. Another drawback of previous works was that it only caters to specific groups of individuals such as stress among youths, stress due to the workplace, etc. and fails to generalize. To overcome the issues related to previous works done, this study proposes a transformer-based deep learning approach for automating the feature extraction phase and classifying a user's state into three classes baseline, stress, and amusement.

Keywords: Stress recognition · Deep learning · Transformer · WESAD · Mental health

1 Introduction

E-governance aims to foster digital ecosystems in all areas, including health. The delivery of healthcare services and the administration of the public health system can be enhanced as information and communication technology (ICT)

F. Ortiz-Rodríguez et al. (Eds.): EGETC 2022, CCIS 1666, pp. 117–125, 2022.
https://doi.org/10.1007/978-3-031-22950-3_10

advances. Stress recognition is vital for improving efficiency in health care delivery, extending health care to remote regions, and providing higher quality at a lower cost. Individuals from different walks of life and different ages can experience stress. In recent times presence of stress among individuals can be seen more. Stress may be caused by various reasons like financial problems, family problems, occupational difficulties, relationship complications, etc. Teens may experience stress due to behavioral changes and negative thoughts. During the COVID-19 pandemic, due to the complications caused by the pandemic, stress was experienced by individuals [9] due to various reasons such as loss of livelihood and loss of loved ones. Stress may act as an ignition for various mental health disorders and it may also amplify existing mental health disorders [12]. Mental health disorders such as depression, anxiety, etc hamper the daily lives of individuals. It can negatively affect how an individual feels, their way of thinking, and also how an individual acts. Nowadays, digital technologies are being used for the efficient monitoring and diagnosis of various health problems. Recently, governments have taken several initiatives for digital mental health care systems [4] and stress recognition may act as a starting point for such digital mental health care systems.

The human body shows different psychological and physiological changes based on different situations. Happiness is mainly because of the release of dopamine which is a neurotransmitter in the central nervous system. During stress, several physiological changes occur in the body such as increased heart rate, increased sweating, and increased blood pressure. Capturing these physiological changes by using sensors embedded into smart wearable devices is an effective way of determining a user's physical and mental state. Smart wearable devices can be worn in various parts of the body; it may be the wrist, chest, eyes, ears, full-body, etc. According to IEC[1](The International Electrotechnical Committee), wearable smart devices are divided into the following defined categories: near-body electronics, body-worn electronics, inside the body electronics, and textiles with electronic components. The different products that fall under the above-divided categories by IEC are namely smartwatches, wristbands, fitness trackers, smart glasses, body-worn sensors, smart textiles, etc. With the help of various sensors embedded in smart wearable devices, stress recognition in a user can be done in real-time and in a continuous manner. This is one of the main advantages of stress recognition using smart wearable devices. The physiological data from smart wearable devices are obtained through sensors such as electrocardiogram (ECG) which records cardiac electrical activity, electroencephalogram (EEG) which records brain electrical activity, electromyogram (EMG) that records muscle activity, Blood Volume Pulse (BVP), electrodermal Activity (EDA) that records sweating level, respiration rate (RESP), electrooculogram (EOG) that records eye movements, body temperature (TEMP), etc. The physiological data obtained from these sensors has paved an automatic and efficient way for determining and keeping track of a user's affective state. This work explores a transformer-based deep learning model for the recognition of stress using physiological data obtained from sensors.

---

[1] https://teslasuit.io/detailed-wearables-classification-by-teslasuit-team/.

2   Literature Review

Recognition of stress through different approaches have been done in previous works such as image-based approach, video-based approach, speech-based approach, multimodal physiological data-based approach, etc. These approaches uses various machine learning algorithms to predict the class [1,2,15]. In recent times, sufficient development in the human-computer interaction field can be seen. One such technology that has seen a rise in recent years is wearable technology. Stress recognition through wearable sensors [3] has come out as an effective way as various physiological data from these sensors helps in automated stress recognition in an accurate and precise manner.

WESAD, a multimodal dataset was open-sourced by Schmidt et al. [14]. For the preparation of this dataset, they made use of 15 individuals and the subjects were put under various conditions such as stress, amusement, meditation, neutral, etc. For recording physiological data from the subjects, they used two wearable devices one was a chest-worn device (RespiBAN) and the other was a wrist-worn device (Empatica E4) and recorded various data such as electrocardiogram data, blood volume pulse, body temperature, respiration rate, etc. They have tested this dataset by extracting important features from the raw data and applying various classical machine learning algorithms such as k-nearest neighbor (kNN), decision tree (DT), linear discriminant analysis (LDA), adaboost (AB), etc. Indikawati et al. [7] proposed a system that helps in the classification of stress levels using multimodal data from wrist-worn device, Empatica E4. They implemented three different classification algorithms such as logistic regression (LR), DT, and random forest (RF) and considered it as a four-class classification problem. Their personalized stress detection system using random forest classifier reported the highest accuracy of 88%-99% on 15 different subjects. Hsieh et al. [6] used dominant features based on EDA for stress detection. They employed f1-score as assessment metric and offered numerous improvements to attain better f1-scores, such as less overlapping signal segmentation and additional signal processing characteristics. Murugappan et al. [11] proposed a user-independent model for stress detection and for this purpose they experimented with several classical machine learning algorithms such as random forest, extra-trees, etc. Garg et al. [5] used ECG, TEMP, RESP, EMG, and EDA sensor data for classifying users physiological conditions (baseline vs stress vs amusement and stress vs non-stress) and used various classical machine learning algorithms such as kNN, LDA, RF, AB, and support vector machine (SVM) [13,17] to do so. Tiwari et al. [16] used SMOTE (Synthetic minority over-sampling technique) to handle the problem of class imbalance and experimented with various classical machine learning algorithms such as LDA, RF, etc.

After going through related works in this area of research following drawbacks are generally found:

– Most of the works used classical machine learning algorithms that require manual extraction of features. This task is not possible without the presence of domain experts.

– Most of the works are involved with building personalized stress detection systems that may fail to generalize.

For addressing the research gaps in existing literature, an end-to-end automatic approach for stress recognition is presented in this work.

3 Proposed Methodology

3.1 Model Architecture Description

As mentioned above, this work focuses on a deep learning approach which helps in automating the feature extraction process. The proposed deep learning model architecture involves the use of the following layers (Fig. 1).

1-D Convolutional Neural Networks or 1-D CNNs. The kernel or filter slides along one dimension. This kind of CNN's are generally preferred when dealing with time-series data. The mathematical equation for convolution operation is given by Eq. 1 where i represents the number of filters or kernels, u is filter or kernel, and f is input feature.

$$v = \sum_i u_i f \tag{1}$$

Multihead Attention. The transformer architecture was first introduced by Vaswani et al. [18]. The attention module in transformer does its computations numerous times in parallel, and each of them is referred to as an attention head. All of the attention calculations from different heads are combined together to generate a final attention score. Equation 2 is the mathematical formulation for calculation of attention score and where Q, K, V are vectors, S represents softmax function, and d_k is dimension of the key vector (K)

$$Attention(Q, K, V) = S(\frac{QK^T}{\sqrt{d_k}})V \tag{2}$$

Layer Normalization. It normalises the prior layer's activations for each instance in a batch. It employs a transformation that causes all preceding layer activation values to have a mean value near to 0 and a standard deviation close to 1.

Dropout. The term "Dropout" means dropping out units i.e. the role of the dropout layer is to randomly set input units to 0. The dropout layer helps in preventing overfitting.

Global Average Pooling 1D. It takes a 3D tensor (batch size * input size * input channels) as input and computes the maximum value among the input channels for each input size.

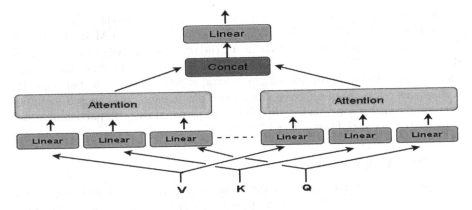

Fig. 1. Multihead attention

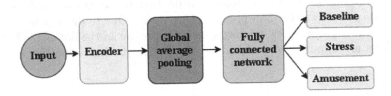

Fig. 2. Transformer model architecture

Fully Connected Network. A network where neurons in a particular layer receives input from all the neurons of the previous layer and also provides outputs to all the neurons of the next layer.

3.2 Implementation Details

Transformer encoder consists of different layers such as 1-D CNN, multihead attention, layer normalization, and dropout. The input is given to the encoder and the encoder chooses what elements of the input to focus on that will help predict the output. The output of the encoder is fed into global average pooling layer and then its output is provided as input to the feed-forward fully connected network as shown in Fig. 2. A softmax activation function is used as activation in the last layer of the fully connected network that outputs the probabilities for each class. The loss function used is cross-entropy loss and the optimizer used is rectified adam (RAdam) [10].

4   Experiments

4.1   Dataset

WESAD [14] dataset consists of data from chest-worn device (RespiBAN) and wrist-worn device (Empatica E4). For experimentation purpose, data from only chest-worn device is used. The raw signals are sampled 700 Hz for RespiBAN. The attributes of the RespiBAN device data are EDA, ECG, EMG, TEMP, and RESP and these attributes correspond to the sensors from where physiological data is recorded. The data is labeled into three classes: baseline, stress, and amusement. Baseline is considered as a neutral affective state of the participants, amusement refers to an affective state when participants are exposed to funny content (basically short video clips), and in stress state, the participants are exposed to trier social stress test (TSST) [8].

4.2   Data Preprocessing

Data preprocessing plays a crucial role in feeding data into deep learning model. A window size of 5 s was set for the raw data from sensors with a window shift of 2 s. Random noise may be present in the data due to physical limitations of the sensors and may lead to uncertain predictions, so random noise components are removed in the data preprocessing phase. Due to discrepancies in the data recording phase, a few missing values are present in the dataset. The missing values are imputed with the mean of two neighboring values for a certain instance.

4.3   Model Training

After data preprocessing stage, the data is splitted in the ratio of 90:10 to training and validation set. The transformer model is of 216,631 parameters out of which 216,519 are trainable parameters and 112 are non-trainable parameters. The number of epochs for training is set to 15 with early stopping. Figure 3 shows the plot of training and validation accuracy and Fig. 4 shows the plot of training and validation loss for each epoch.

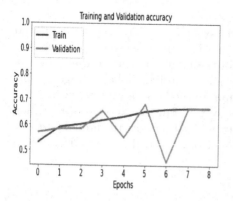
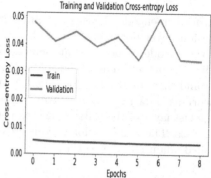

Fig. 3. Plot of training and validation accuracy obtained with respect to epoch

Fig. 4. Plot of training and validation loss obtained with respect to epoch

4.4   Performance Metrics

This section discusses the metrics used for evaluation of the proposed model.

Precision. In general terms, it means accurate predictions made by the algorithm. Precision is the ratio of the number of true positives (TP) and the total number of positives (i.e sum of TP and false positive (FP)).

$$Precision = \frac{\sum TP}{\sum(TP + FP)} \tag{3}$$

Recall. It means how many values that were positive are predicted to be positive. A recall is the ratio of the number of TPs and a sum of TP and false-negative (FN).

$$Recall = \frac{\sum TP}{\sum(TP + FN)} \tag{4}$$

Accuracy. It is one of the most used metrics for the evaluation of classification models. Accuracy is the percentage of predictions the model predicted correctly.

$$Accuracy = \frac{\sum(TP + TN)}{\sum(TP + FP + TN + FN)} \tag{5}$$

F1-Score. It is the trade-off between precision and recall and is the harmonic mean of precision and recall.

$$F1 - score = 2\frac{\sum(precision \times recall)}{\sum(precision + recall)} \tag{6}$$

5   Results and Discussions

The transformer-based deep learning model is trained on physiological data acquired from multiple sensors installed in the chest-worn device, such as ECG, EDA, etc. The model outputs a class label (baseline, stress, and amusement) and this gives an automated method of determining whether or not a user is under stress. Table 1 shows the classification report for all the class labels (baseline, stress, and amusement) comprising of various metrics such as Precision, Recall, Accuracy, and F1-Score. Weighted denotes that the contribution of each class to the average is weighted by each class size. Accuracy of 68.24% and weighted f1-score of 62.48% is achieved by the model.

Our proposed method has been compared with previous work [5] that has used only chest-worn sensor data from the WESAD dataset and classifies a user's state into three classes i.e. baseline, stress, and amusement for fair comparison and it is shown in Table 2. The attributes that were used by them are EDA, ECG,

Table 1. Classification report

Class	Precision	Recall	F1-score
Baseline	0.6823	0.9158	0.7820
Stress	0.6966	0.6184	0.6551
Amusement	0.3684	0.0260	0.0486
Accuracy			**0.6824**
Weighted	0.6353	0.6824	**0.6248**

Table 2. Comparison of our proposed method with previous work on chest-worn sensor data

Method	Reference	Accuracy (%)	F1-score (%)
SVM	[5]	59.56	59.64
AB	[5]	64.34	63.82
LDA	[5]	67.06	50.44
kNN	[5]	65.00	58.14
RF	[5]	67.56	**65.73**
Proposed method	Our model	**68.24**	62.48

EMG, TEMP, and RESP. They have used various classical machine learning algorithms such as SVM, AB, LDA, kNN, and RF. RF has achieved the highest accuracy (67.56%) and f1-score (65.73%) as reported by them. Our proposed method achieves the highest accuracy when compared with the methods used by Garg et al. [5].

6   Conclusion

Stress recognition is an essential aspect of digital health care system as stress may lead towards causing or exacerbating mental health problems. In this study, we have proposed a transformer-based deep learning model that classifies a user's affective state and provides an automatic approach to stress recognition. Our proposed method automates the manual feature extraction phase and provides a generalized stress recognition approach that is not constrained to any particular group of individuals. The model reported an accuracy of 68.24% and weighted f1-score of 62.48%. Our future work will be focused on improving the performance (accuracy and weighted f1-score) of the model and also handling the problem of class imbalance. Code files are available at: https://github.com/orchidchetiaphukan/stress/_recognition/_Xmer.

References

1. Bijalwan, V., Semwal, V.B., Singh, G., Crespo, R.G.: Heterogeneous computing model for post-injury walking pattern restoration and postural stability rehabilitation exercise recognition. Expert Syst. **39**(6), e12706 (2022)

2. Bijalwan, V., Semwal, V.B., Singh, G., Mandal, T.K.: HDL-PSR: modelling Spatio-temporal features using hybrid deep learning approach for post-stroke rehabilitation. Neural Process. Lett., 1–20 (2022). https://doi.org/10.1007/s11063-022-10744-6

3. Can, Y.S., Arnrich, B., Ersoy, C.: Stress detection in daily life scenarios using smart phones and wearable sensors: a survey. J. Biomed. Inform. **92**, 103139 (2019)

4. Díaz-Castro, L., Arredondo, A., Pelcastre-Villafuerte, B.E., Hufty, M.: Governance and mental health: contributions for public policy approach. Revista de Saude Publica **51**, 4 (2017)

5. Garg, P., Santhosh, J., Dengel, A., Ishimaru, S.: Stress detection by machine learning and wearable sensors. In: 26th International Conference on Intelligent User Interfaces-Companion, pp. 43–45 (2021)

6. Hsieh, C.P., Chen, Y.T., Beh, W.K., Wu, A.Y.A.: Feature selection framework for XGBoost based on electrodermal activity in stress detection. In: 2019 IEEE International Workshop on Signal Processing Systems (SiPS), pp. 330–335. IEEE (2019)

7. Indikawati, F.I., Winiarti, S.: Stress detection from multimodal wearable sensor data. In: IOP Conference Series: Materials Science and Engineering, vol. 771, p. 012028. IOP Publishing (2020)

8. Kirschbaum, C., Pirke, K.M., Hellhammer, D.H.: The 'trier social stress test'-a tool for investigating psychobiological stress responses in a laboratory setting. Neuropsychobiology **28**(1–2), 76–81 (1993)

9. Lakhan, R., Agrawal, A., Sharma, M.: Prevalence of depression, anxiety, and stress during COVID-19 pandemic. J. Neurosci. Rural Pract. **11**(04), 519–525 (2020)

10. Liu, L., et al.: On the variance of the adaptive learning rate and beyond (2019). https://doi.org/10.48550/ARXIV.1908.03265, https://arxiv.org/abs/1908.03265

11. Murugappan, R., Bosco, J.J., Eswaran, K., Vijay, P., Vijayaraghavan, V.: User independent human stress detection. In: 2020 IEEE 10th International Conference on Intelligent Systems (IS), pp. 490–497. IEEE (2020)

12. Pittenger, C., Duman, R.S.: Stress, depression, and neuroplasticity: a convergence of mechanisms. Neuropsychopharmacology **33**(1), 88–109 (2008)

13. Reza, M.D.R., et al.: Automatic diabetes and liver disease diagnosis and prediction through SVM and KNN algorithms. In: Hassanien, A.E., Bhattacharyya, S., Chakrabati, S., Bhattacharya, A., Dutta, S. (eds.) Emerging Technologies in Data Mining and Information Security. AISC, vol. 1300, pp. 589–599. Springer, Singapore (2021). https://doi.org/10.1007/978-981-33-4367-2_56

14. Schmidt, P., Reiss, A., Duerichen, R., Marberger, C., Van Laerhoven, K.: Introducing wesad, a multimodal dataset for wearable stress and affect detection. In: Proceedings of the 20th ACM International Conference on Multimodal Interaction, pp. 400–408 (2018)

15. Singh, G., Chowdhary, M., Kumar, A., Bahl, R.: A personalized classifier for human motion activities with semi-supervised learning. IEEE Trans. Consum. Electron. **66**(4), 346–355 (2020)

16. Tiwari, S., Agarwal, S.: An optimized hybrid solution for IoT based lifestyle disease classification using stress data. arXiv preprint arXiv:2204.03573 (2022)

17. Tiwari, S., et al.: Applications of machine learning approaches to combat COVID-19: a survey. Lessons from COVID-19, 263–287 (2022)

18. Vaswani, A., et al.: Attention is all you need. In: Advances in Neural Information Processing Systems, vol. 30 (2017)

Emergency Supply Chain Management

Volodymyr Skitsko👤 and Mykola Voinikov(✉)👤

Kyiv National Economic University named after Vadym Hetman, 54/1 Prospect Peremogy,
Kyiv 03057, Ukraine
skitsko@kneu.edu.ua, mykola.voinikov@kneu.ua

Abstract. Last years demonstrated to the world the importance of emergency supply chain management, mainly because under catastrophic events, a rapid demand change (or even the creation of demand) is observed, which is significant to meet since often unmet demand may cost human lives or the environmental damage. Emergency supply chain management can be considered at different levels: strategic (goals, focus, risk management); e-governance (software, hardware); specific tools, and mathematical models for solving particular problems. In the paper, we look at a five-index transportation problem in the conditions of the catastrophe regarding the transportation of different types of goods from several origins to several destinations through several warehouses where the sorting and packing are done by several vehicles in a limited time. The exponentially increasing complexity required the application of alternative methods of solving transportation problems, and a genetic algorithm turned out to be a matching candidate. The steps of the genetic algorithm are presented, and certain essential aspects of solving such problems with a genetic algorithm are specified, such as guaranteeing the solutions stay in the feasible region after the genetic operator's application. The proposed algorithm allows getting a suboptimal solution or even the optimal one in an acceptable time. Besides, we look at e-governance and possible sources of collecting data for the problem-solving process so that having implemented the algorithm as a part of a decision-making system, the researcher can in real-time import the datasets and experiment with parameters, allowing for fast and high-quality solutions.

Keywords: Multi-index transportation problem · Genetic algorithm · Problem solving under emergency

1 Logistics Problems Under Emergency

The recent occasions demonstrated the danger of neglecting the catastrophic difficult-to-predict events which may lead to rapidly increasing (or creating of new) demand for vital goods, and, as it often happens, only the government can meet such demand because of such factors as its exclusive capabilities, collaboration with other governments, access to resources. In the scientific literature, such hard-to-predict events, which are not likely to happen but can lead to significant losses, are generalized in the black swan theory [1].

Black swan events, according to criteria given by the author [1], have the following characteristics: they are hard to predict for an expert; they lead to significant losses;

F. Ortiz-Rodríguez et al. (Eds.): EGETC 2022, CCIS 1666, pp. 126–140, 2022.
https://doi.org/10.1007/978-3-031-22950-3_11

after the occasion, in retrospective, it seems that the events have a rational explanation as if it could be predicted. In correspondence with the theory [1], we should not focus on predicting black swan events but instead build the robustness for the catastrophic events of different kinds. However, as per e-governance systems and specific tooling, the perfectly built infrastructure allows us to utilize itself both under circumstances of black swan events and in day-to-day operations.

On the scale of the globe, the black swan events happen relatively often, which can be proved by reviewing at least the most known black swans of the past century. The most known black swans of the last century are the First World War, the Second World War, the Chornobyl nuclear power plant accident, the September 11 attacks, COVID-19, and the Russian invasion of Ukraine. But there are thousands of other black swans such as the Haiti Earthquake, the Indian Ocean Earthquake, the Bhola Cyclone, and other disasters.

The black swan events often cause logistics problems, such as an unexpected rise in demand or disruption of the existing supply chains.

For example, the Chornobyl nuclear power plant accident caused the demand for personal protective equipment for liquidators and the resources needed for catastrophe liquidation, such as sand, different constructions, and chemical substances. Then, besides, arose the need for people's evacuation.

The September 11 attacks primarily required the transportation of people to the hospitals and special medical equipment since the hospitals were not expecting such a splash: the need for transportation of blocks and other constructions.

COVID-19 caused massive demand for mechanical ventilators, the number of which was limited. Besides the medical equipment, there was a deficit of personal protective equipment for medical personnel and masks for people to prevent further virus spreading. Needless to say, a lot of supply chain disruptions have occurred.

The Russian invasion of Ukraine has increased the demand for many different goods such as medicine and vital good for citizens, particularly in the hotspots; medicines for cancer patients and other potential who need the medicine regularly to continue their everyday life; medicine and ammunition for the soldiers; the need to transport gas by routes because of destroyed oil depots. Moreover, there was a need to create evacuation plans for hotspot territories.

As we can see, black swan events indeed tend to cause the logistics problems, which can easily be explained that any catastrophe requires some resources for its liquidation at least. Therefore, any government needs to mitigate the risks and be ready for some, at least common scenarios.

Supply chain management under emergency manages the flow of goods and services and includes all processes that transform raw materials into final products, but those flows exist due to catastrophic events and may involve time constraint. Also, the supply chain management under emergency can be split into two phases: mitigation and active.

The mitigation phase involves the actions that allow lowering the risks and the potential damages and developing the tools, systems, and stocks that can be helpful once the black swan event has occurred.

The active phase is the phase in which the black swan event has already happened, and we should focus on minimizing damage. All the tools, systems, plans, and stocks designed in the previous phase are used in this phase. Unfortunately, sometimes during the active phase arise new and unseen problems. For those cases, the handling tools happen in real-time. But the well-planned mitigation phase can cover most of the problems. That's why it is essential to develop tools that can help during the active phase of supply chain management under emergency.

To minimize the probability of specific events happening and mitigate the black swan events results, a government should consider different scenarios and the handling of the results. Therefore, it is essential to consider not only the most common potential problems but also those which can occur with low probability but may have a considerable impact. The supply chain management under emergency for a government can be viewed from different abstraction levels, which can be presented as a hierarchical structure (see Fig. 1).

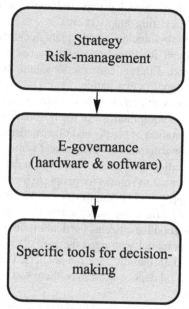

Fig. 1. The levels of supply chain management under emergency [source: created by authors]

Strategic risk management on the governmental level involves all the decision-making centers, including the governmental, regional, and local ones. On the governmental level, the strategy is developed, which outlines the focus domains, and defines the risk-management process. In the real world, some unique agency is created for those functions. For example, Federal Emergency Management Agency [2] operates in the United States as an agency that must mitigate the results of the catastrophes and develop a risk-management strategy; worth mentioning that the Federal Emergency Management Agency has a broad risk-management program, which even ensures that the insurance is affordable for the population.

E-governance, both hardware and software, involves using information technologies for governmental services and exchanging information between government, citizens, and businesses. Addition, such technologies are essential in supply chain management under emergency since those information technologies allow the collection of the required data for problem-solving and transfer of the data to decision-making places.

Specific tools for decision-making. Those are the particular methods and mathematical models that solve specific problems and can be applied to the decision-making process. For those tools, a range of requirements is presented. In particular, they should allow getting the solution of high quality in a reasonable time using the available data. If necessary, the model can be adjusted, but the usual actions require clarity, speed, and efficiency in an emergency. Those characteristics also apply to mathematical methods and models based on algorithms of collective artificial intelligence and evolutionary modelling.

2 Literature Review

In the modern literature, the research on supply chains under catastrophic events and the mathematical models to solve arising problems is done by such authors as Zarghami S.A., Rachida A., Sankar K. Roy, Berkoune D., Iran R. Xavier, Chern C. C., and others.

In the paper [3], the authors develop a quantitative vulnerability assessment method and a vulnerability index based on the joint entropy of centrality values, which can be interpreted as a risk of disruption of the supply chain. The results conclude that the increase in network homogeneity through decentralization yields lower vulnerability and builds extra robustness into the networks.

Authors [4] addressed the problem of transportation of goods in a limited time, which can arise due to catastrophic events, and proposed to solve such problem by applying transportation problem. In the real world, it refers to determining the number, the position, and the mission of required humanitarian aid distribution centers within a disaster region. The objectives of the problem are to minimize the total transportation duration, minimize the number of staff required that operate in the distribution centers and minimize uncovered demand within the affected area. The authors proposed an epsilon-constraint method to solve the problem that generates the exact Pareto front of a complex three-objective location-transportation problem.

In the paper [5], the authors propose to reduce transportation time and cost by including the corresponding parameters in the objective function of the transportation problem. Unlike the previous author's approach [4], including time as an objective function allows to receive the solution even if it does not satisfy the specified time constraint but only approximates those values. The presented approach may be helpful in the transportations where the time is essential but not crucial.

In case of a natural disaster, where physical infrastructure, such as roads and bridges, is often destroyed, and transport capacity is extremely limited or even non-existent, authors [6] propose to use helicopters and present a mathematical model to minimize the total transportation time, which includes the time of operations and the time of mobilization of aid resources.

By designing a heuristic algorithm called the Emergency Relief Transportation Planning Algorithm, the work [7] aims to find feasible routes to deliver medical countermeasures at a target location considering time, physical, human resources, and capacity limitations. The algorithm allows to group and sort demands of the needed goods, the due dates, the possible shared capacities, and the distances from the demand nodes to the depots.

Solving transportation problems using a genetic algorithm is researched in the works of William H. et al., Berkoune D. et al., Renaud J. et al., and Berkoune D. et al.

The work [8] focuses on solving transportation problems using a genetic algorithm. The research presents steps to solve the classic transportation problem with the use of a genetic algorithm as well as focuses on some transportation problem-specific nuances, for example, initialization of the initial population or providing the obtainment of a feasible solution.

In real case scenarios, the classical transportation problem is not that common since the information technologies allow us to collect data, which can be used for problem-solving; multi-index transportation problem allow us to include additional factors. Solving multi-index transportation problems using a genetic algorithm is research in the work [9]. The authors focus on the initialization of the initial population and propose the application of different genetic-algorithm-specific aspects such as elitist function, which allows not to lose the fittest solution among all generations.

A genetic algorithm for transportation problem which is aimed to deal with realistic situations is developed in the work [10]. Authors claim the algorithm to produce near optimal solutions in relatively short computation times and is fast enough to be used interactively in a decision-support system, providing high-quality transportation plans to emergency managers.

In the paper [11], transportation of goods in a supply chain from manufacturer to customers through distribution centers is solved, using a two-stage fixed-charge distribution problem. In addition, a genetic algorithm is used for a separate single-stage fixed-charge transportation problem.

For the last two decades, the literature on emergency logistics has collected many methods to measure the risks, the logistic systems reliability measuring methods, and the mathematical models to solve problems that can arise from catastrophic events. Besides, some works focus on solving transportation problems with a genetic algorithm. However, there are still some gaps on combining the five-index transportation problem with time constraint using a genetic algorithm and the required actions to imply the results in the real world. In our work, we focus on increasing the number of factors, use time constraints and look at how the implementation of such tools can be used in realistic scenarios.

3 Problem Description

Let's take a look at a potential problem caused by catastrophic events which can be solved with the use of e-governance and specific tooling.

Unforeseen enormous demands cause the creation of new supply chains and intensification of the existing ones, which occur not only with the limitation of the financial resources but also with the temporal ones; in most cases, the time resource is crucial and even lifesaving.

To satisfy the demand, we should create a transportation plan that encounters different types of goods, origins, destinations, warehouses, and types of vehicles. In this case, we can formulate it as a five-index transportation problem regarding the transportation of different types of goods on several types of vehicles from some origins to some destination points through the warehouses where some manipulations to the goods can be done (packing, sorting).

The transportation problem, in its classical representation, is a linear programming problem where the objective consists of minimizing the transportation cost of a given homogeneous good from some origins to some destinations [12].

A solution to the transportation problem is a transportation plan, which represents a matrix with the amounts for transportation from a specific origin to a particular destination. The critical characteristic of the transportation problem is the satisfaction of the transportation problem's restriction, which guarantees that the transportation is actual and can be executed in the real world. The restrictions of the classic transportation problem are the availability of goods in origins and the demand at the destination. Elements of the matrix are called the plan's component and represent the number of goods that should be transferred from a specified origin to a particular destination [12].

Classic transportation problem does not support including additional factors such as types of vehicles, warehouses, etc. However, a multi-index transportation problem can be used, which can include several factors. As said before, the present problem description can be suited to the five-index transportation problem with the additional restrictions by the time.

A transportation plan for the five-index transportation problem is a five-dimensional matrix that contains the plan's components, which encounter all the indexes. Also, to include the time, the researcher should collect the data about the trip time for certain combinations and impose the corresponding restrictions on those measurements.

It is worth mentioning that earlier, the multi-index transportation problem was not researched enough since the implementation of such problems required significant computing resources and the need to enter all the data manually. Nevertheless, the development of informational technologies enabled the solving of multi-index transportation problems; digitalization allowed us to add a data source to problem-solving tools right from the initial source, using an application programming interface (API).

Some APIs, a researcher, are public and can be used by any researcher for some fee or even for free. For example, for calculating the required time, a researcher may want to use some mapping platform such as Mapbox [13] or Google Maps [14].

Moreover, some APIs are confidential. For example, those can be governmental data or data from some partner business company. Therefore, the vital thing to keep in mind while implementing such an algorithm is security: we should put the data and security as the key priority since the data leak may lead to unexpected results.

The transportation problems are usually solved in the literature with the simplex algorithm, a systematic procedure for testing the vertices as a possible solution, and with iterations to improve such a solution.

The problems with the multiple indexes require significantly more time and computing resources to solve since the problem's complexity increases exponentially based on the number of indexes [15]. Therefore, for such problems, the classic optimization methods, which can give a precisely optimal solution, lose their efficiency since the time required to solve such problems is not acceptable. That is why it is essential to find the method to solve multi-index transportation problems within an adequate time to obtain suboptimal or even optimal results.

An excellent example of the described methods is the evolutionary algorithms, particularly a genetic algorithm.

4 Genetic Algorithm

A genetic algorithm is an evolutionary algorithm for solving optimization search problems, which can produce high-quality solutions by relying on biologically inspired operations such as mutation, crossover, and selection. A genetic algorithm works with several potential solutions at each step of its functioning and applies the principles of biological evolution, allowing the improvement of solutions over generations [16].

First, let us define the terms of the five-index transportation problem in the context of a genetic algorithm. A chromosome is a transport plan; a gene is a plan's component - an amount of transportation of certain goods from a specific origin to a particular destination through a certain warehouse using a specific vehicle; a population is the collection of chromosomes that function on some generation of the algorithm.

Special attention should be given to the fitness function, which corresponds to the objective function in terms of transportation problems. A fitness function has a huge significance in a genetic algorithm since this is the function that allows assessing the level of goodness of the chromosome, thus choosing the fittest ones based on those scores for the future generations. For the classic approach, the objective function can be taken as a fitness function.

A genetic algorithm uses encoding of the solution, which may vary based on the problem. The common encodings are binary one, permutation (for ordering problems), value encoding (real numbers), and tree encoding [16]. To solve the transportation problem, it is appropriate to use real values encoding. Real values in chromosomes represent the plan's component. While encoding the transportation problem with the real values, the form of the encoded genes will be represented as a multi-dimensional matrix with integers.

Outline of the classic genetic algorithm [16]:

1. Initialization of initial population;
2. Assessment of the current population's fitness scores;
3. Check the stop criteria (go to step 8 if satisfied);
4. Selection of the chromosomes to the mating pool;
5. Application of the genetic operators;
6. Forming the population for the next generation;
7. Go to step 2;
8. Choosing the fittest chromosome as a result.

The steps of the genetic algorithms for solving transportation problems are the same as in classical genetic algorithms, but for each step, there are some additions to transportation-problem-specific aspects, which will be described below.

Step 1. Initialization of initial population. The initialization of initial population of the chromosomes in a genetic algorithm has on purpose the obtainment of the first generation, which then produces the next ones by applying the genetic operators.

It is crucial to produce the initial population with diverse genetic material, since the problem of reaching low diversity is one of the key problems of the genetic algorithm [16], even not considering initial population itself. That's why the usage of classical methods of creating the initial plan for transportation problems are not appropriate for genetic algorithm application. For this purpose, some method should be used, which randomly creates chromosomes, which are the feasible solutions of the transportation problem. The approaches to create such chromosomes are describes in [8, 9].

As mentioned before, to encode the chromosome, we use the natural numbers. To demonstrate the example of a chromosome, let us assume we are solving the problem with two vehicles, two types of goods, two origins, two warehouses, and two destinations. The visualization of a chromosome for solving the problem with the specified indexes may look as follows (see Fig. 2).

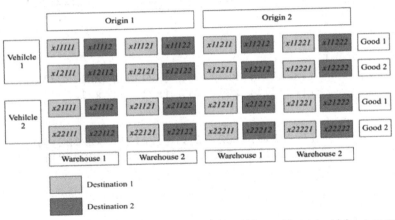

Fig. 2. Chromosome visualization for transportation problem with two vehicles, two types of goods, two origins, two warehouses and two destinations [source: created by authors]

We use a two-dimensional table (Fig. 2) to illustrate how the combination of specific rows and columns forms the groups of indexes, which in the real world has a specific interpretation (some vehicle, good type, or any other index). A cell in the table corresponds to a gene. The genes are marked as an "x", followed by the combination of indexes from the transportation problem. For example, the gene "x12122" contains the transportation of the second good from the first origin to the second destination on the first vehicle through the second warehouse. To be more precise, let us explain the indexes in a different example, where we have five values for each index. Thus, the first chromosome is "x11111", and the last one is "x55555", and some in the middle, for example, "x12345", represent the transportation on the first vehicle of the second type of good from the third origin to the fifth destination through the fourth warehouse.

It is worth mentioning that the increase in index values will expand the number of rows and/or columns for Fig. 2. Adding a vehicle would cause appending two more rows, a different origin would cause appending additional four columns, and so on.

To operate with the chromosome in programming implementation, it's reasonable to use multi-dimensional arrays, the indexes of which correspond to the indexes of the transportation problem. The chromosome for the problem with exact dimensions as in the Fig. 2, stored in memory as a five-dimensional array, has the following structure:

```
[
    [
        [
            [[x11111, x11112], [x11121, x11122]],
            [[x11211, x11212], [x11221, x11222]]
        ],
        [
            [[x12111, x12112], [x12121, x12122]],
            [[x12211, x12212], [x12221, x12222]]
        ]
    ],
    [
        [
            [[x21111, x21112], [x21121, x21122]],
            [[x21211, x21212], [x21221, x21222]]
        ],
        [
            [[x22111, x22112], [x22121, x22122]],
            [[x22211, x22212], [x22221, x22222]]
        ]
    ]
]
```

The elements of the bottom-level array represent genes. For presentation purposes, the names of the genes are used, while indeed, those genes contain the number, representing the amount of good to be delivered for certain indexes combination. In computer science, array indices usually start at 0 in most of programming languages. That's why to receive, for example, "x12122", we need to we need to access array's [0][1][0][1][1] element.

To generate the mentioned above structure for the initial population (based on [9]), the program may be described by the following pseudocode:

```
new_chromosome = five-dimensional empty array
restrictions = object, containing limits for each index

procedure generate:
  for each gene of new_chromosome
    if gene is not last for any of restrictions
      gene = random(0, min among restrictions)

      // subtract left limits for each index
      restrictions = restrictions - gene
    else
      // assign to the last restriction value
      gene = restriction

if chromosome is not valid
  goto generate
else
  return chromosome
```

Step 2. Assessment of the current population's fitness scores. As mentioned before, the fitness function for solving transportation problems is the objective function of the transportation problem. In the classic transportation problem, the objective function contains only the minimization of the total transportation cost. However, it is possible to include additional objectives to the fitness function [5], such as the number of used vehicles, time, etc.

The pseudocode for the fitness function:

```
tariffs = five-dimensional array with fees (input)
time_costs = five-dimensional array with time (input)
fitness_function = 0
chromosome = five-dimensional array with genes

for each gene of chromosome
  // multiplication is performed with the tariff
  // and time_costs particularly for the current gene
  gene_fitness = gene * tariffs + gene * time_costs
  fitness_function = fitness_function + gene_fitness

return fitness_function
```

Step 3. Check genetic algorithm stop criteria. For solving the five-index transportation problem, the researcher can choose the criterion for stopping the genetic algorithm based on the parameters on the problem and the goals from the existing methods. In the literature, among available stop criteria are [16]: 1) the number of generations; 2) the time of the algorithm functioning; 3) the acceptable range of the fitness function (cost and time); 4) plato for specified number of generations; 5) specified number of chromosomes in all generations.

Our research considers the number of generations as stop criteria for the genetic algorithm.

The pseudocode for checking the stop criteria:

```
max_generations = number with max generations (input)
generation_index = index of current generation

if generation_index equals to max_generations number
  return fittest chromosome
else
  continue
```

Step 4. Selection of the chromosomes to the mating pool. The chromosomes from the mating pool are the chromosomes that participate in the forming of the next generation by applying to them genetic operators. The selection method can be chosen by the researcher as well from the existing ones [9, 16]: 1) roulette-wheel selection; 2) tournament selection; 3) rank selection; 4) elitism selection, etc.

Different methods of selection may have different efficiency based on the parameters of the problem. That's why it is important to take into account the parameters of the problem and test different solutions while implementing the algorithm for usage.

The pseudocode for selection:

```
mating_pool = empty array
population = array, containing current generation
population_size = number (input)

for population_size times
  first_candidate = random chromosome from population
  second_candidate = random chromosome from population
  winner = fittest among 1st and 2nd candidate

mating_pool.add(winner)
```

Step 5. Application of the genetic operators. For solving transportation problem, the application of both genetic operators are appropriate: mutation and crossover.

The crossover operation allows producing children based on parents by exchanging genetic material (genes) in an established way. The points of exchange may also be determined by the researcher. It is possible to make such breakpoints by some index, for example, by origin index (odd or even). For the transportation problem, we use the multi-point crossover, which exchanges only the genes with the same interpretation in the real world. So, for example, the gene "x12122" of the first parent can be exchanged for the gene "x12122" of the second parent but can't be exchanged for "x12222".

Pseudocode for crossover:

```
child = five-dimensional array

for each gene of child
  if gene is odd
    gene = 1st parent's corresponding gene
  else
    gene = 2and parent's corresponding gene
```

The mutation operation is used to prevent losing the diversity of the genetic material. It chooses a random gene of the chromosome and changes to the random values (from zero to the highest values, allowed by restrictions).

Pseudocode for mutation:

```
restrictions = object, containing limits for each index
chromosome = five-index array
mutated_gene = random gene from chromosome

mutated_gene = random(0, min among restrictions)
```

The genetic operator is chosen randomly with the specified crossover rate (value from 0 to 1). Mostly the crossover rate equals the values close to 1 [16], meaning that nearly 100% of operations will be done with the crossover operator. However, if the genetic material loses diversity very quickly, the researcher may try lowering the crossover rate.

Step 6. Forming the population for the next generation. The chromosomes obtained as a result of applying the genetic operators create a new generation. However, some chromosomes may not satisfy all the restrictions (go out of its feasible region). The chromosome is included in the next generation only once the one is in the feasible region.

If the chromosome is out of the feasible region, we can apply the special procedure, which evenly distributes the restrictions deviation to its genes until it satisfies the restrictions.

Pseudocode of the procedure of returning chromosome to feasible region:

```
restrictions = object, containing limits for each index
chromosome = five-dimensional array with genes

for each gene of chromosome
  restrictions = restrictions + gene

restrictions_deviations = object, containing arrays
for all restrictions
    restrictions_deviations = genes sum - restriction
// decrement or increment genes by 1 till the deviation
// is eliminated
while all restrictions_deviations do not equal to 0
  for all genes
    if deviation is positive among all restrictions
      gene = gene - 1
    else deviation is negative among all restrictions
      gene = gene + 1
```

Step 7. The Same as Step 2.

Step 8. Choosing the fittest chromosome as a result of the genetic algorithm. In the classic genetic algorithm, we choose the chromosome with the highest fitness function value. However, the fittest chromosome among all generations may be lost. To prevent it, we can use the elitist approach [9], which checks on each iteration the best chromosome of the generation, and if it is fitter than the current elitist - it replaces the elitist. In the end, we return to the elitist as a result of the problem.

Pseudocode of the elitist function:

```
current_elitist = five-index array
fittest_in_generation = five-index array, fittest
chromosome in the current generation

if fittest_in_generation is fitter than current_elitist
  current_elitist = fittest_in_generation
```

Then the pseudocode of the checking the stop criterion will be as follows:

```
max_generations = number with max generations (input)
generation_index = index of current generation

if generation_index equals to max_generations
  return elitist
```

The program implementation of the genetic algorithm for solving similar problems may be a part of the system of the e-governance, which is responsible for logistics. Ideally, a manager should be able to control the process and adjust the parameters such a population size, crossover rate, stop criteria or selection method, which leads to extracting maximum results from the mathematical model. The alternative is to write an algorithm that will change the parameters and try to get the best results.

5   Conclusions

Black swan events happened throughout human history in different forms, such as natural disasters, wars, and accidents, causing supply chain breaks and creating new supply chains under the condition of emergency. The role of logistics in the black swan event is hard to overrate since the result of such events utterly always requires certain goods to deal with them.

Black swan events cannot be predicted, but the risk-management strategy and the results mitigation can be developed. That is why the government should encounter supply chain management under emergency.

The main difference between supply chain management under emergency and the regular supply chain management is that exists the time constraints and the management process can be split into two phases: the mitigation phase (develop strategies, systems, tools, and stocks) and the active one (the application of the mitigation phase results or development of tools for new problems in real-time).

Supply chain management under emergencies can be viewed on different levels of abstraction, such as strategic risk management on the governmental level, e-governance, including software and hardware, and specific decision-making tools. In the paper, we focus on e-governance by looking at how it can be used for specific tools and on the specific tool which solves the logistics problem of transportation.

In the paper, we come up with the representation of a problem that may occur as a result of a black swan event, where the different types of goods should be delivered from several origins to several destinations through several warehouses where the sorting and packing are done by several vehicles in a limited time.

The classical methods to solve transportation problems lose their efficiency since the time with the growth of the number of indexes increases exponentially, thus actualizing the need to search for new solutions that can allow obtaining good results in an acceptable time. A suitable example of such a method can be a genetic algorithm.

A genetic algorithm works with several potential solutions at each step of its functioning and uses the mechanisms which resemble the natural evolution, allowing to obtain a good solution (or even optimal) in a reasonable time. The steps of a genetic algorithm for a five-index transportation problem with time constraints are described in the article. Also, for each step, the possible program implementation is presented.

Specific ambiguous processes, which are omitted in the literature, are described, such as the procedure for returning a chromosome to the feasible region in detail in pseudocode. Without such a procedure, obtaining a feasible solution is nearly impossible, which is why it is essential to describe it in detail.

The five-index transportation problem with time constraints can be a part of a decision-making system, which uses real-time data from different sources such as maps and governmental or business APIs. However, some configurations for the problem itself should be configurable since some problems are unique and may need extra configuration. Except for the transportation problem, the parameters for a genetic algorithm may also be configurable for a searcher, allowing to find better results.

In the scope of using a genetic algorithm for solving multi-index transportation problems, the influence of parameters change is one of the exciting and low-discovered topics which deserves separate research. Also, in further works, we plan to focus on other logistics tools and methods to solve them efficiently.

References

1. Terje, A.: On the meaning of a black swan in a risk context. Saf. Sci. **57**, 44–51 (2013). https://doi.org/10.1016/j.ssci.2013.01.016
2. Federal Emergency Management Agency Homepage. https://www.fema.gov/
3. Zarghami, S.A., Dumrak, J.: Unearthing vulnerability of supply provision in logistics networks to the black swan events: applications of entropy theory and network analysis. Reliab. Eng. Syst. Saf. **215** (2021). https://doi.org/10.1016/j.ssci.2013.01.016
4. Rachida, A., Monia, R., Jacques, R.: An exact solution approach for multi-objective location–transportation problem for disaster response. Comput. Oper. Res. **41**, 83–93 (2014). https://doi.org/10.1016/j.cor.2013.08.001
5. Sankar K.R., Gurupada, M.: Minimizing cost and time through single objective function in multi-choice interval valued transportation problem. J. Intell. Fuzzy Syst. **32**(3), 1697–1709 (2017)
6. Xavier, I.R., Bandeira, R.A., Bandeira, A.P., Campos, V.B., Silva, L.O.: Planning the use of helicopters in distribution of supplies in response operations of natural disasters. Transp. Res. Procedia. **47**, 633–640 (2020). https://doi.org/10.1016/j.trpro.2020.03.141
7. Chern, C.C., Chen, Y.L., Kung, L.C.: A heuristic relief transportation planning algorithm for emergency supply chain management. Int. J. Comput. Math. **87**(7), 1638–1664 (2009). https://doi.org/10.1080/00207160802441256
8. William, H., Ping, J.: A genetic algorithm for generalised transportation problem. Int. J. Comput. Appl. Technol. **22**(4), 190–197 (2005) DOI: https://doi.org/10.1504/IJCAT.2005.006959
9. Skitsko, V., Voinikov, M.: Solving four-index transportation problem with the use of a genetic algorithm. Logforum **16**(3), 397–408 (2020). https://doi.org/10.17270/J.LOG.2020.493
10. Berkoune, D., Renaud, J., Rekik, M., Ruiz, A.: Transportation in disaster response operations. Socioecon. Plann. Sci. **46**, 23–32 (2012)
11. Antony, A., Chandrasekharan, R.: A genetic algorithm for solving the fixed-charge transportation model: two-stage problem. Comput. Oper. Res. **39**(9), 2016–2032 (2012). https://doi.org/10.1016/j.cor.2011.09.020
12. Halley, K.: The solid transportation problem. Ops. Res. **10**, 448–463 (1962)
13. Mapbox Homepage. https://www.mapbox.com/
14. Google Maps Homepage. https://www.google.com/maps
15. Ron, S.: The efficiency of the simplex method: a survey. Manage. Sci. **33**(3), 301–334 (1987)
16. Luke, S.: Essentials of Metaheuristics, second edition, p. 242. Lulu (2013)

Public Budget Simulations with Machine Learning and Synthetic Data: Some Challenges and Lessons from the Mexican Case

David Valle-Cruz[(✉)] [iD], Vanessa Fernandez-Cortez [iD], Asdrúbal López-Chau [iD], and Rafael Rojas-Hernández [iD]

Universidad Autónoma del Estado de México, Santiago Tianguistenco, Mexico
{davacr,vfernandezc,alchau,rrojashe}@uaemex.mx

Abstract. Public resources are always limited and must be sufficient to meet a country's needs in the short term. The budget process is reflected in the structure of the Revenue Law Initiative based on the question: of how much money must be raised, and in the federal spending bill: how will these resources be distributed? Regarding these seminal ideas, this paper explores the potential of machine learning (ML) techniques and synthetic data in public budget simulations. For this purpose, historical data from the Mexican government's federal budget analytics are employed to identify which algorithms perform best in simulating the budget and the challenges in these kinds of practices. Findings discovered that Random Forest was the best-performing algorithm. The paper provides some challenges and lessons for public budgeting with ML and synthetic data. This novel study could assist public budgeting decision-making, simulating scenarios in government.

Keywords: Public budget · Machine learning · Artificial intelligence · Synthetic data · Simulations · Decision-making · Random forest

1 Introduction

Public budgeting is one of the government's wicked problems around the world. As the budgeting decision process becomes more critical, artificial intelligence (AI) benefits construction, such as consistency, uniformity, and decision formalization could help justify and improve the capital budgeting process accountability [21].

Public resources are always limited and must be sufficient to meet a country's needs in the short term. This process for obtaining and distributing these resources is ex-pressed in the Revenue Law Initiative, and the Federal Expenditure Budget Bill. When planning the budget, the global and national economic situation is considered, especially the estimated growth of the Gross Domestic Product (GDP), the price of a barrel of oil, the exchange rate, inflation, international interest rates and the growth of a nation [20].

F. Ortiz-Rodríguez et al. (Eds.): EGETC 2022, CCIS 1666, pp. 141–160, 2022.
https://doi.org/10.1007/978-3-031-22950-3_12

In order to make decisions and be aware of possible risks to economic stability and growth. AI includes various techniques that attempt to simulate the behavior of living beings. One of the techniques mostly adopted by global organizations is machine learning (ML) [3,7]. ML refers to the automated detection of meaningful patterns in data. In the last two decades, it has become a popular tool in almost any task that requires extracting information from large data sets [8,25]. Nowadays, we are surrounded by ML-based technology; e.g. security in credit card transactions by software that learns to detect fraud. ML is also used in scientific applications such as bioinformatics, medicine, astronomy, and economics [16,18]. A common feature of all these applications is that, unlike more traditional uses of computers, in these cases, due to the complexity of the patterns to be detected, a human programmer cannot provide an explicit and detailed specification of how these tasks should be executed. Furthermore, ML techniques has the capacity to learn from different kinds of data and recognize patterns impossible to detect by humans. ML algorithms make it possible to work in resource-scarce environments and represent a strategic tool for organizations in the fourth industrial revolution. In this way, ML in public administration can support better decision-making, reinforce existing good practices, and provide evidence to support decision-making [1,6].

For this reason, there is the potential for machine learning to support government decision-making for resource allocation, generating alternative solutions that cannot always be found with traditional methods [11,23]. Some examples of this can be found in countries such as Japan, India, and U. K. since they are considering using AI to make policy decisions based on data analysis through ML techniques [12,17]. Governments need to adjust their budgets, and if ML could generate models for better decision-making, it would be beneficial [24]. Although it is not about technology doing everything, ML is a powerful tool to assist in decision-making hand in hand with expert knowledge [21,22].

Regarding these ideas and considering that a challenge faced by decision-makers in the public sector is the proposal of possible or prospective scenarios in budget projects with a lack of data. This paper aims to simulate public budget branches with ML techniques and synthetic data in order to provide experiences and potential lessons for decision-making in the public sector. To achieve this, the authors use historical data from the Mexican government's federal budget analytics to identify which type of ML algorithms have better performance in budget simulations. These kinds of experiments could assist decision-making on public budgets, simulating future scenarios in government, especially in contingencies, where governments must make quick and decisive decisions. The paper is divided into five parts, including the foregoing introduction. The second section presents the literature on ML and public budgeting. The third section describes methods based on ML algorithms and synthetic data useful for public budget simulations. The fifth section presents findings. The final section shows conclusions, limitations, and future work.

2   Machine Learning and Public Budgeting

2.1   Machine Learning and Public Budgeting Research

Public finances are finite, this was especially notorious during the COVID-19 crisis and the Ukraine-Russia war. For this reason, the government spending priorities have been overwhelmed by rescue and recovery efforts. For policy and decision-makers in many countries, one impediment to innovating fiscal policy could be the lack of data and information on the causal chains from a policy to its impact on society and the economy. In this regard, well-trained ML models can enable rapid and quantitative predictions and scenarios of policy impact. The combination of advanced statistics, good quality data, and processing power have the potential for ML models to find patterns that connect inputs and outputs [21]. These models are suitable where there is no clear definition and discernible direct connection between inputs and outputs; for complex multi-solution problems such as public policies and budgets or with data-poor scenarios.

Despite its potential, ML effects in the economic policy field have been mainly exploratory. However, the experimentation and development of ML models have a plethoric scope, as never before, due to the processing power of personal computers and the development of open source, easy-to-use libraries in programming languages such as R and Python [12,22]. The advantages of integrating ML algorithms into budgeting processes have to do with building powerful models capable of accurately fore-casting the impact of public spending decisions through simulations and scenarios. Over time, with more data and training, these ML models will improve at identifying causal mechanisms, providing more accurate predictions and guidance. Accurate impact forecasting will enable governments to confidently allocate spending in ways that promote targeted and sustainable outcomes [10].

Fiscal policies and public finances are the most direct and impactful levers to support socio-economic activities and trajectories. Our ability to better inform and monitor public spending is key to promoting fiscal policies that generate welfare and public value. Expanding access to these resources could improve transparency, accountability, and effectiveness of public spending and its impact on our not-so-distant future [4]. Also, public budgeting is at the core of any government, as decisions about resource use affect all areas of public policy and government programs. ML techniques have the potential to improve the public budgeting process. While the potential advantages of using intelligent algorithms for optimization in the private sector have been studied, there are also potential benefits that are unique to the public sector, especially improved decision-making. In this regard, ML has the potential to support in generating of workable solutions to better understand differences between policy priorities and budget allocations, as well as the causes of those differences [10].

ML in administration and its implications for society has attracted widespread interest from researchers and practitioners. Public budgeting could be considered one of the pivotal internal functions of the administration; therefore, it is necessary to under-stand how ML algorithms could affect this function.

In this regard, Valle-Cruz, Gil-Garcia, and Fernandez-Cortez [23] explored the AI techniques potential in the public budget allocations to different programs and policies. Their findings suggest that government decision-makers should consider encouraging investment in social and economic development, as well as increasing the budget in non-programmable expenditures to activate the economy [4].

In Italy, the accounts of local authorities are analyzed to verify data accuracy and the accounting system sustainability. The large number of municipalities and entities to be audited create a complicated analysis process, which has traditionally been carried out by the individual magistrate and his staff. In recent years, specific legislative measures have been adopted requiring authorities to input relevant information digitally into a system that facilitates data collection, interpretation, and review. The new system eases data collection, but all the document and data analysis are a challenge. To improve the audit work, Puglia has implemented advanced data analysis and ML techniques that allow processing large volumes of information and analyzing massive amounts of data [19].

In this regard, ML has the potential to solve various problems faced by revenue and finance agencies. By optimizing processes, ML makes public finance management and tax administration more efficient and helps agencies meet the constant demand to do more with less. Improving controls and detecting anomalies in large data volumes helps reduce accounting errors, identify risks and prevent tax fraud and financial crime. In addition, automating routine processes allows agencies to focus human input on what matters, i.e., using information from data to make better decisions.

ML, robotic process automation, and natural language processing feed into different data sources. For their results to be valuable, the data supporting them must be reliable, consistent, transparent, and available on time [2]. Moraes and colleagues [13] analyze applications of a civic initiative to monitor public spending by federal deputies in Brazil. The authors apply the same ML technologies employed by Google, Microsoft, and Netflix to monitor the use of compensation funds granted to parliamentarians and share the information in a form accessible to anyone; in this regard, the citizenry can supervise and audit such spending, with a minimum of knowledge.

Publicity is a fundamental and structuring principle of public administration, standing out as a supervision instrument and a social control mechanism. In Brazil, public managers are required by law to be accountable and transparent with public spending, the comptroller and public finance court is responsible for monitoring and ensuring that the information provided is clear and complete. Barros de Jesus and colleagues [5] present a comparative study between Support Vector Machine, Naïve Bayes, and Logistic Regression models to classify public spending according to its purpose, identifying some branches omitted by managers. The model built detected 124 unpublished records totaling of 3.1 million dollars.

For the Mexican context, the government invested in technologies such as robots and automation to process the information, cross-reference invoicing data, and at the slightest non-compliance detected, send requirements to the taxpayers' mailbox. ML techniques allows data collection from electronic invoices. It is used to formulate expectations and trends concerning its analysis results, allowing pattern recognition. Furthermore, it allows electronic billing data to be grouped into mathematically formed algorithms; when the program is executed, it develops a series of rules to analyze the data in detail [9]. Despite all this, ML techniques should not necessarily be used to make final decisions automatically but rather to provide insights and identify possible opportunities and contrasting scenarios that managers can evaluate and incorporate into their decision-making processes.

2.2   The Mexican Public Budget

The budget's purpose is to allocate resources to redefine the public service concept, combat corruption, guide resources to the highest national public life priorities and reorient public policies towards programs and projects that require an allocation that enhances the scope of their actions and contributes to development with well-being [15]. Public budget classification could be divided into four categories [14].

- *Programmatic.* Classifying public expenditures into two types of resources: first used to implement and execute specific government plans and programs generally associated with the provision of public goods and services; and second used as general expenditures unrelated to any concrete program. Expenditures are classified as programmable and non-programmable.
- *Administrative.* This category of expenditures is consolidated according to the entity or administrative unit responsible for spending. The accountable units for spending can be grouped into three major groups: federal government, parastatal sector or entities of direct budgetary control, and the entities responsible for exercising non-programmable spending. Each branch includes other responsible units that depend on them, such as the Ministries, the General Directorates, the Coordinating Offices, Area Directorates, Sub-Directorates, etc.
- *Functional.* Aggregating the budget expenditure by type of public functions and related to the provision and supply of public goods.
- *Economic.* In this classifying the budget organizes expenditures by object, according to the economic nature of the spending, whether it serves to maintain the cur-rent operating process of the State, or to maintain or expand its scale of operation, the infrastructure, and the public patrimony. This classification divides expenditures in current and capital expenditure.

The budgeting process consists of seven stages [20]:

- *Planning.* The purpose of this stage is to ensure that money is allocated to achieve the country's vision established in the National Development Plan.
- *Programming.* During this stage, the budgetary program the entities and the re-sources needed to meet their objectives are defined. The process is reflected in the structure of the Revenue Law Initiative.

- *Budgeting* describes the amount, form of distribution, and destination of public resources of the three main branches of government (Executive, Legislative and Judicial), autonomous agencies, such as the Electoral Institute and the National Human Rights Commission, as well as transfers to state and municipal governments.
- *Exercise and control.* Once the Expenditure Budget has been approved by the Chamber of Deputies, the agencies and entities of the Federal Public Administration are responsible for exercising the resources allocated to them under the calendar determined for this purpose.
- *Follow-up* consists of generating the necessary information on the progress of indicator goals and the use of resources allocated to programs. This stage makes it possible to evaluate strategies and adapt them to changing circumstances (contingent situations) and contributes to decision-making with quality information for the allocation and reallocation of spending.
- *Evaluation* is the systematic and objective analysis of programs to determine the relevance and achievement of their objectives and goals and their efficiency, effectiveness, quality, results, impact, and sustainability. For evaluations to be truly objective and used to improve programs, they are carried out by external evaluators who are experts in the field.
- *Accountability.* This stage is to report on results, correct deficiencies, and audit, promote an open government that fosters accountability.

In this research, the authors explore the potential of ML techniques and synthetic data to simulate the administrative classification by branch analyzing the first four stages.

3   Methods

3.1   Data Collection

We downloaded data from the Mexican government's federal budget analytics. The accessible data covers from 2005 to 2021 and is available on the Ministry of Finance and Public Credit portal: https://www.pef.hacienda.gob.mx/es/PEF/Analiticos_PresupuestariosPEF. These data were used to train the ML models. Prediction results were compared with data contained in the reports of the 2022 volumes of the federal budget (https://www.pef.hacienda.gob.mx/es/PEF2022/analiticos_presupuestarios) (See Table 1).

In this way, the best algorithms for each category of the public budget were identified and analyzed. Appendices (Table 2) shows descriptive statistics of the public budget analytics.

3.2   Synthetic Data

Enough samples are necessary to generate accurate prediction models with the ML methods. In our specific case, there are only 18 samples (one per year) per government dependency. These data correspond to the years 2005 to 2022. In

Table 1. Mexican government's federal budget branches

Branch ID	Branch in Spanish	Branch in English
01	Poder Legislativo	Legislative Branch
02	Oficina de la Presidencia de la Republica	Office of the Presidency of the Republic
03	Poder Judicial	Judicial Branch
04	Gobernacion	Government
05	Relaciones Exteriores	Foreign Affairs
06	Hacienda y Credito Publico	Treasury and Public Credit
07	Defensa Nacional	National Defense
08	Agricultura y Desarrollo Rural	Agriculture and Rural Development
09	Comunicaciones y Transportes	Communications and Transportation
10	Economia	Economy
11	Educacion Publica	Public Education
12	Salud	Health
13	Marina	Navy
14	Trabajo y Prevision Social	Labor and Social Welfare
15	Desarrollo Agrario Territorial y Urbano	Agrarian, Territorial, and Urban Development
16	Medio Ambiente y Recursos Naturales	Environment and Natural Resources
17	Procuraduría General de la Republica	Office of the Attorney General of the Republic
18	Energia	Energy
19	Aportaciones a Seguridad Social	Social Security Contributions
20	Bienestar	Welfare
21	Turismo	Tourism
22	Instituto Nacional Electoral	National Electoral Institute
23	Provisiones Salariales y Económicas	Salary and Economic Provisions
24	Deuda Publica	Public Debt
25	Previsiones y Aportaciones para los Sistemas de Educacion Básica Normal Tecnológica y de Adultos	Provisions and Contributions for the Basic, Technological, Normal, Technological, and Adult Education Systems
27	Función Publica	Public Function
28	Participaciones a Entidades Federativas y Municipios	Contributions to Federal Entities and Municipalities
30	Adeudos de Ejercicios Fiscales Anteriores	Debts from Previous Fiscal Years
31	Tribunales Agrarios	Agrarian Courts
32	Tribunal Federal de Justicia Administrativa	Federal Court of Administrative Justice
33	Aportaciones Federales para Entidades Federativas y Municipios	Federal Contributions for Federal Entities and Municipalities
34	Erogaciones para los Programas de Apoyo a Ahorradores y Deudores de la Banca	Expenditures for Programs to Support Savers and Bank Debtors
35	Comisión Nacional de los Derechos Humanos	National Human Rights Commission
36	Seguridad y Protección Ciudadana	Security and Citizen Protection
37	Consejería Jurídica del Ejecutivo Federal	Legal Counsel of the Federal Executive
38	Consejo Nacional de Ciencia y Tecnología	National Council of Science and Technology
40	Información Nacional Estadística y Geográfica	National Statistical and Geographic Information
41	Comisión Federal de Competencia Económica	Federal Economic Competition Commission
42	Instituto Nacional para la Evaluación de la Educación	National Institute for the Evaluation of Education
43	Instituto Federal de Telecomunicaciones	Federal Telecommunications Institute
44	Instituto Nacional de Transparencia Acceso a la Información y Protección de Datos Personales	National Institute of Transparency Access to Information and Protection of Personal Data
45	Comisión Reguladora de Energía	Energy Regulatory Commission
46	Comisión Nacional de Hidrocarburos	National Hydrocarbons Commission
47	Entidades no Sectorizadas	Non-Sector Entities
48	Cultura	Culture
49	Fiscalía General de la Republica	Office of the Attorney General of the Republic

initial experiments, we found that predictions were inaccurate with these scanty samples. Therefore, a linear interpolation was applied to generate synthetic samples. These were used to build predictive models. We observe that this approach improves the performance of the models according to R-squared (R^2), Mean Absolute Error (MAE), Mean Squared Error (MSE), Mean Absolute Percentage Error (MAPE), and Explained Variance Score (EVS). Linear interpolation is one of the simplest methods to generate synthetic data. The underlying model assumes that the relationship between two consecutive samples have the form:

$$z = \alpha x + (1 - \alpha)y \tag{1}$$

where

α is a real number in the interval [0, 1]
x, y are samples from data set
z is the sample generated

The number of samples generated between two consecutive years was eleven. The values of α are computed with $\frac{n}{12}$ where n = 1, 2, ..., 11. After applying this interpolation method, the number of synthetic samples generated was 187. Therefore, the data set contains 205 instances.

3.3 Machine Learning Algorithms

Experimentation is based on testing the potential of ML techniques in public budgets. The algorithms used are briefly explained below.

Random Forest. Random forests (RF) classifier belongs to the category of ensemble methods. In these, the predictions of some base classifiers are aggregated, and the prediction resulted is computed using a voting scheme. This arrangement of base classifiers improves the classification accuracy if the errors committed for each classifier are uncorrelated concerning the other classifiers' errors within the ensemble and if in addition each classifier has an error rate lower than 0.5. RF is an ensemble composed of base classifiers that are all decision trees. This classifier achieves high performance in many applications and is robust to noise in data.

To reduce or avoid the correlation between errors rates of decision trees in a RF, randomization is usually applied. For example, each base classifier can be trained with a subset (randomly chosen) of samples of the training data set; select randomly a subset of attributes to compute the best split point in the training of decision tree; linear attributes combinations randomly chosen can be used.

Support Vector Machines. Support Vector Machines (SVM) is one of the most popular methods for classification in ML. SVM was developed originally for the classification task; currently, there are also implementations for regression, clustering (one-class problems), and transductive SVM.

The original idea of the SVM classifier is to find a linear decision boundary with maximum margin; clearly, SVM has a geometric inspiration in its conception. The problem of computing this linear decision boundary, or in other words, finding the optimal separating hyperplane, yields a formulation of an optimization problem, specifically, a quadratic programming problem (QPP). In real-world classification problems, it is necessary the use of transformations of data; through special non-linear functions known as kernels. In addition, it is essential to allow a few misclassifications of some instances during the construction of the model to avoid over-fitting.

LSTM. Recursive Neural Networks (RNNs) are one model that consider not only the current data input but also previous states (historical information) of the model itself to make predictions. RNNs can process inputs of any length (such as time series) without requiring changing the number of its components (layers).

A well-known issue of RNNs is that the gradient explodes or vanishes as the number of hidden layers increases or when the length of the input is large, this is due to the multiplications that take place during the calibration of the synaptic weights in the optimization method within the backpropagation algorithm. To cope with the problem of gradient explosion, it can limit to a maximum value set a priori (Gradient clipping) or use second derivatives to optimize the synaptic weights. To prevent the gradient from becoming zero: some elements called gates are used to form units, add-ed to modify the cell state (memory) of RNNs. The gates use the previous state and the current input to generate the appropriate responses. These gates are the following:

- Input or update gate. It computes which values will be updated and which ones will remain unchanged.
- Forget gate. Its function is to decide whether a part of the information is discarded or not.
- Output gate. Computes the next value of the cell state (hidden state) of the RNN.
- Two important units are GRU (Gated Recurrent Unit) and LSTM (Long Short-Term Memory). These units improve the performance of RNNs, making them capable of facing long-term temporal dependencies.
- LSTM can be considered a special type of RNN, designed to work with long-term sequences. GRU was designed for the same purpose but to attend the vanishing gradient problem.

3.4   Data Pre-processing

Public budget analytics are obtained as a time series, that is, a set of ordered values collected at successive moments. Figure 1 shows a non-real-world example of a simple univariate time series. Meanwhile, for training a ML model for

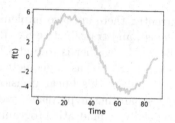

Fig. 1. Example of a time series

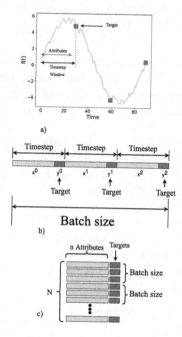

Fig. 2. Transformation of time-series into a supported format for training prediction models

prediction, the input must be a set of vectors, each associated with real value as a target. Therefore, a proper transformation is required. It is explained in Fig. 2: a) shows the range of values (time-step) from which the first vector and its target are obtained; b) shows a batch of the values of vectors and their corresponding targets. This number of samples is called the batch size; finally, c) shows a data set with a suitable structure for training machine learning models.

3.5 Comparison and Simulation

For the data analysis, the amounts were transformed from Mexican pesos to percent-ages, considering as 100% the total amount of the expenditure budget for each year. In this regard, the budget percentage that each branch represents was obtained. By presenting the data as a proportion of the budget expenditure, the comparison between years is easier, and the increase or decrease with respect to other years is clearly identified.

Next, an annual comparison was made of the public budget branches proportion to determine their degree of variation. This allowed to understand the yearly increases in percentage terms for each analyzed factor.

Then, the three ML algorithms were tested (RF, SVM and LSTM), performing measurements to understand the performance of each algorithm by means of R^2, MAE, MSE, MAPE and EVS. The best models were selected for the simulation of the year 2022 based on real and synthetic historical data from the years 2005 to 2021. It was also performed a simulation for the year 2023, the same with historical real and synthetic data from 2005 to 2022.

Furthermore, a comparison of the verified data for 2022 was made with the simulated data. Finally, a simulation of the budget by the object of expenditure (branches) for the year 2023 was performed.

4 Findings

The analysis presented in this paper has some implications and lessons that may be useful for the public budgeting process and decision-making based on ML and synthetic data. This can be a new and functional area of public budgeting based on analytical and algorithmic processing. We consider that, through ML, public budget simulations can be performed by analyzing previous allocations (previous situations and historical data). In this research, we assumed that the government allocated re-sources in the best possible way in previous periods despite the contingencies and considering the economic events, circumstances, and challenges faced at that time. Therefore, ML techniques have the potential to learn from these decisions and the simulations it generates, considering previous experiences. The main findings are presented below.

4.1 Machine Learning Algorithms and Data Analysis

We found that RF was the best performing technique (See Appendices: Table 3). Although LSTM is a robust and sophisticated technique, it did not perform well and did not fit well with the data from our experiments. LSTM has the potential to provide better results with a large amount of data or with other kinds of data. For this reason, RF was selected for most simulations. SVM was only used to simulate data related to national defense and federal contributions for federal entities and municipalities. LSTM was discarded for this stage of the simulations. Regarding the ML algorithms and data analysis, there is the potential to generate synthetic data to facilitate simulations. Since the interval between each time series data is large (one year), it is possible to generate synthetic data for intermediate times. The differences created do not affect the final value of each interval but have the potential to help in the training process of the regressors. LSTM is an algorithm that uses short and long-term memory and does not allow the generation of satisfactory results, compared to RF and SVM, for small data sets.

4.2 Public Budget Simulations

The annual public budget branches' percentage differences (See Appendices: Table 4) were used to improve the results of the simulations. For the 2022 and 2023 simulations, the averages of public budget branches' annual percentage difference (See Appendices: Table 5) were used. Findings show a 4.16% difference between real data ($5,445,515,741,818.00) and ML simulation ($5,218,881,946,851.66). Although this is a relatively small error and acceptable for discussing interesting simulations, it could be improved by generating synthetic data with other AI techniques or exploring other ML algorithms. Our simulation for the year 2023 results in a total of $5,710,420,884,384.90, and each budget's detail branch can be found in the Appendices: Table 5.

4.3 Public Budget Process

For the *planning stage*, it is considered that one of the principal government problems is the efficient allocation of resources to achieve the country's economic development and the population welfare. Therefore, the planning of the expenditure budget must be strategic, operative, and participatory; to detect the population's needs, considering the objectives to be achieved. Nowadays, there are several means of communication between the government and the citizens, where the population expresses its needs, complaints, and suggestions. An example of these means of communication is social media, in this regard, governments can detect where resources should be allocated. There are ML techniques that facilitate the sentiment and content analysis in social media, in addition to allowing the perception of citizens' sentiment towards budgetary decisions made by the government.

For the *programming stage*, it is essential to consider that public resources are always limited and must be sufficient to meet a country's needs in the short term. These needs are met through budgetary programs, to which resources are allocated to meet the objectives established in the planning stage. One tool on which the government can rely for the resources' efficient allocation is through optimization algorithms or evolutionary techniques to distribute available resources, learning from historical data and finding the scenario that best fits to promote the benefit of society.

The *budgeting stage* describes the amount, form of distribution, and destination of public resources of the government branches. Expenditures are consolidated according to the entity or administrative unit responsible for its execution. These groups give rise to identifying the responsible entities for each branch of spending. It should be noted that for these branches, public resources are also limited and must be sufficient to achieve the objectives established for each of them. Governments must seek tools to support and verify that the decisions made for the allocation expenditure budget are suitable for achieving the objectives set out in the planning stage. Each agency decides the allocation of the resources provided by the government. For this reason, ML techniques chosen for simulations may be different since each branch has different allocation priorities. In our findings, SVM was only used to simulate data related to the national defense branch and federal contributions for federal entities and municipalities; for the rest of the agencies or branches RF works better.

For the *exercise and control stage*, the expenditure budget is adjusted to the previously formulated planning process, in this regard, the agencies do not spend only for exercising the resources they were approved but there is a logic behind it that they must follow punctually through the actions they execute. In this regard, control refers to not exercising spending arbitrarily but achieving results and promoting the efficient use of resources. However, contingent events are causing a change in the allocation of the expenditure budget, which consequently leads to the next stage.

In the *follow-up stage*, the necessary information is generated on the progress of the goals established in the planning and on the use of the resources allocated to the pro-grams; it evaluates the strategies and adapts them to the changing circumstances, contributing to decision making. An example of these contingent events was the COVID-19 pandemic, in which the government was forced to allocate resources to acquire vaccines and strengthen the health sector, leaving out some planned expenditures. Therefore, governments need tools that allow them to make the best decisions quickly and efficiently, through the simulation of scenarios, to face the contingencies that arise.

4.4   Data Driven Decision-Making

Data-driven decision-making is faced with having simulations that have quality results and can provide reliable scenarios. The most sophisticated ML techniques as LSTM require a large amount of data to perform well. However, sometimes it is not possible to have enough data. For this reason, the generation of synthetic data for decision-making is a feasible path in the absence of sources that allow generating both statistical models and those based on ML.

5   Conclusions, Limitations, and Future Work

This paper analyzed the potential of machine learning (ML) and synthetic data generation for public budget simulation in Mexico. Given the lack of time-series data for each branch of the public budget, this type of practice can be a feasible option. ML techniques combined with synthetic data can effectively deal with the complexity and data scarcity, helping organizations keep up with changes, mitigate risk, and create value.

When planning the budget, the global and national economic situation is considered, contemplating different economic factors. The experience and results obtained with scenario-based expenditure budget simulations could provide guidelines for the decisions to be made to achieve the country's economic growth due to its expenditure distribution.

ML combined with synthetic data has the potential to be a tool for detecting pattern that occurred in the past and generate simulations comparable to the current situation. It could facilitate decision-making based on experience, considering the most favorable scenario to solve certain problems.

Future directions will be based on analyzing data from different sources, which will allow the generation of more accurate models capturing the behavior of diverse factors of the public budget.

Although in this paper only simulations were carried out with data from Mexico's public budget, some data related to economic growth, inflation, inequality, and the exchange rate can be added. It is also possible to explore the potential of stronger ML techniques to provide more accurate, useful, and practical simulations for decision-making in the public sector.

A Appendix

Table 2. Descriptive statistics of the public budget analytics

Branch ID	Min	Max	Mean	Median	Standard deviation	Skewness	Kurtosis
01	6.36E+09	1.56E+10	1.16E+10	1.24E+10	2.83E+09	−0.47	−0.96
02	8.05E+08	2.30E+09	1.75E+09	1.80E+09	3.97E+08	−0.89	1.22
03	2.10E+10	7.14E+10	4.83E+10	5.02E+10	1.74E+10	−0.11	−1.43
04	3.42E+09	7.71E+10	3.46E+10	2.10E+10	3.04E+10	0.31	−1.89
05	4.03E+09	9.00E+09	6.87E+09	7.53E+09	1.55E+09	−0.37	−1.24
06	2.02E+10	4.62E+10	3.36E+10	3.44E+10	8.66E+09	0.16	−1.36
07	2.40E+10	1.13E+11	6.18E+10	6.52E+10	2.43E+10	0.20	−0.42
08	4.76E+10	9.21E+10	6.99E+10	7.14E+10	1.41E+10	−0.15	−0.83
09	3.37E+10	1.26E+11	7.93E+10	8.45E+10	2.87E+10	0.07	−0.81
10	6.26E+09	2.12E+10	1.32E+10	1.42E+10	5.36E+09	0.23	−1.44
11	1.28E+11	3.38E+11	2.51E+11	2.68E+11	6.63E+10	−0.60	−0.85
12	3.40E+10	1.45E+11	1.07E+11	1.22E+11	3.39E+10	−0.97	−0.11
13	8.64E+09	3.55E+10	2.24E+10	2.46E+10	8.38E+09	−0.21	−1.11
14	3.19E+09	4.33E+10	8.47E+09	4.37E+09	1.10E+10	2.26	5.44
15	4.44E+09	2.66E+10	1.31E+10	1.09E+10	8.43E+09	0.36	−1.56
16	2.13E+10	6.80E+10	4.46E+10	4.51E+10	1.49E+10	0.14	−1.21
17	8.14E+09	1.73E+10	1.34E+10	1.36E+10	3.40E+09	−0.23	−1.69
18	2.33E+09	4.85E+10	1.77E+10	1.54E+10	1.70E+10	0.64	−1.04
19	2.36E+09	9.61E+11	3.57E+11	3.25E+11	2.66E+11	0.67	0.32
20	2.37E+10	7.86E+11	1.90E+11	1.09E+11	2.37E+11	1.78	2.36
21	1.15E+09	1.51E+11	2.46E+10	5.21E+09	4.44E+10	1.93	3.27
22	3.92E+09	2.68E+10	1.22E+10	1.18E+10	5.69E+09	0.71	0.98
23	6.87E+09	1.42E+11	7.55E+10	6.58E+10	4.90E+10	0.03	−1.56
24	1.13E+11	5.41E+11	2.68E+11	2.40E+11	1.21E+11	1.00	0.95
25	3.32E+10	5.43E+11	1.14E+11	4.69E+10	1.63E+11	1.94	2.91
27	1.25E+09	5.41E+10	9.51E+09	1.46E+09	1.92E+10	1.88	2.43
28	9.02E+08	9.51E+11	4.59E+11	4.94E+11	2.72E+11	−0.15	−0.12
30	4.28E+09	9.20E+11	1.42E+11	1.56E+10	3.05E+11	1.91	2.70
31	5.75E+08	2.34E+10	4.02E+09	9.25E+08	7.52E+09	1.96	2.98
32	8.31E+08	2.86E+09	1.80E+09	1.85E+09	6.99E+08	−0.01	−1.56
33	2.55E+09	7.78E+11	4.23E+11	4.51E+11	2.33E+11	−0.54	−0.23
34	1.10E+10	7.36E+11	1.27E+11	2.06E+10	2.52E+11	1.88	2.49
35	7.08E+08	5.13E+10	7.63E+09	1.42E+09	1.55E+10	2.01	3.48
36	1.73E+09	6.34E+10	2.58E+10	2.61E+10	2.11E+10	0.41	−0.91
37	7.21E+07	5.00E+08	1.33E+08	1.17E+08	9.12E+07	3.66	16.75
38	8.14E+09	3.40E+10	2.27E+10	2.52E+10	9.02E+09	−0.31	−1.21
40	4.55E+09	2.25E+10	9.75E+09	7.79E+09	5.20E+09	1.47	1.73
41	2.97E+08	6.18E+08	5.13E+08	5.08E+08	9.43E+07	−1.08	2.28
42	6.13E+08	1.06E+09	9.55E+08	1.02E+09	1.92E+08	−1.46	4.78
43	6.97E+08	2.00E+09	1.61E+09	1.77E+09	4.67E+08	−0.73	−0.29
44	8.77E+08	2.00E+09	1.21E+09	9.38E+08	4.81E+08	0.93	−0.64
45	2.53E+08	1.10E+09	5.56E+08	4.00E+08	3.31E+08	0.69	−1.27
46	2.20E+08	3.50E+08	3.02E+08	3.20E+08	5.60E+07	−0.65	−1.44
47	2.15E+08	1.48E+10	7.71E+09	1.14E+10	7.07E+09	−0.20	−2.64
48	8.79E+09	1.40E+10	1.09E+10	9.28E+09	2.59E+09	0.41	−3.19
49	1.24E+10	1.73E+10	1.44E+10	1.29E+10	2.34E+09	0.41	−3.08

Table 3. Selected machine learning algorithms

Branch ID	R^2	Best	MAE	Best	MSE	Best	MAPE	Best	EVS	Best	Selected
1	0.9999	RF	0.0026	RF	0.0026	RF	0.0159	RF	0.9999	RF	RF
2	0.9606	RF	0.0165	RF	0.0165	RF	0.0244	RF	0.808	SVM	RF
3	0.9566	RF	0.0189	RF	0.0189	RF	0.0315	RF	0.0613	SVM	RF
4	0.9792	RF	0.0261	RF	0.0261	RF	0.2665	RF	0.9806	RF	RF
5	0.9725	SVM	0.0314	RF	0.0314	RF	0.2332	RF	0.9678	RF	RF
6	0.9876	RF	0.0155	RF	0.0155	RF	3.0577	SVM	0.9876	RF	RF
7	0.9484	SVM	0.0527	RF	0.0527	RF	0.1465	SVM	0.1465	SVM	SVM
8	0.9971	RF	0.0048	RF	0.0048	RF	0.0619	RF	0.9972	RF	RF
9	0.9381	RF	0.0325	RF	0.0325	RF	0.0627	RF	0.9415	RF	RF
10	0.9894	RF	0.0172	RF	0.0172	RF	0.0801	RF	0.9915	RF	RF
11	0.9995	RF	0.0052	RF	0.0052	RF	0.1271	RF	0.9995	RF	RF
12	0.9959	RF	0.0091	RF	0.0091	RF	0.2742	RF	0.9959	RF	RF
13	0.9916	RF	0.0134	RF	0.0134	RF	3.3891	SVM	0.9928	RF	RF
14	0.998	RF	0.0059	RF	0.0059	RF	0.0401	RF	0.9981	RF	RF
15	0.9932	RF	0.0093	RF	0.0093	RF	4.8515	RF	0.9933	RF	RF
16	0.9807	RF	0.0191	RF	0.0191	RF	1.287	RF	0.9808	RF	RF
17	0.9144	RF	0.0309	RF	0.0309	RF	6.34E+12	RF	0.9159	RF	RF
18	0.8902	RF	0.0394	RF	0.0394	RF	1.10E+14	RF	0.8918	RF	RF
19	0.992	RF	0.0135	RF	0.0135	RF	1.035	RF	0.9922	RF	RF
20	0.9084	SVM	0.042	RF	0.042	RF	4.08	SVM	0.5264	RF	RF
21	0.8831	SVM	0.0321	RF	0.0321	RF	0.564	RF	0.6948	RF	RF
22	0.8029	RF	0.0367	RF	0.0367	RF	0.734	RF	0.8052	RF	RF
23	0.8116	SVM	0.0463	RF	0.0463	RF	4.247	SVM	0.6552	RF	RF
24	0.7342	RF	0.0651	RF	0.0651	RF	1.75	RF	0.7401	RF	RF
25	0.8773	RF	0.0201	RF	0.0201	RF	0.057	RF	0.5664	SVM	RF
27	0.9777	RF	0.0281	RF	0.0281	RF	0.595	RF	0.9827	RF	RF
28	0.9903	RF	0.0094	RF	0.0094	RF	5.54E+01	SVM	0.9904	RF	RF
30	0.8705	SVM	0.034	RF	0.034	RF	0.0774	RF	0.7391	RF	RF
31	0.6254	SVM	0.0593	RF	0.0593	RF	1.86E+02	SVM	0.0505	RF	RF
32	0.6343	SVM	0.0625	RF	0.0625	RF	1.8445	RF	0.5625	RF	RF
33	0.9416	SVM	0.0481	SVM	0.0481	SVM	0.2513	SVM	0.2513	SVM	SVM
34	0.8774	RF	0.0358	RF	0.0358	RF	11.9671	RF	0.8822	RF	RF
35	0.8999	RF	0.0236	RF	0.0236	RF	1.7503	RF	0.9002	RF	RF
36	0.9945	RF	0.0026	RF	0.0026	RF	5.57E+02	SVM	0.9947	RF	RF
37	0.9253	SVM	0.0518	RF	0.0518	RF	2.99E+09	RF	0.6631	RF	RF
38	0.6811	RF	0.0368	RF	0.0368	RF	0.9926	RF	0.6974	RF	RF
40	0.9666	SVM	0.0296	RF	0.0296	RF	0.056	RF	0.1473	SVM	RF
41	0.473	SVM	0.0438	RF	0.0438	RF	1.01E+14	RF	0.4779	RF	RF
42	0.9763	RF	0.0208	RF	0.0208	RF	6.34E+11	RF	0.9775	RF	RF
43	0.87	SVM	0.0473	RF	0.0473	RF	1.70E+14	RF	0.8079	RF	RF
44	0.9122	SVM	0.0474	RF	0.0474	RF	1.63E+12	RF	0.8533	RF	RF
45	0.9223	RF	0.0338	RF	0.0338	RF	3.97E+11	RF	0.9237	RF	RF
46	0.892	RF	0.026	RF	0.026	RF	8.74E+10	RF	0.892	RF	RF
47	0.9997	RF	0.0029	RF	0.0029	RF	3.21E+11	RF	0.9997	RF	RF
48	0.7635	SVM	0.0502	RF	0.0502	RF	4.19E+11	RF	0.7252	RF	RF
49	0.9897	RF	0.0063	RF	0.0063	RF	2.12E+11	RF	0.9897	RF	RF

Table 4. Annual public budget branches' percentage differences

Branch ID	2022	2021	2020	2019	2018	2017	2016	2016	2015	2014	2013	2012	2011	2010	2009	2008	2007	2006	2005
1	0.28%	0.31%	0.29%	0.29%	0.38%	0.38%	0.39%	0.39%	0.38%	0.37%	0.41%	0.40%	0.40%	0.40%	0.41%	0.45%	0.43%	0.44%	0.45%
2	0.02%	0.02%	0.02%	0.04%	0.04%	0.05%	0.05%	0.05%	0.07%	0.07%	0.07%	0.07%	0.07%	0.07%	0.08%	0.08%	0.09%	0.10%	0.10%
3	1.35%	1.48%	1.45%	1.42%	1.74%	1.83%	1.74%	1.74%	2.20%	1.51%	1.58%	1.55%	1.49%	1.43%	1.42%	1.42%	1.44%	1.50%	1.48%
4	0.11%	0.12%	0.13%	1.36%	1.57%	1.54%	1.84%	1.84%	0.23%	2.25%	0.71%	0.86%	0.64%	0.35%	0.42%	0.34%	0.29%	0.30%	0.24%
5	0.17%	0.17%	0.19%	0.19%	0.22%	0.21%	0.21%	0.21%	0.23%	0.23%	0.24%	0.22%	0.23%	0.25%	0.23%	0.27%	0.28%	0.29%	0.28%
6	0.39%	0.42%	0.51%	0.50%	0.65%	0.71%	0.78%	0.78%	1.35%	1.26%	1.55%	1.68%	1.52%	1.53%	1.60%	1.60%	1.96%	1.74%	1.90%
7	1.91%	2.33%	2.02%	2.09%	1.98%	1.83%	1.97%	1.97%	2.03%	1.96%	2.07%	2.02%	1.95%	1.84%	1.91%	1.75%	1.84%	1.67%	1.69%
8	1.02%	1.02%	1.02%	1.46%	1.76%	1.86%	2.32%	2.32%	2.63%	2.49%	2.56%	2.59%	2.88%	3.09%	3.09%	3.23%	3.34%	3.26%	3.41%
9	1.20%	1.16%	1.17%	1.49%	2.07%	2.23%	2.87%	2.87%	3.60%	3.56%	2.93%	3.10%	3.38%	3.38%	3.17%	2.93%	2.24%	2.16%	2.59%
10	0.07%	0.14%	0.13%	0.20%	0.23%	0.25%	0.40%	0.40%	0.60%	0.64%	0.69%	0.68%	0.64%	0.60%	0.62%	0.54%	0.47%	0.49%	0.49%
11	6.70%	7.01%	7.01%	6.88%	6.87%	7.06%	8.28%	8.28%	8.69%	8.77%	8.84%	9.14%	9.01%	8.85%	8.78%	8.71%	8.68%	8.80%	9.00%
12	3.56%	3.02%	2.77%	2.78%	3.00%	3.21%	3.61%	3.61%	3.84%	3.91%	4.14%	4.12%	4.11%	3.78%	3.71%	3.48%	3.18%	2.71%	2.40%
13	0.69%	0.74%	0.72%	0.72%	0.77%	0.69%	0.75%	0.75%	0.77%	0.74%	0.74%	0.71%	0.71%	0.67%	0.70%	0.67%	0.63%	0.59%	0.61%
14	0.47%	0.49%	0.62%	0.97%	0.10%	0.09%	0.70%	0.70%	0.63%	0.15%	0.20%	0.21%	0.14%	0.22%	0.25%	0.26%	0.27%	0.28%	0.34%
15	0.24%	0.34%	0.34%	0.42%	0.41%	0.42%	0.70%	0.70%	0.63%	1.99%	1.92%	1.99%	2.00%	1.95%	1.97%	1.96%	1.66%	1.37%	1.73%
16	0.75%	0.65%	0.64%	0.69%	0.92%	0.95%	1.52%	1.52%	1.94%	0.52%	0.54%	0.54%	0.47%	0.50%	0.54%	0.54%	0.53%	0.61%	0.57%
17	0.86%	0.00%	1.04%	0.34%	0.40%	0.42%	0.08%	0.08%	0.09%	0.10%	0.08%	0.12%	0.13%	0.13%	1.91%	1.81%	1.87%	1.75%	1.86%
18	0.00%	0.00%	0.00%	0.61%	0.06%	0.06%	0.08%	0.08%	0.08%	0.10%	0.18%	0.19%	0.20%	0.17%	0.17%	0.18%	0.42%	0.53%	0.48%
19	20.05%	19.93%	18.56%	17.57%	17.11%	16.96%	15.13%	15.13%	14.30%	14.57%	13.89%	13.38%	12.70%	12.50%	9.88%	9.55%	10.97%	11.33%	10.41%
20	5.50%	3.98%	3.90%	3.37%	2.61%	2.78%	2.99%	2.99%	3.26%	3.34%	3.24%	3.08%	3.14%	3.37%	2.98%	2.51%	2.17%	1.70%	1.67%
21	1.21%	1.23%	1.21%	1.29%	1.35%	1.37%	1.37%	1.37%	1.34%	1.41%	1.47%	1.56%	1.74%	1.84%	2.14%	2.12%	2.28%	2.12%	2.54%
22	0.36%	0.56%	0.36%	0.20%	0.10%	0.10%	0.42%	0.42%	0.53%	0.35%	0.37%	0.54%	0.41%	0.36%	0.53%	0.69%	0.42%	0.76%	0.45%
23	2.47%	2.64%	2.83%	0.34%	0.59%	0.40%	3.87%	3.87%	3.63%	3.65%	2.62%	2.30%	1.93%	2.77%	3.62%	2.60%	2.95%	0.69%	0.45%
24	10.66%	11.22%	11.57%	12.14%	11.57%	10.99%	9.76%	9.76%	9.18%	9.23%	9.56%	9.36%	9.37%	9.80%	9.35%	10.04%	10.58%	11.65%	11.14%
25	1.11%	0.80%	1.23%	1.21%	1.29%	1.35%	1.37%	1.37%	1.34%	1.41%	1.47%	1.56%	1.74%	1.84%	2.14%	2.12%	2.28%	2.12%	2.54%
27	0.03%	0.03%	0.03%	0.04%	0.05%	0.05%	0.04%	0.04%	0.04%	0.04%	0.05%	0.05%	0.04%	0.04%	0.07%	0.08%	0.09%	0.59%	0.50%
28	18.72%	19.11%	20.45%	20.56%	19.85%	19.60%	18.54%	18.54%	17.30%	17.32%	18.18%	18.32%	19.28%	18.58%	18.79%	20.08%	18.53%	18.61%	19.21%
30	0.55%	0.67%	0.46%	0.49%	0.42%	0.62%	0.44%	0.44%	0.46%	0.47%	0.51%	0.52%	0.53%	0.56%	0.22%	0.05%	0.05%	0.89%	0.05%
31	0.02%	0.06%	0.05%	0.02%	0.02%	0.02%	0.07%	0.07%	0.03%	0.03%	0.03%	0.04%	0.03%	0.03%	0.04%	0.03%	0.05%	0.04%	0.01%
32	0.05%	0.06%	0.06%	0.02%	0.02%	0.02%	0.07%	0.07%	0.07%	0.07%	0.07%	0.07%	0.07%	0.07%	0.07%	0.06%	0.06%	0.07%	0.08%
33	15.25%	16.13%	16.33%	16.45%	16.83%	17.20%	16.84%	16.84%	16.86%	16.36%	17.46%	17.50%	17.62%	17.64%	17.31%	18.55%	18.99%	18.69%	19.11%
34	0.71%	0.23%	0.93%	1.15%	0.93%	0.95%	0.56%	0.56%	0.31%	0.35%	0.46%	0.45%	0.58%	0.58%	1.35%	1.51%	1.55%	2.37%	2.24%
35	0.03%	0.03%	0.04%	0.04%	0.05%	0.05%	0.04%	0.04%	0.04%	0.04%	0.05%	0.05%	0.04%	0.04%	0.04%	0.04%	0.05%	0.59%	0.50%
36	1.71%	1.32%	1.29%	1.15%	0.00%	0.00%	0.00%	0.00%	0.00%	0.00%	1.40%	1.47%	1.39%	1.36%	1.44%	0.00%	0.78%	0.00%	0.00%
37	0.00%	0.00%	0.02%	0.04%	0.00%	0.00%	0.00%	0.00%	0.00%	0.00%	0.00%	0.00%	0.00%	0.00%	0.02%	0.05%	0.05%	0.00%	0.01%
38	0.54%	0.55%	0.55%	0.55%	0.67%	0.71%	0.93%	0.93%	0.96%	0.03%	0.86%	0.79%	0.69%	0.67%	0.68%	0.60%	0.53%	0.57%	0.57%
40	0.20%	0.16%	0.06%	0.27%	0.19%	0.19%	0.21%	0.21%	0.24%	0.24%	0.18%	0.18%	0.18%	0.37%	0.33%	0.00%	0.00%	0.00%	1.44%
41	0.01%	0.01%	0.01%	0.01%	0.02%	0.01%	0.01%	0.01%	0.01%	0.01%	0.00%	0.00%	0.00%	0.00%	0.00%	0.00%	0.00%	0.00%	0.00%
42	0.00%	0.00%	0.00%	0.04%	0.00%	0.00%	0.03%	0.03%	0.03%	0.02%	0.00%	0.00%	0.00%	0.00%	0.00%	0.00%	0.00%	0.00%	0.00%
43	0.03%	0.02%	0.03%	0.03%	0.05%	0.05%	0.05%	0.05%	0.06%	0.06%	0.00%	0.00%	0.00%	0.00%	0.00%	0.00%	0.00%	0.00%	0.00%
44	0.02%	0.02%	0.02%	0.02%	0.05%	0.05%	0.03%	0.03%	0.03%	0.00%	0.01%	0.00%	0.00%	0.00%	0.00%	0.00%	0.00%	0.00%	0.00%
45	0.00%	0.01%	0.01%	0.01%	0.03%	0.03%	0.01%	0.01%	0.01%	0.09%	0.09%	0.05%	0.05%	0.05%	0.05%	0.05%	0.06%	0.57%	0.57%
46	0.00%	0.00%	0.00%	0.00%	0.01%	0.01%	0.01%	0.01%	0.24%	0.01%	0.18%	0.18%	0.18%	0.18%	0.33%	0.00%	0.00%	0.00%	1.44%
47	0.35%	0.25%	0.29%	0.01%	0.01%	0.01%	0.40%	0.40%	0.00%	0.00%	0.00%	0.00%	0.00%	0.00%	0.00%	0.00%	0.00%	0.00%	0.00%
48	0.28%	0.29%	0.29%	0.26%	0.23%	0.23%	0.00%	0.00%	0.00%	0.00%	0.00%	0.00%	0.00%	0.00%	0.00%	0.00%	0.00%	0.00%	0.00%
49	0.33%	0.36%	0.36%	0.29%	0.32%	0.33%	0.00%	0.00%	0.00%	0.00%	0.00%	0.00%	0.00%	0.00%	0.00%	0.00%	0.00%	0.00%	0.00%

Table 5. Public budget simulations 2022 and 2023

Branch ID	Average percentage differences	Simulation 2022	Simulation 2023
1	0.38%	$14,344,742,509.74	$14,399,382,560.47
2	0.06%	$759,107,051.65	$759,569,522.39
3	1.53%	$71,219,421,780.11	$72,311,156,090.92
4	0.90%	$16,237,369,546.99	$16,383,654,251.12
5	0.23%	$8,459,869,374.66	$8,479,067,575.65
6	1.19%	$20,889,945,643.79	$21,138,384,508.93
7	1.94%	$110,357,053,949.98	$112,496,517,707.06
8	2.39%	$53,099,036,659.70	$54,366,761,384.80
9	2.53%	$63,982,173,365.09	$65,601,443,222.06
10	0.44%	$7,007,683,755.06	$7,038,262,638.61
11	8.18%	$352,946,967,519.03	$381,813,626,066.82
12	3.42%	$140,611,696,795.42	$145,417,993,743.17
13	0.70%	$35,098,136,473.50	$35,345,118,905.46
14	0.26%	$32,878,971,452.74	$32,962,927,038.91
15	0.38%	$18,822,222,469.30	$18,893,095,537.69
16	1.48%	$32,386,040,554.44	$32,865,068,145.26
17	0.35%	Not available	Not available
18	0.74%	$44,563,781,646.86	$44,892,976,629.27
19	11.74%	$1,180,092,758,948.78	$1,318,585,216,385.16
20	5.33%	$242,057,186,785.08	$254,960,018,101.24
21	0.68%	$114,655,074,126.56	$115,430,597,468.64
22	0.40%	$23,739,394,109.70	$23,835,119,498.52
23	2.33%	$118,837,253,653.19	$121,606,543,548.00
24	9.06%	$693,489,242,738.99	$756,288,656,422.87
25	3.24%	$67,877,189,277.24	$70,075,778,912.70
27	0.25%	$4,357,190,605.08	$4,368,001,529.58
28	15.77%	$720,063,116,873.90	$833,623,991,201.60
30	3.59%	$54,081,053,626.54	$56,020,485,924.33
31	0.11%	$1,501,718,537.84	$1,503,326,937.80
32	0.06%	$2,763,005,028.58	$2,764,663,275.75
33	14.61%	$768,884,679,869.14	$881,244,225,785.37
34	3.44%	$37,687,953,233.89	$38,983,111,387.24
35	0.19%	$3,173,921,067.96	$3,180,106,125.58
36	0.76%	$74,746,490,944.43	$75,312,178,747.35
37	0.00%	$142,084,871.16	$142,091,549.78
38	0.70%	$27,784,650,900.25	$27,978,905,193.04
40	0.34%	$7,631,026,262.29	$7,656,682,120.83
41	0.01%	$610,280,620.68	$610,321,477.10
42	0.01%	Not available	Not available
43	0.02%	$1,770,215,451.19	$1,770,583,832.25
44	0.01%	$1,192,139,349.68	$1,192,306,878.84
45	0.01%	$345,455,007.27	$345,476,682.79
46	0.00%	$264,203,149.88	$264,212,026.53
47	0.09%	$15,756,040,536.99	$15,769,970,950.59
48	0.08%	$17,015,343,859.68	$17,028,939,613.54
49	0.10%	$14,699,056,867.63	$14,714,367,279.31

References

1. Alimadadi, A., Aryal, S., Manandhar, I., Munroe, P.B., Joe, B., Cheng, X.: Artificial intelligence and machine learning to fight Covid-19 (2020)
2. Atalla, G., MacDonald, M.: How AI can help governments manage their money better. Digital source (2019). https://www.ey.com/en_gl/consulting/how-ai-can-help-governments-manage-theirmoney-better
3. Coglianese, C., Lehr, D.: Regulating by robot: administrative decision making in the machine-learning era. Geo. LJ **105**, 1147 (2016)
4. Hopp, D.: How machine learning could help make government spending greener (2021). https://unctad.org/es/node/35076, prosperity for all
5. de Jesus, M.B., da Silva, G.L., Ladeira, M., Van Erven, G.C.: Using text mining to categorize the purpose of public spending for the benefit of transparency and accountability. In: 2019 18th IEEE International Conference on Machine Learning and Applications (ICMLA), pp. 263–267. IEEE (2019)
6. Kuziemski, M., Misuraca, G.: AI governance in the public sector: three tales from the frontiers of automated decision-making in democratic settings. Telecommun. Policy **44**(6), 101976 (2020)
7. Lee, C., Lim, C.: From technological development to social advance: a review of industry 4.0 through machine learning. Technol. Forecast. Soc. Change **167**, 120653 (2021)
8. López-Chau, A., Valle-Cruz, D., Sandoval-Almazán, R.: Sentiment analysis of Twitter data through machine learning techniques. In: Ramachandran, M., Mahmood, Z. (eds.) Software Engineering in the Era of Cloud Computing. CCN, pp. 185–209. Springer, Cham (2020). https://doi.org/10.1007/978-3-030-33624-0_8
9. Molina, M.: Así usa el sat la inteligencia artificial para fiscalizar (2022). https://www.elcontribuyente.mx/2022/04/asi-usa-el-sat-la-inteligencia-artificial-para-fiscalizar, el Contribuyente
10. Maia, R., Sharma, H., Hopp, D.: Using machine learning to make government spending greener (2021). https://greenfiscalpolicy.org/blog/using-machine-learning-to-make-government-spending-greener
11. Medaglia, R., Gil-Garcia, J.R., Pardo, T.A.: Artificial intelligence in government: taking stock and moving forward. Soc. Sci. Comput. Rev. 08944393211034087 (2021)
12. Mittal, M., Goyal, L.M., Sethi, J.K., Hemanth, D.J.: Monitoring the impact of economic crisis on crime in India using machine learning. Comput. Econ. **53**(4), 1467–1485 (2019)
13. Moraes, T., Valdevino, A.M., d.N.A.: Serenata de amor: um doce não tão saboroso. Teoria e Prática em Administração (2021)
14. Oracle: qué es el aprendizaje automático (2022). https://www.oracle.com/mx/data-science/machine-learning/what-is-machine-learning/
15. Presupuestaría, T.: Presupuesto de egresos de la federación 2020 (2020). https://www.transparenciapresupuestaria.gob.mx/es/PTP/infografia_pef_2020
16. Raghavendra Sai, N., Aruna Safali, M., Reshma, G.: Machine Learning for All. Walnut Publication
17. Thennakoon, A., Bhagyani, C., Premadasa, S., Mihiranga, S., Kuruwitaarachchi, N.: Real-time credit card fraud detection using machine learning. In: 2019 9th International Conference on Cloud Computing, Data Science & Engineering (Confluence), pp. 488–493. IEEE (2019)

18. Tiwari, S., et al.: Applications of machine learning approaches to combat Covid-19: a survey. Lessons from COVID-19 263–287 (2022)
19. Tritto, N.M.: Improve budget analsyis with machine learning, data analytics. Int. J. Gov. Auditing 40 (2020)
20. de la Unión, C.: Presupuesto de egresos de la federación (2007). https://www. cefp.gob.mx/intr/edocumentos/pdf/cefp/cefp0582007.pdf, cuaderno de Finanzas Públicas 2007
21. Valle-Cruz, D., Fernandez-Cortez, V., Gil-Garcia, J.R.: From e-budgeting to smart budgeting: exploring the potential of artificial intelligence in government decision-making for resource allocation. Gov. Inf. Q. **39**(2), 101644 (2022)
22. Valle-Cruz, D., Fernandez-Cortez, V., López-Chau, A., Sandoval-Almazán, R.: Does Twitter affect stock market decisions? Financial sentiment analysis during pandemics: a comparative study of the h1n1 and the Covid-19 periods. Cogn. Comput. **14**(1), 372–387 (2022)
23. Valle-Cruz, D., Gil-Garcia, J.R., Fernandez-Cortez, V.: Towards smarter public budgeting? Understanding the potential of artificial intelligence techniques to support decision making in government. In: The 21st Annual International Conference on Digital Government Research, pp. 232–242 (2020)
24. Valle-Cruz, D., García-Contreras, R., Muñoz-Chávez, J.P.: Mind the gap: towards an understanding of government decision-making based on artificial intelligence. In: DG.O 2022: The 23rd Annual International Conference on Digital Government Research, pp. 1–9. ACM Digital Library (2022)
25. Wang, H., Ma, S.: Preventing crimes against public health with artificial intelligence and machine learning capabilities. Socioecon. Plann. Sci. **80**, 101043 (2022)

Open Data Hackathon as a Tool for Increased Engagement of Generation Z: To Hack or Not to Hack?

Anastasija Nikiforova[✉] [ORCID]

Institute of Computer Science, University of Tartu, Narva Mnt 18, 51009 Tartu, Estonia
nikiforova.anastasija@gmail.com

Abstract. A hackathon is known as a form of civic innovation in which participants representing citizens can point out existing problems or social needs and propose a solution. Given the high social, technical, and economic potential of open government data (OGD), the concept of open data hackathons is becoming popular around the world. This concept has become popular in Latvia with the annual hackathons organised for a specific cluster of citizens – Generation Z. Contrary to the general opinion, the organizer suggests that the main goal of open data hackathons to raise an awareness of OGD has been achieved, and there has been a debate about the need to continue them. This study presents the latest findings on the role of open data hackathons and the benefits that they can bring to both the society, participants, and government. First, a systematic literature review is carried out to establish a knowledge base. Then, empirical research of 4 case studies of open data hackathons for Generation Z participants held between 2018 and 2021 in Latvia is conducted to understand which ideas dominated and what were the main results of these events for the OGD initiative. It demonstrates that, despite the widespread belief that young people are indifferent to current societal and natural problems, the ideas developed correspond to current situation and are aimed at solving them, revealing aspects for improvement in both the provision of data, infrastructure, culture, and government- related areas.

Keywords: Civic innovation · Hackathon · Generation Z · Knowledge-based society · Open data · Open government data · Social innovation · Society 5.0

1 Introduction

Open data hackathons are considered a creative and "out-of-the-box" approach to civic innovation, also known as "social innovation", described by an unconventional way of thinking and an openness to create solutions in a new and creative way [1, 2], which are becoming increasingly popular all over the world. The specificity and perhaps the main value of these government-induced open data engagement initiatives [2] is that they bring together people with different backgrounds, experience, knowledge, skills, and expertise [1, 3] in one place for short periods of time, thus supporting intense bursts of creativity [4] to create services or solutions that will benefit the public by

© The Author(s), under exclusive license to Springer Nature Switzerland AG 2022
F. Ortiz-Rodríguez et al. (Eds.): EGETC 2022, CCIS 1666, pp. 161–175, 2022.
https://doi.org/10.1007/978-3-031-22950-3_13

creating a *win-win* scenario for all participants [5]. The diverse skills and knowledge of participants facilitate and promote innovation and learning as participants generate and evaluate ideas from different perspectives [3]. The hackathon provides a solution-oriented environment for the co-creation (collaborative creation) of social services, free from hierarchical constraints. Another important, but not the only, goal of such events is to raise an awareness of the open government data (OGD) among citizens, making them the main input that should be used to create solutions or services within the hackathon, thus indicating their value and unlocking their potential. The definition of open data hackathons before pandemic also referred to the mode in which they were held - an offline, face-to-face competition [2], which changed due to the COVID-19 pandemic, when hackathons turned into a virtual space, and remain to be online events. Citizen engagement in these hackathons can greatly contribute to the uptake and adoption of OGD as a whole [6]. In addition, as suggested in [5, 7], organizing hackathons or digital innovation competitions is an opportunity for aspiring entrepreneurs to collaborate with external partners, promote new ideas and launch a new start-up.

Another popular trend is the organization of hackathons for participants representing Generation Z (Gen Z), which is and should be an interesting target audience, considered to have the best digital capabilities [8] being so-called *"digital natives"*, because they have never experienced life before the Internet [9], which, along with social media, became part of their daily lives and socialization [10]. This makes Gen Z to be unique, since no other generation has lived in the era when technology is so readily available at such a young age [9]. In the context of Gen Z, a recent study [11] inspected OGD as a governance strategy as a potential factor in promoting millennial and Generation Z trust in government institutions. They found that OGD has a positive impact on millennials and Gen Z satisfaction with public outcomes and trust in institutions. In this way, the authors encourage civil servants to implement open data strategies to improve youth attraction and involvement in democratic institutions. Open data hackathons can be an excellent opportunity to be used. This is even more so considering motivation factors for participating in hackathons defined in [6], where 4 of 5 factors – intrinsic motivation, extrinsic motivation, effort expectancy, social influence, and data quality – are considered valid by default for Gen Z, where only the "data quality" is not met by default but can be seen as a test item that Gen Z is likely to be able to evaluate. Therefore, in line with the argument proposed in [6] – citizen engagement is one step further than the use of OGD, this study suggests that Gen Z engagement may be the next towards revealing and solving societal issues and pointing out challenges related to OGD.

The OGD hackathon for Gen Z participants has been held annually in Latvia since 2018, but the organizers believe that the goal of hackathons to raise an awareness of OGD has been achieved, and the debate about the need for their further organization has been ongoing on for the past two years. This study aims to highlight the need for Gen Z hackathons as a source of feedback, identifying opportunities for improvements, and seeking ideas for the development and maintenance of a sustainable and citizen-oriented smart city and *knowledge-based society 5.0*. The latter – *Society 5.0* or super smart society also referred to as society of imagination – is seen as the next from of the society defined as *"imagination society, where digital transformation combines with the creativity of diverse people to bring about "problem solving" and "value creation" that lead us to sustainable development"* as defined in [12] and is characterized by 5 key areas: (1) *problem solving and value creation*, (2) *diversity*, (3) *decentralization*, (4) *resilience*, (5) *sustainability and environmental harmony*. It is also expected to contribute to the achievement of the Sustainable Development Goals (SDG) adopted by the United Nations, both sharing the same objectives.

To meet the objective of the study, this paper will first establish the role of open data hackathons by examining current research on the topic. It aims to demonstrate various perspectives, including the benefits that open data hackathons can bring. This is done by carrying out systematic literature review (SLR). Then, empirical research of 4 case studies of open data hackathons for Generation Z participants held between 2018 and 2021 in Latvia is conducted to understand which ideas dominated and what were the main results of these events for the OGD initiative, and whether the COVID-19 led to a decrease in the diversity of solutions developed expected by the organizers. It demonstrates that, despite the widespread belief that young people (in Latvia) are indifferent to current societal and natural problems, the ideas developed correspond to current problems and are aimed at solving them, revealing aspects for improvement in both the provision of data, infrastructure, culture, and government related areas that will allow moving towards a sustainable, resilient, and innovative knowledge-based society or *Society 5.0* and a smart city. The analysis is conducted by the hackathon mentor, which should affect positively the interpretability of the results. The results clearly indicate the need for further organization as a source of feedback from the most modern cluster of society, identifying opportunities for improvements and seeking ideas for a more coherent and robust understanding of how open data crisis-management can be established and maintained. This idea was originally presented in [13].

The paper is organized as follows: Sect. 2 provides an overview of the existing body of knowledge with reference to a SLR and its results, Sect. 3 provides an overview of Gen Z open data hackathons in Latvia, analyses ideas developed in 5 editions of this hackathon and observations made by participants on the OGD initiative, as well as the observations made by mentor, while Sect. 4 concludes the paper.

2   Related Research

To identify relevant literature for study, forming the knowledge base, a systematic literature review (SLR) was conducted. This was done by searching digital libraries covered by Scopus and Web of Science (WoS) that index well-known publishers of peer-reviewed literature such as ScienceDirect (Elsevier), Springer, Emerald, ACM, IEEE, Taylor & Francis, Sage, Wiley-Blackwell, Oxford University Press, Cambridge University Press etc. These databases were queried for keywords (1) *""hackathon" AND ("Open Government Data" OR "open data" OR "OGD") AND ("Generation Z" OR "Gen Z)"*, (2) *""hackathon" AND ("Open Government Data" OR "open data" OR "OGD")"*, (3) *"("Open Government Data" OR "open data" OR "OGD") AND ("Generation Z" OR "Gen Z)"*. These search terms were applied to the article title, keywords, and abstract to limit the number of papers to those, where these objects were primary research object rather than mentioned in the body, e.g., as a future work. Only articles in English were considered, while in terms of scope, both journal articles, conference papers, and chapters were studied. The first search returned no results, i.e., there are no studies on the open data hackathons discussed in the context of Gen Z. The 2nd query resulted in 38 articles in Scopus and 5 in WoS. After comparing the resulting sets and eliminating duplicates, 39 studies remained for their further examination covering either open data hackathons or open data in the context of the Gen Z. The third query resulted in one article – [11] referred to in the Introduction. In terms of the research area, these studies tend to be different, i.e. in Scopus, most studies belong to Computer Science (24 of 38), Social Sciences (14), Business, Management and Accounting (6), Engineering (5), Mathematics (5), and Decision Sciences (4), while in WoS – Computer Science (3 of 5), Public Administration (2), Geography (1), Government Law (1), Information Science Library Science (1). These studies are diverse in nature – from testing an idea during a hackathon as an experiential setting representing different domains in which to gather feedback, exploring trends in a specific area such as developing software or a strategy to set up a start-up, to conceptualizing the motivation for participating in hackathon etc. They mostly indicate the high and varied value of hackathons both for the organizers, i.e., for the government enabling *"government as a model of an open data activist"* [6], participants, and for society. Let discuss them in more detail.

In [5] the authors examine goals and design strategies that contribute to the successful execution of open data hackathons to understand the co-ordination between the multiple stakeholders and improve the execution of open data hackathons and innovation competitions. The outcomes indicate that the most critical design strategy was the involvement of mentors in the event and the level of support provided to nascent entrepreneurs to accelerate their creativity, develop applications, and launch their prototypes on the market. The authors argue that prior studies have not thoroughly concentrated on the planning and assessment processes of these competitions, stressing that scholars have not compared the execution of different strategies in many hackathons or digital innovation competitions rather focusing on the actions that the organizers of a specific hackathon have implemented or the challenges they have faced.

Yuan and Gasco-Hernandez [14] address a gap in research that refers to open innovation outcomes and contribution to public value creation by referring to open data hackathons in US. It defines the concept of open innovation as the leverage of external resources and knowledge provided by citizens or other stakeholders for innovation to help solve public problems, which contributes to the creation of public value. They found that open data hackathons promote *procedural rationality*, also called *procedural legitimacy*, *democratic accountability*, and *substantive outcomes*. They also emphasize that *citizen engagement* and *participation*, as well as *network building* are more important than physical products or solutions as the outcomes of open innovation initiatives.

Jaskiewicz et al. [15] investigated the opportunities of leveraging a hackathon format to empower citizens by increasing abilities to use open data to improve their neighbourhoods and communities. The discussion presented is based on five case studies of civic hackathons organized in five European cities. The research revealed specialized learning and collaborative alignment as two mutually complementary aspects of the learning processes involved, which were achieved with the help of high-fidelity and low-fidelity prototypes, respectively. The study identified three key factors needed to sustain social learning ecosystems beyond the hackathon events, and with the purpose of democratizing smart city services. These factors include (a) *supporting individuals in obtaining specific expert knowledge and skills*, (b) *building/nurturing data-literate activist communities of practice made up of citizens with complementary set of expert skills*, and (c) *enabling members of these communities to prototype open-data services.* The twofold purpose originally formulated for civic hackathons considered (O4C) was to support citizens in discovering new opportunities for meaningful open data applications, and *bottom-up, community-driven learning* and *sharing of data literacy skills.* These goals are closely interlinked. This allowed them to develop a general framework that promises to serve as a guideline for defining relevant key performance (KPI) and behavioural indicators to assess learning in future civic hackathons. The framework considers (a) *individual learning,* (b) *community capacity,* and (c) *learning through prototyping* as three mutually enforcing learning activities within civic hackathons. However, study by Molinari [16] argues that initiatives such as the O4C better articulate some of the psychosocial dimensions that explain the resistance to data disclosure, especially on the part of public administration, the impact of political culture on the management of public goods, the aims and motivations of the stakeholders involved, guided by different interests and competencies, and the role of outside advocacy groups.

Carroll and Beck [17] demonstrated that hackathons provide insights into practices and goals, where water quality was the subject of their interest, i.e., diverse local initiatives for water quality testing and threat mitigation were identified during the hackathons, allowing problems to be framed and brainstorm session to be organized to collectively discuss possible solutions. This allowed them to introduce, or rather co-design, the concept of *platform collectivism* as an alternative to *platform capitalism,* concluding that the gathering and sharing community watershed data is an inherently collective endeavour that co-produces community engagement and water security.

Purwanto et al. [2] explored the motivations of citizens to be engaged in hackathons by conducting a case-study of open data hackathons that represent to one particular domain – agriculture or farming. They found out that a list of factors motivate citizens to participate in OGD hackathons constituting a framework of citizens' motivation to engage in open data hackathons: (1) *intrinsic motivation,* represented by constructs such as fun and enjoyment and intellectual challenge, (2) *extrinsic motivation,* constituted by performance expectancy or relative advantage and learning and developing skills, (3) *effort expectancy* related to the ease of use, (4) *social influence* related to influence from a social relationship and contributing to societal benefits, and (5) *data quality* with the reference to accuracy. With the reference to this study, it should be noted that 4 of 5 factors describing motivation can be considered valid by default for Gen Z, where only the "data quality" defined as *"data that are fit for use by data consumers"* is not met by default but can be seen as a test item that Gen Z is likely to be able to evaluate.

Gama [18] argues that hackathons, while being a very promising idea, tend to suffer from several problems, such as (1) *functional requirements defined for applications in civic hackathons identified based on needs, interests or experience of developers instead of societal needs,* (2) *concerns about the quality of the software,* i.e. the quality of the developed service or solution, (3) *poor organization and task management,* (4) *issues related to release and maintenance of the developed solution.* The investigation was conducted by surveying participants in three civic hackathons. The 3rd assumption was not proven with a partly rejection of the fourth assumption, if the maintenance of the developed item was the case for the vast majority of participants and at least version control tools were employed, however, as regards the release, it really turned out that most of the developed prototypes were not finished and, in many cases, abandoned, especially those that are not recognized as winners. Bad or low quality of the developed software was also rejected, as the authors saw traces of design and testing practices. However, there was evidence to support claims that civic apps are based on the experience of developers rather than the actual needs of citizen, where roughly half of the respondents indicated that the requirements for their apps were based only on their experience. This result, however, cannot be generalized, as 40% of the participants in two of three hackathons studied did additional (online) research.

Mainka et al. [19] discussed the role of hackathons in the development of mobile applications (*m-apps*) using OGD collectively, intended to solve urban problems, as it is not known whether the output of hackathons leads to value-added city services, as well as challenges that governments face in making open data available. The latter, i.e., the challenges of making OGD available can be seen as both (1) *a political challenge* where politicians are afraid of losing their monopoly in public affairs, (2) *a legal challenge* associated with *security*, *privacy* and *copyright* as key arguments of "protecting" data from the public, (3) *governance challenge* – motivation to open data and the need to collaborate with business and citizens, (4) *human resource challenge* related to the variety of skills required to prepare data suitable for reuse, which is seen as a complex task, (5) *IT infrastructure challenge*, making online services available to the public, and (6) *IT budget challenge*, with the reference to cases where the government implements charging models for their data. Their investigation showed that most hackathons gather people, who are programmers or designers, which is not in line with the cities / urban open data vision, i.e., most citizens do not feel affiliated to join hackathons. It is still unclear whether hackathons are really capable of changing something and involving citizens in governmental processes, although people come together as a community and develop public services, which can help make the whole city and its residents smarter.

There are also studies confirming the power and usefulness of intensive team-oriented hackathons for the development of previously unseen services or solutions, such as Data & Analytics Framework (DAF) [20], Biomedical Data Translator program ("Translator") [21], a planning tool for farmers that compiles crop calendars, agroclimatic data, and historical records of production enabling geospatial navigation of agricultural activities and crowdsourced updates of calendars ("CropPlanning") [22]. They also make it possible to define requirements for further developments, as was the case for a system called "Theophrastus" [23] designed to assist biologists in their research on species and biodiversity, which supports automatic annotation of documents through entity mining, and provides services using Linked Open Data (LOD) in real-time.

To sum up, while the topic of hackathon is relatively popular in the literature with some studies devoted to open data hackathons and datathons, conducted SLR indicates a scientific gap in the knowledge on the Gen Z role in them making this study unique.

3   Gen Z Open Data Hackathon

This section is devoted to Gen Z open data hackathons in Latvia. First, it provides a brief overview of the general structure of hackathons. It then provides an overview of the ideas developed between 2018 and 2021. It then discusses issues identified by participants related to open data, infrastructure etc., data on which were collected through interviews with participants during the hackathon during the post-pitch Q&A session.

Open data hackathons for representatives of Gen Z are held annually in Latvia, where the first edition took place in 2018. They are organized by the Latvian Association of Open Technologies in cooperation with governmental/public agencies, including the entity responsible for the OGD in Latvia, namely the Latvian Ministry of Environmental Protection and Regional Development (VARAM) as part of the jury or organizer, depending on the edition. Their main idea, as defined by organizers but also found in the literature [24], is to raise awareness of OGD, thereby facilitating an increase in their use by this cluster of citizens representing the future and development of the country.

Compared to the traditional hackathon model, including the model referred to in the previous section, these hackathons are longer, i.e., the participants are given several weeks to make their solutions and services as polished as possible. This is also the case because the hackathon takes place in the autumn during the fall semester, which tends to negatively impact participation rates if the traditional hackathons model is chosen. This form of hackathons, being closer to virtual hackathons is generally found to be a good way of promoting inclusiveness and digital participative collaboration [25]. This also allowed the organizers to switch to the fully virtual/online mode in 2020 (due to pandemic) relatively easy. In short, participants apply for a hackathon, then they get together to develop their idea, gather teammates (if not done before), brainstorm, get some knowledge from the hand-outs and workshops delivered by the organizers, mentors, partner etc., and then present their ideas at a very high-level during the first pitch session. This pitch session allows participant to receive initial feedback from mentors, organizers, and other participants, as well as to ask their questions on the sketched idea. This also allows the organizers to recommend or assign mentors to teams depending on the idea and the nature of the questions (theoretical or practical, technical etc.). Then, teams work independently on their own outside of the event, organizing their work independently and communicating with the mentors, who guide them. Then two or three weeks later (depending on the edition), the second pitch session is organized, when progress, i.e., the mock-up or prototype is demonstrated and elaborated on by participants, allowing mentors to see "from idea to solution" progress and sustainability of the service, including its significance and value for the economy, society etc. After the pitch session, a team of mentors selects the most promising solutions and services to be presented at the hackathon final – usually 10 teams, which bring together a wider audience, including, but not limited to, industry representatives. They are sometimes specially invited by the organizers and mentors, depending on the nature of the developed services to get the attention of relevant stakeholders, thereby trying to prevent the idea from being abandoned or discarded, which is a common problem of hackathons [5, 26, 27], and increasing chances to get the support – technological, financial etc. Participants are provided with another portion of feedback on their solutions and/or services, where mentors share their experience and suggestions, and also allow them to choose the right direction for their ideas and suggestions for monetizing them. Then, a week later, the final pitch session takes place, where selected solutions are presented, considering previously received feedback, where the final decision is made on the winners at the level of hackathon and supporters, where the latter can be public agencies or business representatives. All in all, these hackathons last approximately 1 month.

3.1 Ideas Developed over 5 Editions

This section discusses ideas developed in Gen Z open data hackathons between 2018 and 2021 in Latvia. This is done using a qualitative approach analysing the data collected by the organizers of the hackathon, including the author, who is the mentor of this hackathon. Thus, this study provides an analysis made from the mentor perspective with its direct involvement/participation, which allows a more accurate interpretation of the data collected and the observations made.

Open Data Hackathon of 2018. The year 2018 was characterized by the predominance of solutions related to mobility and transport aimed at simplifying route planning, bicycle parking – finding a spot or requesting/voting for organizing a new one. However, planning of leisure time for both tourists (by means of crowdsourcing) and local citizens, and recommenders for choosing of place of living depending on the location and level of crime, and the determination of a kindergarten with the shortest queues for a child, were also popular. While most of them are something fairly typical for open data-based solutions regardless of the country, although contributing to its sustainable development or improvement of daily routines (being also in line with most SDG), the latter – the determination of a kindergarten with the least queues was of very important for young parents in that year, where there was an expressed issue with finding kindergarten and very limited information about the process making it very non-transparent.

Open Data Hackathon of 2019. In 2019, the question of how to choose the best place to live based on the nearest infrastructure and prices was popular, while solutions different from 2018 were an open data-based tool for a unified assessment of Latvian schools and a forecast of their future development being especially relevant for Latvia that year, given poor results shown in examinations and the upcoming education reform. Last but not least, there was a solution to simplify the search for a medical institution and corresponding doctors for patients with a focus on rare diseases, which was a very timely solutions given the digitization of medical services and the development of national e-health system, which at first raised a lot of concerns among citizens.

Open Data Hackathon of 2020. The 2020 hackathon was the first edition that took place in an online mode six months after the start of the pandemic. Although it was assumed that all solutions will be related to the fight against the pandemic and crisis management, this was not the only case considered by the participants. Moreover, COVID-19 was more seen as factor to be considered in solutions to allow leisure planning mostly for citizens, but for some teams, for tourists, with the reference on how to recover the tourism during and after pandemic (to identify the least crowded areas, places, or routes), since the tourism is of high economic value for Latvia. There was an expressed popularity of solutions that allow young people to choose a university or profession based on current statistics on their salaries, employment etc. Some ideas were influenced by the call of the organizers to test the data prepared for their further publication on the national OGD portal (after the feedback collected about them) – data of the Register of Enterprises of the Republic of Latvia. Some ideas were oriented on preventing climate change, with two more solutions dedicated to agriculture. All in all, only two solutions focused on the COVID-19 only - interactive maps based on the current rate of a spread of the disease and the consequences by regions.

Open Data Hackathon of 2021. The 2021 hackathon was defined by the organizers as an open geospatial data hackathon, encouraging participants to use the geodata available. This edition dominated by solutions focused on regional development and urban planning, with a focus on identifying problem areas to be addressed in an appropriate regional development plan. Some of the proposed solutions refers to the gamification design, or at least the use of game elements, which is also in line with current trends set by both theoreticians and practitioners [28]. One solution was dedicated to waste management, with 4 more floods and fire forecasts and their risk assessment, air quality and pollution monitoring, with another for planning bicycle routes considering the landscape and infrastructure appropriateness. Likewise in 2020, only 1 solution was purely COVID-19 related, suggesting the creation of a single source for crawling, and presenting all information related to COVID-19, with one more considering its consequences - internet coverage outside the capital of Latvia for those who work from other regions with much more limited access to the internet (if any). The solution mentioned above – a single source of information related to the pandemic, would gather all informative materials about the current situation that would be provided to users in a visual manner, supplementing these data and relevant visualizations with forecasts/predictions of risk to be affected by COVID-19 in various regions, which should be achieved by means of using neural networks. In addition, the team planned a built-in chatbot and the opportunity to get in touch with users of the service, sending out the most critical notifications about changes in the regions of interest. Although the idea of this solution overlaps with the solutions currently available, it was presented before the actual creation of such a website in Latvia, thereby indicating the interest of citizens (even so young) in solutions of this nature, especially given that the idea presented is more advanced compared to the introduced. The latter was also recognized by the developers of the above solution. This demonstrates the potential of open (government) data and is in line with the potential of the OGD to transform the society into a Society 5.0 - society of imagination.

3.2   Key Observations Reported by Participants

The above discussed structure of hackathons allowed to gather a feedback or observations made by participants while working with the open data and the portal on which they are accessible. These data were collected through interviews with participants during the hackathon during a post-pitch Q&A session. Unfortunately, this feedback was collected as a result of unstructured interviews during short Q&A sessions without the possibility of further communication and collecting more detailed feedback, which should definitely be the case of hackathons as this is a great opportunity to get an opinion of someone who actually used the data from their locating, downloading, discovering, distilling, scrutinizing, refining, with their further transformation into a prototype, including the design and development of such, and has more likely encountered challenges that are valid for open data and the open data portal (also in line with [6]).

Nevertheless, the feedback collected is in line with expert assessment of the Latvian OGD and portal [29], being also in line with evidence found in the literature [5]. More precisely, the main critical feedback or the issues identified by the participants are:

(1) *poor data quality*, where both the quality of the metadata and the data, i.e., the content of the data (completeness, accuracy, credibility), were referred to;
(2) *outdated data* with the reference to the issues related to the *timeliness* of data and *data recency*, which tend to be violated;
(3) data in some datasets tend to be *poorly structured*;
(4) the *lack of "valuable data"* found to be the most frequently reported issue;
(5) the *inability to use data through API*.

Data quality and data credibility/reliability that was a topic of interest for decades, has become more topical in the context of OGD, which tend to suffer from low quality. At the same time, there is limited research on open data quality with reference to the content of datasets with a higher interest in metadata quality or defining open data quality as the compliance with open data principles, lacking a data management and data quality management perspective. The rise in the popularity of this topic was observed during pandemics, when data on COVID-19 became a very hot topic for both researchers, practitioners, including small and medium-sized business (SME) and citizens. This proves again that although the availability of data is a prerequisite, a shift *"from quantity to quality"* should be made. This is especially important given that it is not always clear who is responsible for this – the owners of the data portal, government, the publishers of the data, or data user, who should analyze data quality analysis prior their use.

For the lack of "valuable data", commonly referred to as "high value data", the 2021 hackathon provided evidence that not only the imagination of citizens or users and the desire to create value form the OGD for society matters, but also the diversity of data. However, not only the content of the data matters here, but also the readiness of the country under consideration for digitization at all levels. It has been shown that in the case of Latvia, especially the latter – the level of digitization – is in some cases insufficient for the development of some crisis management services. More precisely, one of the ideas was to develop an application that would allow citizens to plan the use of public transport, tracking not only its timetable/schedule and current location (whether it arrives on time or is delayed), but also the number of people in it to avoid overcrowding. This would allow an assessment of the need to travel at a specific time and vehicle when transport is overcrowded and the ability to choose another vehicle or time to reach their destination in a safer way, thus allowing both individuals and the general public to be protected from maintenance in an overcrowded vehicle. On the one hand, there are open data available on the OGD portal, where registrations of an e-ticket are fixed, which is partially in line with the objective, but they are not provided in real-time, which significantly reduces their value and contradicts with the modern trends regarding OGD, because only approximate data can be obtained, by analyzing historical data, instead of real-time data. In addition, although they would allow to fix the number of passengers who have just entered the transport in question, these data still do not provide actual data on the number of passengers, since passengers who have exited the transport are not recorded. However, this could be addressed by either equipping transport with sensors to monitor the number of passengers entering and leaving, thereby allowing for real-time and accurate data that would create value, or by other advanced solutions such as computer vision, as suggested participants of the hackathon. It should be mentioned that the question of the need to integrate sensors into transport was discussed in Latvia before the pandemic, but it was decided not to implement them. The crisis has highlighted the emerging need of smart solutions, including urban data, and the need to follow current trends. It also points on the complexity of the OGD ecosystem, which cannot be separated from other areas of national development.

The lack of API pointed to in earlier editions of the hackathons (2018–2019) seems to be at least partly resolved, which proves the current state of the OGD. More precisely, the owners of the OGD portal have ensured that all datasets provided in.*csv* format are automatically supplemented with the ability to retrieve them through the API.

All in all, hackathons indicate or assign some prerequisites to data, according to which the data available must comply with principles such as machine-readability, timeliness, and data currency, requiring regular updates of the data, high data quality and data relevance being a valuable asset for business and society, as well as these data should be easy to retrieve, i.e., API support becomes almost a prerequisite.

Although the feedback was collected through unstructured interviews with no opportunity to collect more detailed feedback, the observations made by the participants are consistent with expert assessment, suggesting that the hackathon can be a valuable asset for the government and public agencies to get rich and relevant feedback on the current state and identify opportunities for improvement, which can sometimes be accompanied by recommendations. The value of these also lies in the fact that this information comes from real data users making it possible to look at it from citizen's lens.

3.3 Key Implications from Hackathons: A Mentor's Perspective

Although Generation Z is associated with the term "*digital natives*", the point to be considered, however, is the age of the current representatives of Gen Z, which is relatively low and, as a result, some limitations arise from it. In other words, some of them do not hold a secondary school diploma, which automatically makes them less prepared for the classical hackathon's paradigm, where participants come together for hours or days to develop solutions in many cases having relevant skills and experience – being in line with findings that in most cases participants of hackathons tend to be developers or software engineers. This requires some efforts on the part of mentors and organizers, as well as the organization of practical workshops, which, however, although provides support and some basic knowledge, cannot substitute a real experience.

This leads to the fact that some ideas are not implemented or remain at the level of a sketch or mock-up, while there are many – those presented in the final, which are already working prototypes. It should be emphasized that the exclusion of the developed ideas depending on the level of their implementation should not be decisive, where the maturity of the general idea is of higher importance, which is especially true considering the age of the participants. In other words, according to the existing body of knowledge, if an idea is mature enough and proves its societal or business value, it deserves consideration even in final, when it can be presented for a wider audience and help participants find supporters – technological, business etc., who will help to implement it and monetize, thereby revealing the full potential of the idea and hackathons in general. Otherwise, the risk of abandoning the idea, and project discontinued is high as proves both the experience and literature [18]. This is also in line with [24], according to which the key take-away of hackathons should not only awareness raising or physical products as outcomes [14], where *citizen engagement* and *networking* are most relevant. Latvian hackathons have also proven to be events that allow businesses and government *to see gaps in the current state-of-the-art of both social, technical, and sociotechnical nature*, and get ideas on how they can be addressed presented by participants representing the most modern part of society, with relevant ideas that are one step ahead of the ideas proposed within entities – businesses or government. The question is *whether the representatives of these entities are open to the proposed solutions* or rather resistant to these changes and to the realization of the reality regarding the problems identified.

Regarding the prototypes developed during the hackathons, although it can be speculated that they are be developed not only by the participants, but also by other people not participating in the hackathon for the sake of the needed competence, i.e., parents, students etc., most participants demonstrate their expertise during pitch sessions and progress discussions with mentors, providing some evidence that the Gen Z are digital natives. These participants are characterized not only by the high level of knowledge and skills showed in the development of their prototypes, but also by the acquisition of new knowledge and skills in a very short terms, e.g., when they are suggested to turn to another technology. Nonetheless, there are some gaps in their knowledge, such as version control of their solutions or (an accurate) licencing of published source code, that older participants more likely have – although even this is argument is sometimes posed under question [18]. This together with the current body of knowledge about Gen Z and specificities of learning methods they require, which should be significantly different from those used for previous generations born in less technologically developed world, being integrated with various games, mobile apps [10], allows to define the proposition that *a hackathon can also serve as a part of the educational process* [13].

4 Conclusions

In promoting the use of open data, governments sought to be seen not (only) as "*government as a platform*", but also as "*a government as an open data activist model*", in which the government not only provides an open data infrastructure but also promotes its use by citizens, the private sector, or the government itself [6], often organize activities in the form of a hackathon contests, where citizens (and businesses) compete to pitch an idea or the design for a service [30]. However, the role of these hackathons is not always obvious. Many see them only as a form of raising awareness of OGD and the corresponding portal, and once this goal seems to be achieved, there tend to be a debate about the need to continue their organization. This is also the case for Latvia and open data hackathons for Generation Z seen as the future of our society.

The aim of this paper was to highlight the need for open data hackathons and hackathons for Gen Z as the most modern part of the society, including their role as a source of feedback, identifying opportunities for improvement, and seeking ideas for sustainable and citizen-centric development and maintenance of the smart city and knowledge-based society. To achieve this goal, this study first conducts a SLR, thereby building a knowledge base of what is currently known about open data hackathons, in particular, in the context of Gen Z, known as *digital natives*. It was revealed that although the topic of hackathon is relatively popular in the literature, and young people make up the majority of the participants, with some studies devoted to open data hackathons, there is a scientific gap in knowledge, including the role of Gen Z in (open) data hackathons.

Then, an empirical study of 4 open data hackathons for Generation Z organized in Latvia was carried out to understand which ideas dominated and what were the main results of these events for the OGD initiative. An analysis of the developed ideas, solutions, and services, i.e., regardless of the stage of output maturity, whether it is a mock-up or a working prototype, indicates that, despite the widespread opinion about the indifference of young people to current societal and natural problems, developed ideas correspond to the current situation and relevant problems for the country aimed at solving them. This study also confirms the results presented in [19], i.e., while it remains unclear whether hackathons are truly capable of making a difference and engaging citizens in government processes, it is clear is that people come together as a community and develop or co-create governmental services, which also contributes to the digital and open data literacy of participants. This can help make the whole city and its residents smarter, as well as identify and suggest improvement to public services even if there is little open data, although they should be sufficiently structured, of high quality [31] and represent high-value data, also potentially capable to contribute to the development of a value-creating, sustainable open data ecosystem [32]. It also allows to suggest that this form of citizen engagement facilitates the shift or transition from the *Information Society*, known as *Society 4.0*, to *Society 5.0*, or what Verhulst et al. [33] call "*Collective Intelligence*", also known as "*wisdom-of-crowd*" [34].

This study rejects the organizer's assumption that the COVID-19 pandemic will lead to a decrease in the diversity of solutions, where the pandemic was seen as a factor to be considered when presenting different solutions and services, including crisis management services. The results clearly point to the need for further organization as a source of feedback from the most modern cluster of society. In other words, they should not be organized to raise awareness of open data alone, where not only citizen engagement and network building or physical products or solutions as outcomes of open innovation initiatives [14, 24] are important, but also the ability to identify opportunities for improvements in the provision of open data, infrastructure, culture, and government areas that will allow and facilitate movement towards a sustainable, resilient, innovative knowledge-based society and a smart city, seeking for a more robust understanding of how open data crisis management can be established and maintained.

Acknowledgement. This research has been funded by European Social Fund via IT Academy programme (the University of Tartu).

References

1. Toros, K., et al.: Co-creation of social services on the example of social hackathon: the case of Estonia. Int. Soc. Work **65**, 593–606 (2020)
2. Purwanto, A., Zuiderwijk, A., Janssen, M.: Citizens' motivations for engaging in open data hackathons. In: Panagiotopoulos, P., et al. (eds.) ePart 2019. LNCS, vol. 11686, pp. 130–141. Springer, Cham (2019). https://doi.org/10.1007/978-3-030-27397-2_11
3. Pe-Than, E.P.P., Herbsleb, J.D.: Understanding hackathons for science: Collaboration, affordances, and outcomes. In: Taylor, N.G., Christian-Lamb, C., Martin, M.H., Nardi, B. (eds.) iConference 2019. LNCS, vol. 11420, pp. 27–37. Springer, Cham (2019). https://doi.org/10.1007/978-3-030-15742-5_3
4. Taylor, N., Clarke, L.: Everybody's hacking: Participation and the mainstreaming of hackathons. In: CHI 2018, pp. 1–2. Association for Computing Machinery (2018)
5. Kitsios, F., Kamariotou, M.: Digital innovation and entrepreneurship transformation through open data hackathons: design strategies for successful start-up settings. Int. J. Inform. Manage. 102472 (2022, in press)
6. Purwanto, A., Zuiderwijk, A., Janssen, M.: Group development stages in open government data engagement initiatives: a comparative case studies analysis. In: Parycek, P., et al. (eds.) EGOV 2018. LNCS, vol. 11020, pp. 48–59. Springer, Cham (2018). https://doi.org/10.1007/978-3-319-98690-6_5
7. Nolte, A.: Touched by the Hackathon: a study on the connection between Hackathon participants and start-up founders. In: 2nd ACM SIGSOFT International Workshop on Software-Intensive Business: Start-ups, Platforms, and Ecosystems, pp. 31–36 (2019)
8. Basantes-Andrade, A., Cabezas-González, M., Casillas-Martín, S.: Digital competences relationship between gender and generation of university professors. Int. J. Adv. Sci., Eng. Inform. Technol. **10**(1), 205–211 (2020)
9. Prensky, M.: Digital natives, digital immigrants part 2: do they really think differently? On the Horiz. **9**, 1–6 (2001)
10. Szymkowiak, A., Melović, B., Dabić, M., Jeganathan, K., Kundi, G.S.: Information technology and Gen Z: the role of teachers, the internet, and technology in the education of young people. Technol. Soc. **65**, 101565 (2021)
11. Gonzálvez-Gallego, N., Nieto-Torrejón, L.: Can open data increase younger generations' trust in democratic institutions? a study in the European Union. Plos one **16**(1), e0244994 (2021)
12. World Economic Forum: Modern society has reached its limits. Society 5.0 will liberate us. https://www.weforum.org/agenda/2019/01/modern-society-has-reached-its-limits-society-5-0-will-liberate-us/ (2019). Accessed 10 Jun 2022
13. Nikiforova, A.: Gen Z open data hackathon – civic innovation with digital natives: to hack or not to hack? In: 2022 Ongoing Research, Practitioners, Posters, Workshops, and Projects of the International Conference, EGOV-CeDEM-ePart 2022. CEUR-WS (2022)
14. Yuan, Q., Gasco-Hernandez, M.: Open innovation in the public sector: creating public value through civic hackathons. Public Manag. Rev. **23**(4), 523–544 (2021)
15. Jaskiewicz, T., Mulder, I., Morelli, N., Pedersen, J.S.: Hacking the hackathon format to empower citizens in outsmarting "smart" cities. IxD&A **43**, 8–29 (2019)
16. Molinari, F., Concilio, G.: Culture, motivation and advocacy: relevance of psycho social aspects in public data disclosure. In: Proceedings of the 17th European Conference on Digital Government, pp. 86–95. Academic Conferences and Publishing International (2017)
17. Carroll, J., Beck, J.: Co-designing platform collectivism. CoDesign **15**(3), 272–287 (2019)
18. Gama, K.: Preliminary findings on software engineering practices in civic hackathons. In: 2017 IEEE/ACM 4th International Workshop on CrowdSourcing in Software Engineering, pp. 14–20. IEEE (2017)

19. Mainka, A., Hartmann, S., Meschede, C., Stock, W.G.: Open government: Transforming data into value-added city services. In: Citizen's Right to the Digital City, pp. 199–214. Springer, Singapore (2015)
20. Fallucchi, F., Petito, M., Luca, E.W.: Analysing and visualising open data within the data and analytics framework. In: Garoufallou, E., Sartori, F., Siatri, R., Zervas, M. (eds.) MTSR 2018. CCIS, vol. 846, pp. 135–146. Springer, Cham (2019). https://doi.org/10.1007/978-3-030-14401-2_13
21. Fecho, K., et al.: Sex, obesity, diabetes, and exposure to particulate matter among patients with severe asthma: Scientific insights from a comparative analysis of open clinical data sources during a five-day hackathon. J. Biomed. Inform. **100**, 103325 (2019)
22. Grajales, D.F.P., Mejia, F., Mosquera, G.J.A., Piedrahita, L.C., Basurto, C.: Crop-planning, making smarter agriculture with climate data. In: 2015 Fourth International Conference on Agro-Geoinformatics (Agro-geoinformatics), pp. 240–244. IEEE (2015)
23. Fafalios, P., Papadakos, P.: Theophrastus: on demand and real-time automatic annotation and exploration of (web) documents using open linked data. J. Web Semant. **29**, 31–38 (2014)
24. de Macedo Guimarães, L.B., et al.: Sustainability hackathon: integrating academia and companies for finding solutions for socio-environmental problems. In: Leal Filho, W., Tortato, U., Frankenberger, F. (eds.) Integrating Social Responsibility and Sustainable Development. WSS, pp. 591–607. Springer, Cham (2021). https://doi.org/10.1007/978-3-030-59975-1_40
25. Charvat, K., et al.: Capacity development and collaboration for sustainable african agriculture: amplification of impact through hackathons. Data Sci. J. **20**(1), 23 (2021)
26. Ayele, W.Y., Juell-Skielse, G., Hjalmarsson, A., Johannesson, P., Rudmark, D.: Evaluating open data innovation: a measurement model for digital innovation contests. In: PACIS, p. 204 (2015)
27. Frey, F.J., Luks, M.: The innovation-driven hackathon: one means for accelerating innovation. In: 21st European Conference on Pattern Languages of Programs, pp. 1–11 (2016)
28. Simonofski, A., Zuiderwijk, A., Clarinval, A., Hammedi, W.: Tailoring open government data portals for lay citizens: a gamification theory approach. Int. J. Inf. Manage. **65**, 102511 (2022)
29. Nikiforova, A., Lnenicka, M.: A multi-perspective knowledge-driven approach for analysis of the demand side of the Open Government Data portal. Gov. Inf. Q. **38**(4), 101622 (2021)
30. Sieber, R.E., Johnson, P.A.: Civic open data at a crossroads: dominant models and current challenges. Gov. Inf. Q. **32**(3), 308–315 (2015)
31. Matheus, R., Ribeiro, M.M., Vaz, J.C.: Brazil towards government 2.0: Strategies for adopting open government data in national and subnational governments. In: Boughzala, I., Janssen, M., Assar, S. (eds.) Case Studies in e-Government 2.0, pp. 121–138. Springer, Cham (2015). https://doi.org/10.1007/978-3-319-08081-9_8
32. Van Loenen, B., et al.: Towards value-creating and sustainable open data ecosystems: a comparative case study and a research agenda. JeDEM-eJournal of eDemocracy and Open Government **13**(2), 1–27 (2021)
33. Verhulst, S., Addo, P.M., Young, A., Zahuranec, A.J., Baumann, D., McMurren, J.: Emerging uses of technology for development: a new intelligence paradigm. **6** (2021). SSRN 3937649
34. Bajpai, P.: Challenges and opportunities. In: Deep Eutectic Solvents for Pretreatment of Lignocellulosic Biomass. SAST, pp. 89–93. Springer, Singapore (2021). https://doi.org/10.1007/978-981-16-4013-1_8

Data Visualization Guide for Smart City Technologies

Teresa Cepero[1]([✉])([iD]), Luis G. Montané-Jiménez[1]([iD]),
and Gina Paola Maestre-Góngora[2]([iD])

[1] Facultad de Estadística e Informática, Universidad Veracruzana, Xalapa, Mexico
{mcepero,lmontane}@uv.mx
[2] Universidad Cooperativa de Colombia, Medellín, Colombia

Abstract. Smart city technologies collect and analyze urban data from which they generate visualizations that allow authorities to monitor the city and make more efficient decisions based on evidence. However, visually representing the data by itself does not reveal the visual patterns of interest; each type of visualization has its strengths and limitations that will make it suitable for some purposes and unsuitable for others. In this study, we propose a guide for selecting data visualization techniques to support people who wish to visualize and take advantage of the data available in a city. The guide was developed based on the fundamentals of visualization and considering the data visualization needs for city management. Using the guide will help analysts select effective visualization techniques, thus helping to create communication channels between data and people.

Keywords: Visualization · Urban data · Smart city · Technology

1 Introduction

Smart cities are territories that make intensive use of technology to address the challenges of today's cities, such as overpopulation, mobility, air pollution, emergency management, among others. Formally, smart cities have been defined in different ways. In its beginnings, a smart city was simply conceived as a city that integrates technology into its critical infrastructure to make it more efficient. But the smart city concept has been evolving along with the new aspirations of operations and life in cities. The smart city definition of Washburn et al. [28] emphasizes the use of software and applications to improve city services and citizens' lives. More current studies have extended the definition of smart city by incorporating a sustainable axis. According to Maestre [16], a smart city is a territory characterized by the intensive use of information and communication technologies (ICT) to promote collaboration, efficient use of resources, improve the provision of services, the quality of life of citizens, and the sustainability of the city.

F. Ortiz-Rodríguez et al. (Eds.): EGETC 2022, CCIS 1666, pp. 176–191, 2022.
https://doi.org/10.1007/978-3-031-22950-3_14

A key element in the development of smart cities is the collection of urban data and its use through technology [16]. Smart city technologies are a set of technologies -IoT, open data, big data, cloud computing, among others- that allow city data to be collected, analyzed, and presented to provide an understanding of the elements in a city through a graphical user interface.

The recent proliferation of big data has contributed to the transformation from traditional cities to smart cities. Big data generally refers to large and complex datasets that represent digital traces of human or urban activities. Cities worldwide collect massive amounts of data from the urban environment (e.g., energy infrastructure) and its population (e.g., residents using energy). This data contributes to creating useful content for various stakeholders, including local governments, businesses, citizens, and visitors [14].

A large amount of data is generated in cities, which represents an analysis challenge. Through data visualization, smart city systems transform data into visual representations that make it easy for people to understand the information. Visualization in smart city systems is a key element for communicating information in an understandable and accessible way. However, visually representing the data alone does not reveal the visual patterns of interest; each type of visualization has its strengths and limitations that will make it suitable for some purposes and not for others.

In order to take advantage of the potential of visualization and support the visualization process, previous studies [5, 8, 22] have developed guidelines for data visualization in the urban context. However, these works do not cover the necessary visualization techniques to perform spatial analysis, monitoring performance indicators, and processes carried out in the city. Therefore, they do not provide enough support to make an adequate selection of visualization techniques in some scenarios in a smart city context.

The purpose of this study is to support the data visualization design process through an instrument that guides the selection process of visualization techniques. The instrument for selecting data visualization techniques is a tool developed based on the fundamentals of data visualization and taking into account the needs of data visualization in technologies for city management. The proposed guide presents techniques to monitor indicators; analyze distributions; compare data, groups, and categories; identify ranges; study the parts of a whole (composition); analyze data over time; explore relationships; hierarchical information analysis; spatial analysis; text analysis; represent processes; represent systems; and for the communication of uncertainty and error.

Efficient data visualization relies on people's natural cognitive abilities to detect patterns, helping people analyze city data effectively. Urban data visualization can help local authorities and citizens monitor cities, recognize potential problems, identify appropriate solution alternatives, and generate an insight that supports a decision-making process to determine what actions to take.

This paper is organized as follows: Sect. 2 presents an overview of data visualization used in smart city technologies. This section also includes a review of the available tools for selecting visualization techniques and specific tools for visualizing urban data. Section 3 presents the guide proposal for selecting visualization techniques in the context of smart cities. Finally, Sect. 4 presents the conclusions and future work.

2   Data Visualization in Smart City Technologies

Smart city systems process and analyze data from the urban environment -from its physical and social environment- to provide a picture of current conditions in the city through a graphical user interface. According to an analysis of 34 smart city schemes (tools, frameworks, indices, indicators, and rankings) [24], the most common themes are economy, people, governance, environment, mobility, life, and data. These smart city schemes rely on a diversity of data sources and types. Secondary sources are dominant and include censuses, yearbooks, and historical data records. Primary data sources include questionnaires, interviews, on-site analysis, sensor observations, and cameras. Both sources of information complement each other, so the use of both primary and secondary sources is common. Although in current practice, smart city technologies are strongly oriented toward real-time data sources such as sensors and social networks [2].

Barns [1] analyzed a set of urban data platforms that facilitate data access. According to the author, there are urban data platforms designed to display and visualize information (dashboards), there are also platforms with the aim of facilitating the search and access to data in an open data format (datastores and open data portal), and there are urban data platforms that are geared towards monitoring progress or performance against agreed indicators (CityScore). The datastores and open data portal are designed to facilitate access to datasets related to the city, while the dashboards (see Fig. 1) and CityScore (a type of dashboard focused on monitoring indicators, see Fig. 2) present information on the city in a visual way to facilitate its consultation and interpretation [1].

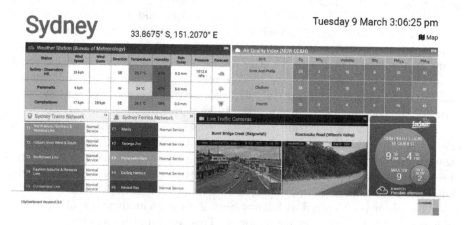

Fig. 1. Sydney dashboard [3]

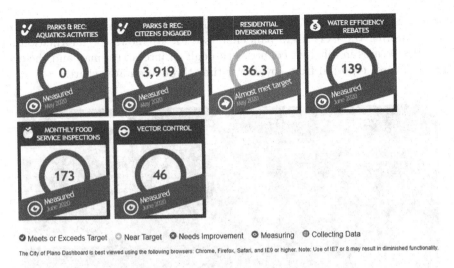

Fig. 2. Plano dashboard [21]

Smart city platforms incorporate different visualization techniques to represent the different types of data they integrate and communicate them to the population and key government actors. It is estimated that there are about a hundred different types of charts [13], although only a small subset are regularly used in both dashboard and smart city system interfaces. Visualization studies in smart city systems [4,6,9,20] show that the main visualization methods are: table, bar chart, histogram, pie chart, line chart, scatter chart, bubble chart, heat maps, and treemap. In addition to the extensive use of the map to represent geospatial information.

Maps are the most used method to represent georeferenced phenomena, which is why it is also the main technique used to represent data in smart city systems. The wide use of maps is due to their usefulness to locate and georeference elements and events in a city, understand urban areas and compare them, analyze routes and trajectories (mainly transport), among other uses [4]. The most commonly used map types are maps with pointers, choropleth maps, and route maps [6]. Using maps, geospatial features - such as grouping patterns - are easier to identify than a table. In order to efficiently communicate information through maps, it is necessary to use a generic and standard graphic language [30].

Given that it is difficult to represent a city's different dimensions and complexity with a single chart, using dashboards that integrate different visualizations is common. A dashboard is a system that collects city data and allows users to consult interactive visualizations that combine data sources and visual models. Thanks to the advantages offered by dashboards to integrate and explore information in a consolidated way, this tool has been applied in various domains in the management of a city, including education, transportation, energy and environment, waste management, water management, climate trace, public health, among others. These dashboards make it easy to explore information with different analysis approaches. For example, the Johns Hopkins University dashboard for monitoring the COVID-19 pandemic (see Fig. 3) shows the information on COVID-19 cases in different countries through an interactive map and the evolution of cases reported from covid over time through an area chart.

Fig. 3. COVID-19 Dashboard [26]

The visualizations integrated into smart city systems can be complemented by multimedia resources such as video clips, photos, and text. The purpose of these so-called annotations is to supplement the visualizations with contextual material [20]. For example, on a map of hospitals in a region, the hospital's photo, telephone number, and opening hours are contextual information that could help citizens.

Smart city management systems share common ground; many systems aim to analyze city data and deliver information. A study of smart cities [14] indicates that a key success factor of using big data in smart cities is the effectiveness of the visualization and delivery of information. In data-driven smart city development projects, data visualizations must be clear and relevant to improve the acceptance of information by citizens, visitors, and local authorities [14].

2.1 Tools to Select Data Visualization Techniques

In the visualization field, there are models [17,27], frameworks [10,25], and manuals [7,11–13] for designing visualizations that represent data in a visual and meaningful way that helps to understand the information. In particular, the manuals [7,11–13] explain the principles for display design and describe the most commonly used techniques.

Few's [7] and Knaflic's [12] manual present a limited selection of visualization techniques that could hardly be used to present the spatial patterns of a city. Koponén and Hildén [13] developed a practical manual for visualization development. This manual includes a classification of visualization techniques into genres to show the variety of visualizations. In this manual, information visualization techniques are grouped into the following genres: information illustration, maps, statistical charts, conceptual charts, network diagrams, and scientific visualizations. Each category includes descriptions of the most used maps and charts and recommendations for their optimal design. However, this manual does not provide enough guidance for choosing an optimal visualization technique.

Kirk [11] classified the most common and useful chart types being used across the visualization field. This classification aims to help the selection of a visualization technique based on what the analyst wants to communicate or understand from the data (angle of analysis). The classification contains five families: categorical, hierarchical, relational, temporal, and spatial. The categorical chart is used to compare categories and distributions of values; the hierarchical chart reveals the relationships and hierarchies of the elements; the relational chart explores correlations and connections; the temporal chart plots trends and intervals over time; and the spatial chart maps spatial patterns [11].

From the classic visualization studies, frameworks and tools have been developed to support the visual design of Internet of Things (IoT) data [22]. Protopsaltis et al. [22] proposed some rules to guide the visualization of IoT data based on the number of variables (one variable, two, or multiple) and the objectives of the visualization process (evaluate relationships, distributions, compare data, and study a composition). For example, Protopsaltis [22] recommends using scatter plots to analyze the relationship between two variables, and for three variables, the use of bubble charts. However, these guidelines are limited to statistical graphs (bar chart, line chart, scatter plot, histogram, among others).

Grainger et al. [8] proposed a framework for environmental data visualization in non-scientific professional contexts that offers guidelines for a user-centered visualization design. This framework is an adaptation of the Sedlmair (2012) framework, a methodology based on the experience from design studies to provide practical human-computer interaction guidance. However, these guidelines are intended to support the design process and do not provide sufficient guidelines for selecting a type of visualization.

Dunne et al. [5] identified preliminary specifications for visual analytics tools for transportation planning using case analysis and interviews with transportation, urban planning, and visualization experts. In terms of visualization, Dunne et al. [5] recommend using interactive tools for data exploration and including map-based views and statistical charts to support understanding geospatial dynamics.

The analyzed works establish the bases for data visualization in smart city technologies. However, some available tools [5,8,13] do not provide the elements to help support effective data representation. There are some tools [7,11] oriented to help evaluate relationships between variables, comparisons between variables, compositions, time series, and spatial patterns. Although these tools and charts can be used to analyze urban data, these tools lack the necessary visualization techniques to monitor performance indicators and promote understanding of the processes carried out in the city.

3 Guide to Selecting Data Visualization Techniques

Based on the fundamentals of data visualization [7,11,13] and considering the needs of data visualization in smart city technologies [4,5,22,24,29], we made an instrument for selecting data visualization techniques.

Before beginning the process of developing a visualization, the analyst must analyze the goals and needs of the users [19]. That is why, before selecting a visualization technique, it is important to ask ourselves: What is our objective (explore the data, communicate, confirm a hypothesis)? What are the user's information needs? What questions should the chart or map answer? The answers to these questions will guide the data selection and representation process. Once the objectives of the visualization are clear, we can search the instrument for the visualization techniques that help analyze the objective information.

The proposed instrument (see Fig. 4 and Fig. 5) organizes the visualization techniques into 13 categories based on the analyses and relationships that the visualizations support. The instrument is made up of the following categories:

- Techniques for monitoring indicators: Visualization methods that show the values of an indicator or a set of indicators. For example, through techniques such as the icon with a number, we can represent indicators and metrics of a city, such as fire response indicators, police responses, employment rate, number of emergency calls answered, etc.
- Techniques for analyzing distributions: Visualization methods that show the frequency and how data is distributed over an interval [7]. For example, through charts such as the histogram and the density plot, it is possible to show the distribution by age of the population, the distribution of income, and the distribution of the time spent to attend requests in an institution, among others.
- Techniques to compare elements, groups, and categories: Visualization methods that help to compare the (quantitative) values of a set of elements or groups. For example, through the bar chart or lollipop plot, it is possible to compare the budget of different institutions, the population in different places, and the production of agricultural products.
- Techniques to identify ranges: Visualization methods that show the variations between the upper and lower limits of a data set [23]. For example, through techniques such as the range chart, we can represent the price range of the products of the basic basket, the salary range of public officials, and the minimum and maximum values of monthly water consumption.
- Techniques to study the parts of a whole: Visualization methods that show the parts, elements, or subcategories that make up a group or whole. They are commonly used to show how something is divided [23]. For example, through techniques such as the pie chart, it is possible to study the percentage of animal production (beef, pork, poultry, etc.), the main industries that generate greenhouse gases, and the main industries that create jobs.

- Techniques to analyze data over time and trends: Visualization methods that show how values change over a period of time (days, months, years, etc.) [7]. For example, through the line chart, we can analyze trends in economic variables (such as the variation in GDP and the value of a currency) and monitor environmental variables such as temperature, humidity, and noise level over time.
- Techniques to explore relationships: Visualization methods that show relationships and connections between elements and variables. Particularly the methods that show relationships -such as the scatter plot, bubble plot, and heat map- help to determine possible correlations between two or more variables, so they are widely used to determine if changes in one of the variables influence the changes of the other [23].
- Techniques for hierarchical analysis: Visualization methods that reveal the relationships and hierarchies of a set of elements [11]. For example, the hierarchical tree diagram is useful to show the composition of the organizational structure of the government.
- Techniques for spatial/geographical analysis: Visualization methods for the spatial exploration of a variable and mapping spatial patterns. Most spatial relationships are presented through maps [7]. Different maps represent information with different levels of detail and spatial limitation. For example, maps with pointers are an excellent option to locate elements and events of interest in the city, such as schools, hospitals, museums, and government offices; while choropleth maps work best to display information by defined spatial regions -such as countries, states, or districts-.
- Techniques for text analysis: Visualization methods for analyzing the frequency of words in a text, that is, a set of charts to represent the most repeated words in a text. They can be used to extract the opinion of citizens in social networks, the analysis of applications in a government institution, and the results of a survey, among other applications.
- Techniques to represent processes: Visualization methods that help explain processes [23]. For example, the progress bar is useful to present the level of progress of a project or procedure.
- Techniques to represent and analyze systems: Visualization methods that help understand the interactions between the elements that make up a system. For example, the block diagram can be used to represent the municipal solid waste and collection system, the water distribution system, or the functioning of administrative systems.
- Techniques for communicating uncertainty and error: Visualization methods are used to communicate or analyze the range of error or uncertainty in a data set. For example, the error bands and band graph could be used to represent the margin of error in sensor readings or survey results.

In order to facilitate the interpretation of data visualization, each chart and map must be accompanied by a descriptive title and graphic references (such as an axis or legend) or text that serve as a reference and help interpret the information. For example, the dashboard of the city of Moncloa (see Fig. 6)

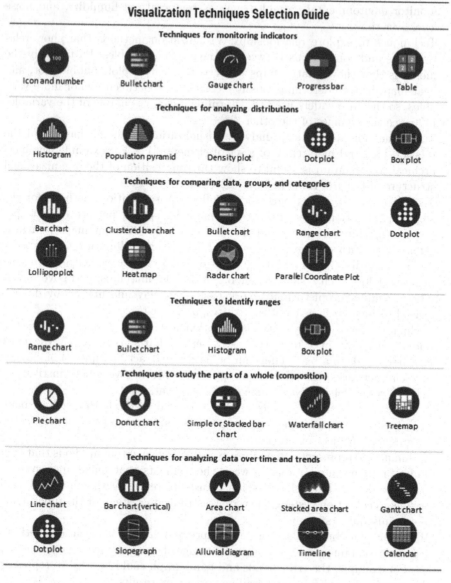

Fig. 4. Visualization techniques selection guide [part 1].

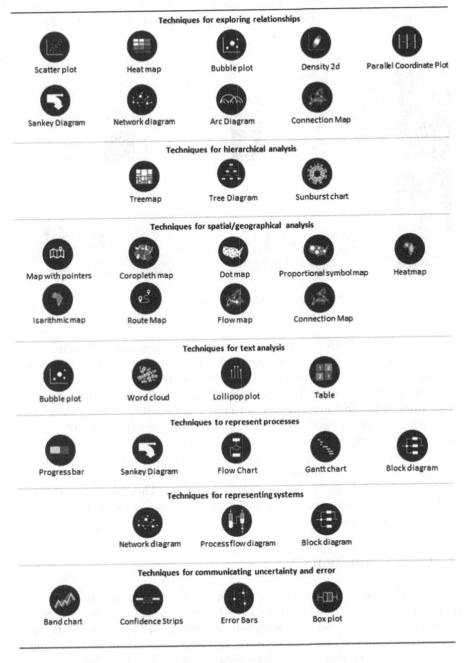

Fig. 5. Visualization techniques selection guide [part 2].

integrates area charts with clearly defined axes and indicators with reference text of the maximum and minimum values. These references provide context and help users interpret the displayed information for environmental variables.

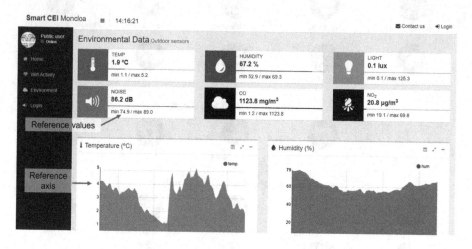

Fig. 6. Dashboard Moncloa [15]

It would be difficult to represent the different dimensions and complexity of an urban problem or phenomenon with a single graph, so we recommend exploring different visualization techniques to analyze various data patterns and multiple variables. For example, it would be challenging to understand the weather's state from just a line graph reporting hourly temperature estimates, which is why weather reports regularly include multiple displays that present temperature, precipitation, and wind speed information.

Using the guide will help select effective visualization techniques in smart city technologies and help develop an understanding of what is happening in the city from data, which helps to make informed decisions. Therefore, an appropriate and efficient data visualization improves and facilitates decision-making among the different city actors [18].

4   User Evaluation

We conducted an exploratory study to examine the clarity, usefulness, and ease of use of the guide for the selection of visualization techniques. For this reason, we carried out a series of tests with software developers to obtain feedback on the perception of the clarity, usefulness, and ease of use of the proposed guide. Five volunteers (two male and three female) participated in this exploratory study, from which two of the participating evaluators were also specialists in data visualization systems.

The study consisted of a series of tests where the volunteers used the visualization guide and then answered a post-test questionnaire to gain some feedback of the perception of usefulness and clarity of the guide. The evaluation sessions was conducted virtually through the Zoom platform. Through this platform, a meeting was held with each evaluator to coordinate the test, establish the evaluation's objective, explain the procedure, request the signing of the informed consent letter, share the link with the test material (description of the scenarios for user experience testing, guide instructions, guide to selecting data visualization techniques, and questionnaire), and a dataset to explore with different visualization techniques.

A scenario was proposed to use the proposed guide for selecting four visualizations. Below is the description of the scenario:

"Consider that you have the task of analyzing the urban data of Mexico City to plan the use of the city's space. The tasks include: analyzing the income distribution in the population, analyzing the population growth in the last hundred years, analyzing the population density in the different regions of the city, and analyzing the air quality in the different regions of the city.

- Select an appropriate visualization technique to represent the population's income distribution.
- Select a suitable visualization technique to represent the population growth for the defined time period.
- Select an appropriate visualization technique to represent the population density in the different regions of the city.
- Select a suitable visualization technique to represent the air quality in the different regions of the city".

After establishing the scenario for selecting a set of visualization techniques, we asked participants to use the guide for choosing visualization techniques by following these steps:

1. Analysts must ask themselves, What is my purpose (to explore data, communicate information, or confirm a hypothesis or assumption)? What are the information needs of users? What questions should the graph or map answer? Answering these questions provides an overview of the purpose of the visualization and will guide the selection process.
2. Once the visualization goals or questions are clear, search the guide for visualization techniques that help reveal target information and patterns of interest.
3. Explore different visualization techniques within the selected category. Sketching can be a useful method to analyze the different visualization techniques.
4. Select the visualization that makes evident the patterns or relationships of interest to users and better support the understanding of the data.

After using the guide to selecting data visualization techniques, participants completed a survey about the clarity, usefulness, and ease of use of the guide. They completed the survey using a 5-point Likert scale (1: Strongly disagree,

2: Disagree, 3: Neither agree nor disagree, 4: Agree, and 5: Strongly agree). In addition, there were a comment box provided in the survey questionnaire to get participants' feedback on their total experience.

5   Results

The results of the evaluation are divided into two parts. The first part corresponds to the questions associated with the clarity and perceived usefulness of each guide category; the second part shows the results regarding the clarity, ease of use, level of detail of the guide, and usefulness in facilitating the selection of visualization techniques.

The exploratory test results show that the guide categories were perceived as easy to understand. As Table 1 shows, we observed a median ranging between 4 and 5, which means that the participants agreed (4) and strongly agreed (5) that the categories of visualization techniques in the guide were clear or easy to understand. Regarding its usefulness, most participants fully agreed (5) that the categories are useful for selecting visualization techniques.

Table 1. Results of the perception of usefulness and clarity of the guide categories

Guide categories	Clarity		Usefulness	
	Median	Sum	Median	Sum
1. Techniques for monitoring indicators	4	20	5	23
2. Techniques for analyzing distributions	5	23	5	24
3. Techniques to compare elements, groups, and categories	5	22	5	23
4. Techniques to identify ranges	4	20	5	24
5. Techniques to study the parts of a whole	4	20	5	22
6. Techniques to analyze data over time and trends	5	23	5	25
7. Techniques to explore relationships	5	23	5	23
8. Techniques for hierarchical analysis	5	22	5	24
9. Techniques for spatial/geographical analysis	4	22	5	24
10. Techniques for text analysis	5	24	5	23
11. Techniques to represent processes	5	24	5	23
12. Techniques to represent and analyze systems	4	21	5	23
13. Techniques for communicating uncertainty and error	4	20	4	20

The results of the general perception of the guide are shown in Fig. 7. The participants agreed and strongly agreed that the guide includes all the key categories to support a data analysis and visualization process. They also agreed that the guide makes it easy to select visualization techniques and is an easy-to-use instrument. However, there were different opinions about the level of detail in the guide. Some volunteers with visualization experience agreed that the guide presents sufficient detail to support a visualization process, while those with less experience disagreed or showed a neutral position. Finally, in the open question, some participants expressed that the guide was easy to use and useful but that it would be desirable to provide a little more detail on each technique; this extra information would help in the selection process.

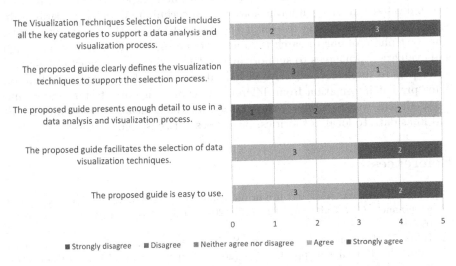

Fig. 7. Results of the perception of the guide

5.1 Conclusions

Cities seeking to move towards a smart city model to take advantage of data need to incorporate technologies that effectively contribute to better analysis and communication of information. This study presents a data visualization techniques selection guide to support the visualization design process in smart systems. We developed the visualization guide based on the fundamentals of data visualization and considering the needs of data visualization in technologies for city management. The proposed instrument presents techniques to monitor indicators; analyze distributions; compare data, groups, and categories; identify ranges; study the parts of a whole; analyze data over time; explore relationships; analyze hierarchical information; for spatial analysis; for text analysis; to represent processes; represent systems, and communicate margin of error.

The visualization techniques selection guide helps to see the options to represent the patterns of interest. This tool does not include an exhaustive list of all visualization techniques. In recent times, new proposals have emerged to represent mobility patterns and city models visually; however, more research is needed on these techniques that provide information on their effectiveness. That is why the instrument comprises a selection of the most used and consolidated visualization techniques that effectively represent information.

The proposed instrument for selecting visualization techniques comprises charts and maps that encode data effectively and accurately. However, there is no foolproof visualization technique. A poor design of a visualization technique can lead to interpretation difficulties and even cause misinterpretation. That is why we recommend the application of visualization design principles and evaluating the effectiveness of interactive visualizations in smart city systems.

The results of the exploratory test show that the guide was perceived as useful and easy to use; however, some participants with little experience in visualization also indicated that more information on each technique would be desirable. In future work, we are going to conduct additional tests with more participants. The next phase of our research is to analyze and integrate visualization design and evaluation principles to support urban data analysts and smart city system developers to implement effective visualizations successfully. Data visualization helps present information from different areas of a city in a faster, easier, and more efficient way to analyze, thus functioning as a means that communicates and links data to local authorities, businesses, citizens, and visitors.

References

1. Barns, S.: Smart cities and urban data platforms: designing interfaces for smart governance. City Cult. Soc. **12**, 5–12 (2018). https://doi.org/10.1016/j.ccs.2017.09.006
2. Batty, M., Hudson-Smith, A., Hugel, S., Roumpani, F.: Visualising Data for Smart Cities. In: IGI Global, pp. 453–475 (2018). https://doi.org/10.4018/978-1-5225-2589-9.ch021
3. Centre, C.F.R.: Sydney dashboard screenshot (2022). http://citydashboard.be.unsw.edu.au/. Accessed 09 Mar 2022
4. Cepero, T., Montané-Jiménez, L.G., Benítez-Guerrero, E., Mezura-Godoy, C.: Visualization in smart city technologies. In: Smart Cities. vol 1555, pp. 86–100. Springer International Publishing, Cham (2022). https://doi.org/10.1007/978-3-030-96753-6_7
5. Dunne, C., Skelton, C., Diamond, S., Meirelles, I., Martino, M.: Quantitative, qualitative, and historical urban data visualization tools for professionals and stakeholders. In: Streitz, N., Markopoulos, P. (eds.) Distributed, Ambient and Pervasive Interactions, pp. 405–416. Springer International Publishing, Cham (2016). https://doi.org/10.1007/978-3-319-39862-4_37
6. Eberhardt, A., Silveira, M.S.: Show me the data! a systematic mapping on open government data visualization. In: Proceedings of the 19th Annual International Conference on Digital Government Research: Governance in the Data Age. Association for Computing Machinery, New York (2018). https://doi.org/10.1145/3209281.3209337
7. Few, S.: Show Me the Numbers, 2nd edn. Analytics Press, Berkeley (2012)
8. Grainger, S., Mao, F., Buytaert, W.: Environmental data visualisation for non-scientific contexts: literature review and design framework. Environ. Model. Softw. **85**, 299–318 (2016). https://doi.org/10.1016/j.envsoft.2016.09.004
9. Habibzadeh, H., Kaptan, C., Soyata, T., Kantarci, B., Boukerche, A.: Smart city system design: a comprehensive study of the application and data planes. ACM Comput. Surv. **52**(2), 1–38 (2019)
10. Isson, J.P., Harriott, J.: Data Visualization Presenting Information Clearly: The CONVINCE Framework, pp. 95–109. John Wiley & Son, Hoboken (2013)
11. Kirk, A.: Data Visualization. SAGE, New York (2016)
12. Knaflic, C.N.: Storytelling with Data: A Data Visualization Guide for Business Professionals. John Wiley, Hoboken (2015)

13. Koponen, J., Hildén, J.: Data Visualization Handbook. Aalto korkeakoulusäätiö (2019)
14. Lim, C., Kim, K.J., Maglio, P.P.: Smart cities with big data: reference models, challenges, and considerations. Cities **82**, 86–99 (2018). https://doi.org/10.1016/j.cities.2018.04.011
15. de Madrid, U.P.: Smart cei moncloascreenshot (2017). http://ceiboard.dit.upm.es/dashboard. Accessed 09 Mar 2021
16. Maestre-Gongora, G.P., Bernal, W.N.: Conceptual model of information technology management for smart cities: SmarTIcity. J. Glob. Inf. Manage. (JGIM) **27**(2), 159–175 (2019)
17. Munzner, T.: A nested model for visualization design and validation. IEEE Trans. Vis. Comput. Graph. **15**(6), 921–928 (2009)
18. Pardo-García, N., Simoes, S.G., Dias, L., Sandgren, A., Suna, D., Krook-Riekkola, A.: Sustainable and resource efficient cities platform - SureCity holistic simulation and optimization for smart cities. J. Cleaner Prod. **215**, 701–711 (2019). https://doi.org/10.1016/j.jclepro.2019.01.070
19. Peddoju, S.K., Upadhyay, H.: Evaluation of IoT data visualization tools and techniques. In: Anouncia, S.M., Gohel, H.A., Vairamuthu, S. (eds.) Data Visualization, pp. 115–139. Springer, Singapore (2020). https://doi.org/10.1007/978-981-15-2282-6_7
20. Pettit, C., Widjaja, I., Russo, P., Sinnott, R., Stimson, R., Tomko, M.: Visualisation support for exploring urban space and place. In: ISPRS Annals of the Photogrammetry, Remote Sensing and Spatial Information Sciences, vol. 1, pp. 153–158 (2012). https://doi.org/10.5194/isprsannals-I-2-153-2012
21. of Plano Government, C.: Plano performance dashboard screenshot (2021). https://dashboard.plano.gov/. Accessed 09 Mar 2021
22. Protopsaltis, A., Sarigiannidis, P., Margounakis, D., Lytos, A.: Data visualization in internet of things: tools, methodologies, and challenges. In: Proceedings of the 15th International Conference on Availability, Reliability and Security. ARES 2020, Association for Computing Machinery, New York (2020)
23. Ribecca, S.: Cátalogo de visualización de datos (2022). https://datavizcatalogue.com/ES/index.html. Accessed 20 May 2022
24. Sharifi, A.: A typology of smart city assessment tools and indicator sets. Sustain. Cities Soc. **53**, 101936 (2020). https://doi.org/10.1016/j.scs.2019.101936
25. Shen, H., et al.: Information visualisation methods and techniques: state-of-the-art and future directions. J. Indust. Inf. Integr. **16**, 100102 (2019). https://doi.org/10.1016/j.jii.2019.07.003
26. Covid-19 dashboard screenshot. Johns Hopkins University (JHU) for Systems Science E.C (2022).https://coronavirus.jhu.edu/map.html. Accessed 13 June 2022
27. Ware, C.: Information Visualization: Perception for Design. Morgan Kaufmann, Burlington (2012)
28. Washburn, D., Sindhu, U., Balaouras, S., Dines, R.A., Hayes, N., Nelson, L.E.: Helping cios understand "smart city" initiatives. Growth **17**(2), 1–17 (2009)
29. Young, G.W., Kitchin, R.: Creating design guidelines for building city dashboards from a user's perspectives. Int. J. Hum.-Comput. Stud. **140**, 102429 (2020). https://doi.org/10.1016/j.ijhcs.2020.102429
30. Zhong, C., Wang, T., Zeng, W., Müller Arisona, S.: Spatiotemporal visualisation: a survey and outlook. In: Arisona, S.M., Aschwanden, G., Halatsch, J., Wonka, P. (eds.) Digital Urban Modeling and Simulation. CCIS, vol. 242, pp. 299–317. Springer, Heidelberg (2012). https://doi.org/10.1007/978-3-642-29758-8_16

A Machine Learning-Based Mobile Chatbot for Crop Farmers

Patience U. Usip[1]([⊠]) [iD], Edward N. Udo[1], Daniel E. Asuquo[1] [iD], and Otobong R. James[2]

[1] Department of Computer Science, Faculty of Science, University of Uyo, Uyo, Nigeria
{patienceusip,edwardudo,danielasuquo}@uniuyo.edu.ng
[2] Computer Science Department, National Open University of Nigeria, Lagos, Nigeria

Abstract. Agriculture remains the basis of the country's economy, providing the main source of livelihood for most citizenry such as food, employment, income and foreign exchange as well as raw materials for the manufacturing sectors. Despite the great need for economic advancement in crop farming, agriculture seems to be limited in some parts of the country as many people go about in search of white-collar jobs due to lack of adequate information and knowledge on the use of modern farming technologies. The inability of farmers in rural and sub-urban areas to access agricultural knowledge and real-time information on latest farming practices to enhance informed decision making related to soil properties, seeds, fertilizers, pests, modern agricultural tools, and agro-best practices leads to poor crop productivity by farmers. This work is aimed at providing a mobile chatbot for crop farmers in Uyo and its environs. The dataset used was obtained from Akwa Ibom State Ministry of Agriculture and farmers using a combination of two classic research methods; questionnaires and interviews. An ontology-based representation of the obtained dataset is used for training the chatbot using a hybridized machine approach that consists of word shuffling and Jacquard Similarity algorithm. The resulting chatbot is a knowledge base that will provide the means of obtaining useful answers to questions, advice and recommendations on specific farming concerns. The use of the chatbot will give government a platform to reach out to famers in the state and obtain feedback on governance through agricultural services.

Keyword: E-farming · Intelligent systems · Mobile chatbot · Knowledge representation · Natural language processing

1 Introduction

Agriculture is an important activity for human survival and has continued for thousands of years [1]. Farming plays a major role in the development of the world because it provides employment opportunities to a greater number of people around the countries of the world and many people depend on it for their livelihood [2]. Most countries depend on agriculture for their gross domestic product (GDP growth. In Nigeria, FAO [3] reports that not less than 70% of the population earns a living through agriculture where they obtain among others food, employment, income, foreign exchange and raw materials for the manufacturing sectors. In spite of the huge availability of crude oil in Nigeria, agriculture remains the central index for measuring the growth of its economy because it serves as the main source of livelihood for most Nigerians. Nigerian farmers today are faced with the problem of low income due to lack of information about government schemes, fertilizers and farming equipment. Some smallholders and marginalized farmers have low awareness as most of them live in remote areas [2].

According to Sawant et al. [4], the advancement of technology in the field of agriculture is to bring about innovations that can assist human beings in their day-to-day business transactions and living. Recently, conversational systems, known as chatbots, have gain popularity and wider attention [5, 6]. Chatbot is a computer program that communicates through text in a humanly manner and provides services to human users in order to accomplish a well-defined goal [2]. It is a latest technology that duplicates human conversation. Khin et al. [7] reports that it is widely used in banking, marketing education, etc. A farmer chatbot is an end-to-end trainable learning model to create a conversational system with minimum error and answer questions about current conditions. Farmers can have conversation with a chatbot and obtain expert advice [8]. Although, agricultural information in mobile connectivity is seeing an exponential growth through information technology services [9], the expert advice does not still get to many famers on time since these technologies are not effectively deployed and remote farmers do not have access to theme [8]. This is because remote farmers continue to depend largely on the handy peer's knowledge to tackle the issues they face.

There are many reasons why farming is becoming less attractive. One of such reasons is the lack of knowledge on modern technologies used in farming; a major problem facing farmers in rural communities [5]. Information, one of the important resources in rural development [10], enhances knowledge gain in farming and can assist small-scale farmers in making timely decisions regarding application of best practices and technologies. Lack of agricultural information is one of the major factors that have greatly limited agricultural advancement in developing countries [11]. This has impacted negatively on the farmer's earnings and opportunities to increase their crop yield. Right information is therefore critical for social and economic activities as it fuels the development of any business. Farmers in remote areas of any part of Nigeria without adequate information related to new technological trends and agricultural practices and who do not have access to enough information on crops, soil properties, seeds, latest tools, fertilizers, etc. as it relates to current agricultural and farming practices, will definitely experience low productivity in crops and livestock [2].

The scope of this work covers Uyo and its environs. Uyo is the capital city of Akwa Ibom State (AKS) in Nigeria. Akwa Ibom State has a land mass of about 8,412 square Kilometres and much arable land in West Africa's rain forest with a population of over 4million people at a density of 350 inhabitants per square Kilometres. Agriculture is the dominant economic activity of Akwa Ibom State and supports about 75% of the state's population. The rural economy of the state is agro-based, and the state is a powerhouse for various agricultural products such as palm oil, cassava, yam, cocoyam, plantain, maize, rice, rubber, and many varieties of fish and other sea food. Factors that favour agriculture in Akwa Ibom State abound such as favourable all-year round climate; abundance of rich fertile soil; talented, skilled, and able-bodied manpower base [12]. Akwa Ibom is basically an agricultural state whose people have always depended on farming for existence, though at subsistent level. In fact, before the era of this oil boom in Nigeria, which has become the country's economic mainstay, the state, then part of the Eastern Region, was a major contributor of palm produce which put the country as the world's number one producer.

Conventionally, agricultural extension officers (AEOs) visit the farming communities within Uyo and its environs to provide training, advice and support to farmers. The inadequate supply of AEOs makes it difficult for many rural farmers to access timely vital farming information for decision making related to soil properties, seeds, fertilizers, pests, modern agricultural tools, and agro-best practices. Lack of access to agricultural knowledge and information on real time basis is the problem bewildering the farmers within our study area. To overcome some of these challenges, a chatbot for crop farmers is proposed using a hybridized machine learning approach, where the farmers can communicate with the chatbot efficiently and obtain correct answers to questions; advice and recommendations on specific farming problems. The application of deep learning-based chatbots is growing rapidly in recent years and is used in many areas like customer support, reservation system and as personal assistant [8].

The rest of the paper is organized as follows. Section 2 reviews relevant literature on access to agricultural information by farmers, web and mobile-based systems for providing advisory services by AEOs, as well as efforts towards development of smart interactive chatbots. It highlights the strength and weakness of previous studies and chat a course for the present study. Section 3 presents the architecture of the proposed hybridize machine learning-based mobile chatbot for crop farmers, and describes its functional components. The sources and methods of data collection as well as the adopted sampling procedure from the study area are also highlighted. In Sect. 4, the algorithmic implementation of the model in Python and the chatbot training approach are demonstrated. Results evaluated using system usability scale are discussed in Sect. 5 while Sect. 6 concludes the paper.

2 Related Works

Several solutions have been proposed to address the issues of inability of farmers in developing countries to access information. These include forums for asking agricultural related questions to experts and peers [13], peer education using participatory video – that is creating videos by farmers and using human-mediated instruction to disseminate these videos to other farmers [14], interactive voice response (IVR) systems – uses a computer-based back-end with a keypad/voice-based input, and audio output to provide farmers with relevant information related to weather, fertilizers and market prices [15, 16] and social networks for farmers [17, 18]. All these were not real-time solutions. Government therefore made tremendous efforts towards the development of chatbot for farmers as early works can be traced back to the web-based farmer's portal [19], to make knowledge accessible to Indian farmers. It is only computer literate farmers that can access the system.

Other researches aimed at reaching out to the local farmers have been undertaken since then. The author in [20] proposed a short message service (SMS)-to-web-system for rural farmers in Uganda to send agricultural questions by SMS to a web-based system. Although the use of the local language increases the chance of system adoption, it lacks flexibility and availability because farmers' questions are interpreted and answered by human beings. Fue et al. [21] developed a web and mobile-based system called "Ushaurikilimo" that allowed farmers to request advisory services from an AEO using either the web-based system or mobile phone. Detailed overview and analysis of the application of SMS in agro-business were provided. The system operated a two-way communication platform between farmers and experts, allowing farmers to ask questions through SMS and get a response from the agricultural expert via SMS. The platform enable farmers to ask for advice on agricultural-related issues like; farm management, livestock keeping, marketing information, and aquaculture. Again, the system depended on the presence of the experts in order for the farmer's problems to be addressed.

In [22], a chatbot called FarmChat was designed to meet the information needs of farmers in rural communities. The system offered information to the farmers by answering their farming-related queries. The researchers developed a knowledge base for potato farming using the kisan call center (KCC) dataset and information collected from formative interviews with smallholder farmers and agri-experts. The authors suggested that conversational agent delivered through mobile-based smart phones could be used as an effective way to improve the information accessible to people with limited computer literacy. As a follow up to earlier recommendations, [23] developed a call center helpline service for farmers to clarify their queries over a mobile phone. This service facilitated a telephonic conversation communication between farmer and extension agent to bridge the information gap. However, these services were only available from 6 am to 10 am. As more people venture into farming the number of questions gradually increased, thereby limiting the call centers' effectiveness in answering all queries on time. Hence, a scalable solution was needed to accommodate the increasing number of queries in a better and efficient way.

The authors in [24] developed a smart chatbot which performed machine learning analysis on all the valuable parameters (weather, season, rainfall and type of soil) needed to increase farmers' yield. The analysis was based on historic data. The system was trained to suggest which crops to grow and the crops to mix for good yield. The system helped farmers in remote places where no connectivity is present to better understand the crop to be grown based on atmospheric conditions and also answer their basic questions on farming. An interactive web-based chatbot named Agribot was developed in [25] to assist farmers in problem-solving such as crop disease detection and weather prediction. This chatbot used a sequence-to-sequence learning, an approach that allows the model to learn the mapping between questions and their suitable response. This system is similar to our proposed system by mode of operation but differs in terms of application platform since our proposed chatbot utilizes smart phone platform. The authors suggested that the chatbot could be more generalized in terms of conversations if the model is trained with a massive amount of data. In [2], a chatbot system, called Agroexpert was developed using pattern matching technique. It provides an interface for farmers to communicate with the chatbot efficiently. The system is a web-based application that has Farmer and Admin login for privacy purposes and acts as a farming assistant that responds to the farmers' queries. If the system does not give answers to the queries, the queries are then forwarded to experts. Vamsi et al. [26] built a chatbot using artificial intelligence (AI) and deep learning (DL) techniques. The chatbot was built in such a way that it would be able to understand users' perspective and then deliver accurate answers. Multiple layered neural networks were constructed in order to process the data.

In [27], an interactive chatbot that allows the consumers of farm produce to communicate directly with the farmers via any social media platform was developed. The customers place their orders by providing all the necessary input. Once the product is ready the farmer delivers it to the consumer. This eliminates the middleman problem and reduces the purchasing price. Manimala et al. [28] developed an interactive chatbot for farmers called "AgriApps" which act as a search engine and ranked as one of the most popular apps among farmers. It has a rating of 4.3 out of 5.0 on Google Play store. This portal brings information about farming resources and government services through an online mobile application to the farmers and also provides a chat option for farmers which enable them to chat with an agricultural expert using this app efficiently. However, as a modeled search engine, the user has to search for a particular piece of information manually and if the user opts to chat with the application operator instead of searching manually, the user has to wait for a significant period of time for a response from the operator. Consequently, the system is not a real-time system as the one proposed in this work. This work leverages on the power of AI to build a solution that can mitigate the limitation of the above systems. In order to achieve this, a machine learning (ML)-based conversational agent (chatbot) which can be utilized on smart mobile phones platform to ease accessibility and automate the process of conversation with the user (farmer) is proposed. Also, the system integrates features like real-time outputs, facilitates farmer-friendly interface to potentially bridge the information gap for the farmers towards a productive agro-business.

3 Methodology

3.1 Study Area Description

This study was conducted in Akwa Ibom State, Nigeria. Akwa Ibom State is located in the coastal South-South region of Nigeria. The state is chosen because of its location and availability of food crops such as cassava. The state is located between latitudes $4°321$ and $5°331$ north and longitudes $7°51c$ and $8°251c$ east. It has a total land area of $7,246$ km^2. It is bordered in the east by Cross River State, in the west by Rivers State and in the South by Abia State. The state under study has a population of about $3,902,051$ with cassava, cocoyam, yam, maize, melon, okra and vegetables (green, fluted pumpkin, water-leaf and bitter leaf) as the main crops grown by farmers. The livestock reared include; sheep, goats, pigs and poultry while fish is also cultured.

The mean annual temperature ranges from 21.1 C to 31.1 C, the rain varies from 1100 mm per annum in the southern part to 800 mm per annum in the northern part. The rainy season starts in late March and ends in October, the dry season stretches from November to early March. The soil type ranges from deep, medium coarse sandy loam over sandy clay loam, weak structure, well drained, porous, moderate moisture and nutrient retention [29]. The above ecological features favored the cultivation of various food crops in the state. The location of Akwa Ibom State is shown in the map of Nigeria in Fig. 1 while the detailed study area is shown in the map of Akwa Ibom State in Fig. 2.

Fig. 1. Map of Nigeria showing Akwa Ibom State

Fig. 2. Map of Akwa Ibom showing detailed study area

3.2 Sources of Data and Data Collection Methods

Two sources of knowledge informed the development of the proposed system;

(i) dataset of farmers' frequently asked questions and answers from Akwa Ibom State Agricultural Development Programmme (AKADEP), and
(ii) findings from a formative study with local farmers and agric-experts.

Before collecting this data, a research permit was obtained from AKADEP. The dataset obtained contains two attributes: query (question) from farmers and response (answer) by the extension officers. In the context of the proposed system, the data collected was restricted to cassava related issues since most farmers around the study area were engaged in cassava farming during the study period. The dataset obtained from AKADEP does not contain a complete dialogue between the farmers and the extension officers, rather a summary of questions and answers provided. To fill this gap, a complementary source of data was needed to verify whether the dataset applies to the local situations around the study area. Semi-structured interviews with farmers and extension officers were conducted in the study area using questionnaires to complement the primary data. The primary data collected from farmers include: (a) socio-economic characteristics (demographic characteristics of the farmers) such as personal variables relating to the farmers (age, sex, marital status, level of education and farming experience of the farmers); (b) measured variables which are presumed to have significant effects on the adoption of chatbot application by farmers such as smartphone ownership, operating system and Mobile App Use for Farm Activities. These measurement variables were adopted from previous study [30] on the adoption of mobile applications by farmers in the study area and modified to suit this study; and (c) Chatbot user experience of the proposed system.

Secondary data were however sourced from Food and Agriculture Organization [4], relevant journals and research reports published by information and technology professionals and agricultural experts. These were to complement the primary data. These data were analyzed using descriptive statistical techniques such as frequencies, means and percentages. After designing the questionnaire, a pilot study was conducted on five randomly selected smartphone owners who either were farmers or had interest in farming and two extension officers from AKADEP. This helped to ascertain the reliability, validity and clarity of the questionnaire. The responses and comments obtained were used to improve the questionnaire for clarity and suitability for this study.

3.3 Sampling Procedure and Sample Size

Multi-stage sampling technique was employed in the selection of respondents (farmers) for the study. In the first stage, the study area (Akwa Ibom state) is segmented into three (3) agricultural zones namely Ikot Ekpene, Uyo, and Eket. The second stage is a random selection of thirty (30) farming communities (villages) from each of the zones, which is proportional to the size of the zone. The proportional factor used is given in Eq. (1) as:

$$N_i = \frac{n_i}{N \times 30} \tag{1}$$

where, N_i = the number of villages to be selected from the zone i, $i = 1, 2, 3$

n_i = the number of village in zone i.
N = the total number of villages in the three zones (#2664).
30 = the desired number of villages selected from the three zones

In the third stage, a random selection of one hundred and eighty (180) farmers from the selected villages/farming communities was made, using the compiled name list of farmers obtained from AKADEP agency. Time and cost were the basis for the sample size. The number of farmers selected from each of the villages was proportional to the size of the village. The proportional factor used is given in Eq. (2). The overall sampling procedure is represented as a tree in Fig. 3.

$$F_i = \frac{n_i}{N \times 180} \qquad (2)$$

where, F_i = the number of farmers to be selected from the villages

n_i = the number of villages in zone i, $i = 1, 2, 3$.
N = the total number of villages in the three zones.
180 = the desired number of farmers selected from the three zones.

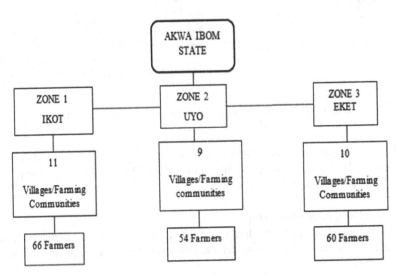

Fig. 3. Study sampling procedure

3.4 Proposed Mobile Chatbot for Crop Farmers

The proposed mobile chatbot uses a retrieval-based model that concentrates on a specific domain. A closed domain of agricultural domain query is taken for implementation.

The system architecture of the deep learning-based mobile chatbot for crop farmers is shown in Fig. 4, with the following modules as key components; Deep machine learning algorithms, natural language processing (NLP), intent recognition algorithm (query), knowledge base (dataset), response generator and user interface. The cassava crop farmers interact with the system through the user interface of their mobile devices to send queries and view generated responses. However, data obtained from identified sources are stored in the knowledge base and typically used to help the ML algorithms define rules for generating outcomes after processing user questions. Word shuffling and Jacquard Similarity algorithms were deployed to develop classifiers for the users' intents. The NLP pre-processing techniques were used to interpret human natural language input to ease understanding of the users' input by the machine (chatbot).

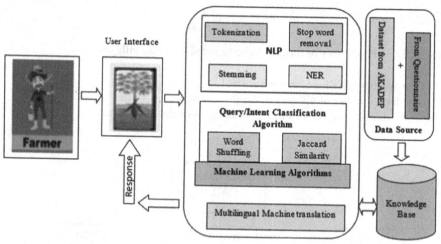

Fig. 4. Architecture of proposed mobile chatbot for crop farmers

The user simply chats with the bot while the administrator has several roles such as editing, updating, deleting and adding information. The architecture of the proposed system comprises of the following modules:

A. **Natural language processing**

The objective of this module is to interpret human natural language input and enable machines (chatbot) to understand the user input. The steps involved in NLP are:

i. **Tokenization**: the process of splitting the input sentences into a list of smaller pieces or tokens. Paragraphs can be tokenized into sentences and sentences tokenized into words [31].

ii. **Noise and stop word removal:** Stop words (noise) are a set of commonly used words in a language which do not provide any meaningful information. Examples of stop words in English are 'a', 'the', 'is' 'are' 'and' etc. The idea behind the removal of stop words is that, by removing low information words from text, we can focus on the important words.

iii. **Stemming**: Stemming refers to the process of reducing words to their stems or root variant. For instance, "computer", "computing", "compute" can be reduced to "comput"; and "walks", "walking" and "walker" reduced to "walk". This process might also benefit the model precision, as the words with the same stem will be treated the same.

iv. **Named entity recognition** (NER): It is a process of detecting the named entities such as crop names from a text. NER helps in recognizing and classifying essential pieces of information from within larger unstructured text-based data into a predefined category such as crop name, disease name, leaf colour, etc.

B. Intent recognition algorithm

To develop the classifier of the user intents (the goal the farmer has in mind when typing in a question to the chatbot), the following machine learning algorithms were considered:

Jaccard similarity algorithm: To be able to use Jaccard Similarity function as the main algorithm for intent identification and selection, we import the package from Python library. This module is used to improve the accuracy of intent recognition and reduce the number of situations where the chatbot will not be able to determine the user's intention and answer his question. The answer to the question that has the highest score of similarity will be retrieved. Figure 5 illustrates the steps of this algorithm.

Jaccard Similarity is defined as an intersection of two documents divided by the union of two documents, which gives the number of common words over a total number of words [32].

The mathematical representation of the Jaccard Similarity is given in Eq. 3.

$$J(doc\_1, doc\_2) = (A \cap B)/(A \cup B) \tag{3}$$

The Jaccard Similarity score (index) is in a range of 0 to 1. If the two documents are identical, Jaccard Similarity is one (1); else the Jaccard similarity score is zero (0) if there are no common words between two documents.

Example:

doc_1 = *"how to apply fertilizer to cassava"*

doc_2 = *"best fertilizer for cassava"*,

To calculate the intersection and union of these two sets of words and measure the **Jaccard Similarity index** between **doc_1** and **doc_2,** the set of unique words for each set of documents is obtained.

doc_1 = {"how", "to", "apply", fertilizer", "to", cassava"}

doc _2 = {"best", "fertilizer", "for", "cassava"}

After parsing these sentences to remove stop words, the following two sets were obtained:

doc_1 = {"how", "apply", fertilizer", "cassava"}
doc _2 = {"best", "fertilizer", "cassava"}

Therefore **Jaccard Similarity index, J**(doc_1,doc_2) is as given in Eq. (4)

$$
= \frac{\{\text{"how", "apply", "fertilizer", "cassava"}\} \cap \{\text{"best", "fertilizer", "cassava"}\}}{\{\text{"how", "apply", "fertilizer", "cassava"}\} \cup \{\text{"best", "fertilizer", "cassava"}\}} \tag{4}
$$

$$
= \frac{\{\text{"fertilizer", "cassava"}\}}{\{\text{"how", "apply", "cassava", "best", "fertilizer", "cassava"}\}}
$$

$$
= 2/6 = .33(33.3\%)
$$

Thus, the Jaccard Similarity index of the two sentences is J(doc_1,doc_2) = 0.33 (33.3%).

In the context of the proposed system, Jaccard Similarity index is used in selecting an output from a library of predefined inputs by comparing the similarity between two or more strings, which we refer to as the source string (S) and the target string (T). Using this algorithm, the user's message (intent) is compared with predefined data in the database of the chatbot and the Jaccard Similarity index is calculated and a value representing how similar the strings are is returned. The range of similarity value is from 0 to 1 and a higher value indicates more similarity.

In any given query, the chatbot compares the statement given by the user with each statement in the database of the chatbot, the statement with the highest similarity value is returned as the best match answer for a given query. The answer returned is a stored predefined data that is best similar to the input question using the value of the Jaccard similarity index.

The threshold value for the response selection is empirically determined to be 75% (0.75), if the ratio value is equal to or more than the threshold, then the user's intention coincide with the predefined input question in the database of the chatbot and a corresponding answer is returned as an output.

The proposed system has a local database to store questions and answers, the database may be updated and new questions can be added by the administrator of the database.

The main steps of the proposed system can be summarized as followed:

- Chatbot obtain farmer's query using user interface (UI).
- Send the query to the NLP for tokenization, stop word removal, stemming and named entity recognition
- The machine learning module takes the structured input from the natural language processing (NLP) and predicts the next best action by extracting the intent from the user massage.
- A notification is sent to the chatbot database to read the farmer's question.
- Calculate Jaccard index between the user question and questions in the database.
- The response generator retrieves the answer to the closest question using Jaccard similarity index of the input text and predefined text.
- If the user's intent is not found, the message: "I don't understand your question" "Please rephrase it" is triggered.

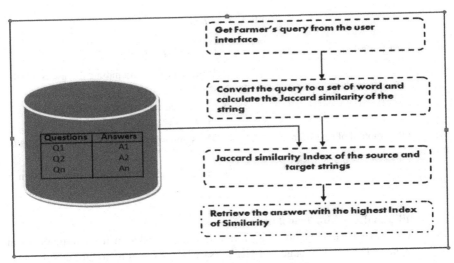

Fig. 5. Jaccard similarity methods

Word Shuffling: In this work we used word shuffling method in expanding the training data. Using this technique, it is possible to move around words while maintaining the grammatical correctness and the meaning of the sentence. Each sentence is tokenized into separate words, then shuffled and gathered back to create a new sentence. The resulting sentence is validated to ensure that they retain grammatical correctness after the transformation, an example is shown in Table 1. The validated sentences will then be used to extend the initial dataset. This is done to ensure that, the training data to have a wider coverage to accommodate wider user intents. When applied to input parts of the dataset (the user's query), the grammatical correctness is not necessary as users can provide inputs that are not correct. When such cases are possible, it can be beneficial to train the chatbot using word shuffling.

Table 1. Sample application of word shuffling technique

Before word shuffling	After word shuffling
Which month is best to plant cassava?	• Which month is best to plant cassava
	• Best month to plant cassava is which
	• To plant cassava which month is best
Which cassava cutting has resistant to mosaic disease?	• What type of soil is best for growing cassava
	• Best for planting cassava is what type of soil
	• What soil type is best for planting cassava
What type of soil is best for growing cassava?	• Which cassava cutting has resistant to mosaic disease

(continued)

Table 1. (*continued*)

Before word shuffling	After word shuffling
	• Resistant to cassava mosaic disease is which cuttings
	• Cassava cutting which has resistant to mosaic disease is
What is the symptom of cassava mosaic infection?	• The symptom of cassava moisaic infection is what
	• Cassava mosaic infection is what symptom

C. **Multilingual machine translation**

The framework seeks to adopt a multilingual translation from farmers' local language to English language and vice versa when responding to farmer's request.

4 Implementation

Python 3.6 was chosen as the main programming language to implement the chatbot. The model will be trained using JSON file named "intents.json", where the information about the typical questions the chatbot should be expecting and their responses is stored. The intents file has all the data that will be used to train the model.

Python was used in backend to handle all the server related activities while the front end of the chatbot is built using google flutter. It is a multi-operating system, user interface, software development kit created by Google to enhance the development of open source application. Flutter can be used to develop applications for android, iOS, Linux, Mac, Windows and any other operating system. The justification for the use of flutter is to mitigate the limitation of existing chatbots, which are platforms dependent. Thus, the proposed system is designed to operate as cross-platform software (multi-platform software or platform-independent software). The implementation process begins with installations of the required python modules and flutter module in the operating system.

4.1 Intents Definition

At this stage some intent and a bunch of messages that correspond to those intents is defined. To achieve this we create a JSON file named "intents.json". The intents.json file is where typical questions the chatbot should be expecting and their corresponding responses are stored. The JSON file maps a list of defined user inputs to a list of outputs.

The sample code for implementation of the intent is shown in Appendix and consists of the following components:

Pattern: The ways in which users usually ask questions relating to a particular tag.
Response: Predefined responses for each tag in the dataset from which the model can choose to respond to a particular question.

4.2 The Chatbot Training Method

The training data is a dataset that is used to teach the chatbot to respond to queries posed by the user. The training data is manually labeled or organized in a way that will enhance the chatbot to respond to queries automatically. In the context of the proposed chatbot, data collected from AKADEP which include frequently asked questions by framers and answers provided by extension officers as obtained during interaction with the AEO is what was used in training the chatbot. The data will be used in training the chatbot to: Identify the user input as one of the listed intents and return an output from the corresponding list of responses. The training dataset contains two attributes: query (question) and response (answer) as shown in Table 2 and the encoded tags given in the Appendix.

Table 2. Sample dataset used in training the chatbot

Question/Query	Answer/Response
What is the best way to apply NPK fertilizer?"	*In a ring, 6 cm wide and 10 cm from the plant*
After how many days, should I harvest my cassava?	*8 weeks after planting*
Which month is best to plant cassava?	*Depending on the cutting you plant, cassava matures between 6–10 months*
What type of soil is best for growing cassava?	*At the beginning of raining season (March to April)*
Which stem are the best for high yield cassava?"	*Cassava grows best on light sandy loam or loamy soil, which are moist and fertile*
	TME 419, TMS 90527 and TME 581 give good yield
Which cassava stem is good for the production of Garri and Fufu?	*Cassava variety TME581 is good for the production of Garri and Fufu due to the low starch content*
What is the maturity time of TM581 cassava stem?	*It matures between 6–8 months*
Which cassava cutting has resistant to mosaic disease?	*The Farmer pride and TME 419*
On harvest, I got small cassava	*Many things may cause this such as; planting time, stem size, variety of the stem, fertilizer used and weeding time*
Tell me the fertilizer is good for my cassava plant?	*NPK is the best fertilizer for cassava*
	In a ring, 6 cm wide and 10cm from the plant

(continued)

Table 2. (*continued*)

Question/Query	Answer/Response
How should I apply fertilizer?	*8 weeks after planting*
When should I apply it? and how many time	*In split doses, one half at or shortly after planting and the rest at 2 to 3 month after planting*
Cassava plant has twisted leaflet with white patches on leaves and twisted distorted leaves	*That is symptom of cassava mosaic infection*
What should I do?"	*Remove all infected plants, this help to reduce source of the disease and monitor the rest of your plants closely, especially those that were located near infected plants. Prepared healthy cutting which will be used to replace the infected plant Using clean planting materials*

5   Discussion of Results

To evaluate the performance and usability of the chatbot, system usability scale (SUS) proposed by Brooke (1996) was used. The SUS is one of the widely used evaluation mechanisms for hardware or software system, it allows the developers to quickly and easily assess the usability of a system. Using this mechanism, participants (farmers) were asked to score the following 10 questions with one of five responses that range from strongly agree to strongly disagree:

i.   *I think that I would like to use this Chatbot frequently*
ii.   *I found the Chatbot unnecessarily complex*
iii. *I thought the Chatbot was easy to use*
iv.   *I think that I would need the support of a technical person to be able to use this Chatbot.*
v.   *I found the various functions in this Chatbot were well integrated.*
vi.   *I thought there was too much inconsistency in this Chatbot.*
vii. *I would imagine that most people would learn to use this Chatbot very quickly.*
viii. *I found the Chatbot very cumbersome to use.*
ix.   *I felt very confident using the Chatbot.*
x.   *I needed to learn a lot of things before I could get going with this Chatbot.*

The results of the above experiment show that, although it was the first time most participants interacted with a chatbot, they generally found the system to be usable due to its friendly user interface and the quality of response. It was found that the system was generally acceptable by the farmers as an information source to satisfy their farming information needs as all participants (users) expressed willingness to use the Chatbot.

To evaluate the accuracy of the system, we used the traditional accuracy concept to evaluate the accuracy of the responses provided by the proposed chatbot. This concept is done by randomly asking (querying) a chatbot with randomly selected questions asked in different ways. We randomly selected forty (40) questions and thirty-four (34) were answered correctly, from this experiment we observed that for most of the input questions given, the system generates good and accurate responses. The average value of accuracy of the system at different levels was taken as the accuracy of the system. Thus, the proposed system shows 85% accuracy and shows signs of improvement as the knowledge base of the chatbot is updating with new inputs and responses. We also observed that as the number of questions increased the accuracy also improved. It was also noted that as we increased the size of the dataset by adding new queries and responses to the knowledge base of the system also improved.

6 Conclusion

A machine learning-based mobile chatbot for crop farmers was presented in this work. A knowledge base that will provide the means of obtaining useful answers to questions, advice and make recommendations on specific farming problems was generated. The use of the chatbot will give government a platform to reach out to famers in the state as farmers in the rural and sub-urban region with mobile devices can interact with the system in any language of their choice.

Acknowledgements. The authors express thanks to Akwa Ibom State Agricultural Development Programme (AKADEP) for providing parts of the dataset used in this work and Management Team of the University of Uyo and National Open University, Nigeria for providing a conducive environment for research.

Conflict of Interest. The authors declare that there is no conflict of interest among them.

Appendix

```
{"intents": [
{"tag": "greeting",
"patterns": ["Hi", "Hey", "Hello"]
"responses": ["Hello", "Hi", "Hi there"]
},
{"tag": "goodbye",
"patterns": ["bye", "see you later", "goodbye"],
"responses": ["See you later", "Have a nice day", "Bye!"]
},
{"tag": "thanks",
"patterns": ["Thanks", "Thank you", "That's helpful", "Thanks for the help"],
"responses": ["Happy to help!", "My pleasure"]
},
{"tag": "about",
"patterns": ["Who are you?", "What are you?", "Who you are?"],
"responses": ["Im farm bot, your farm assistant", "I'm an AI bot"]
},
{"tag": "questions",
"patterns": ["have a question", "I want to ask a question ", "can i ask a    question?
"],
"responses": ["Please tell me your question in order to assist you", "what is your
question, i will answer you "]
}
{"tag": "best practices ",
"patterns": ["How to apply NPK fertilizer?", "give me an idea to apply fertilizer",
"Can you tell me how to apply NPK fertilizer?", "What are the ways to apply NPK
Fertilizer?", "I need a support to apply NPK fertilizer ", "I need a help to apply NPK
fertilizer ", "support me please to apply NPK fertilizer "],
"responses": ["In split doses, one half at or shortly after planting and the rest at 2 to
3 months after planting "]
},
{"tag": "best practices ",
"patterns": ["Which month is best to plant cassava ", "the best month to cultivate
Cassava ", " I want to know the best time to plant cassava "],
"responses": ["At the beginning of raining season (March to April) "]
},
{"tag": "best practices ",
"patterns": ["Which cassava cutting has resistant to mosaic disease?", "tell me mo-
saic resistant cutting?", "I want to know cutting that is resistant to mosaic disease",
"cassava cutting that has resistant to mosaic infection?"]
"Responses": ["farmer pride and TME 419 has resistant to mosaic "]
},
"tag": "best practices ",
```

"Patterns": ["What type of soil is best for growing cassava?", "the best soil for cassava?", "what soil is good for growing cassava?", "tell me the soil type is good for cassava? "]

"responses": ["light sandy loam or loamy soil"]

},

{"tag": "Fertilizer Application ",

"patterns": ["Fertilizer Application ", "how to apply fertilizer", "I want to apply fertilizer" How to apply NPK fertilizer "],

"responses": ["NKP fertilizer can be applied in split doses, one half at or shortly after planting and the rest at 2 to 3 month after planting "," shortly after planting and the rest at 2 to 3 month after planting ", "In a ring, 6 cm wide and 10cm from the plant 8 weeks after planting"]

}

References

1. Channe, H., Kothari, S., Kadam, D.: Multidisciplinary model for smart agriculture using internet-of-things (iot), sensors, cloud-computing, mobile-computing and big-data analysis. Int. J. Comput. Technol. Appl. **6**(3), 374–382 (2015)
2. Vijayalakshmi, J., Pandimeena, K.: Agriculture talkbot using AI. Int. J. Recent Technol. Eng. **8**, 186–190 (2019)
3. FAO: Nigeria at a glance. https://www.fao.org/nigeria/fao%20in-nigeria/nigeria-ata-glance/en/ (2017)
4. Sawant, D., Jaiswal, A., Singh, J., Shah, P.: Agribot - an intelligent interactive interface to assist farmers in agricultural activities. In: Proceedings of IEEE Bombay Section Signature Conference (IBSSC), pp. 1–6 (2019)
5. Ekanayake, J., Saputhanthri, L.: E-AGRO Intelligent chat-bot. IoT and artificial intelligence to enhance farming industry. Agris On-line Pap. Econ. Inform. **12**(01), 15–21 (2020). https://doi.org/10.7160/aol.2020.120102
6. Suman, S., Kumar, J.: Interactive agricultural Chatbot based on deep learning. In: Hemanth, D.J., Pelusi, D., Vuppalapati, C. (eds.) Intelligent Data Communication Technologies and Internet of Things. LNDECT, vol. 101, pp. 965–973. Springer, Singapore (2022). https://doi.org/10.1007/978-981-16-7610-9_70
7. Khin, N.N., Soe, K..: University chatbot using artificial intelligence markup language. In: IEEE Conference on Computer Applications (ICCA) (2020). https://doi.org/10.1109/ICCA49400.2020.9022814
8. Darapanemi, N., Raj, S., Raghul, V., Sivaraman, V., Mohan, S., Paduri, A.: LSTM-RASA Based Agri Fram Assistant for Farmers. arXiv.2204.09717v1[CS-CL]. **11**(1), 1–10 (2022). https://doi.org/10.48550/arXiv2204.09717
9. Chen, A.P.S., Liu, C.W.: Intelligent commerce facilitates education technology: the platform and chatbot for the Taiwan agriculture service. Int. J. e-Educ., e-Bus., e-Manage. e-Learn. **11**(1), 1–10 (2021). https://doi.org/10.17706/ijeeee.2021.11.1.1-10
10. Meyer, H.W.J.: Information use in rural development. The New Rev. Inform. Behav. Res. **4**(1), 109–125 (2010). https://doi.org/10.1080/14716310310001631471
11. Oladele, O.I.: Effect of information communication technology on agricultural information access among researchers, extension agents and farmers in south western Nigeria. J. Agric. Food Inform. **12**, 167–176 (2011). https://doi.org/10.1080/10496505.2011.563229

12. Akwa Ibom Agricultural Development Extension Programmes Annual Report (2019). Akwa Ibom State Ministry of Agriculture and Natural Resources. https://www.aksgonline.com/agric/default.html. Accessed 23 Aug 2022
13. Patel, N., Chittamuru, D., Jain, A., Dave, P., Parikh, T.S.: Avaaj Otalo: a field study of an interactive voice forum for small farmers in rural India. In: Proceedings of the SIGCHI Conference on Human Factors in Computing Systems (CHI'10), pp. 733–742 (2010). https://doi.org/10.1145/1753326.1753434
14. Gandhi, R., Veeraraghavan, R., Toyama, K., Ramprasad, V.: Digital green: participatory video for agricultural extension. In: IEEE International Conference on Information and Communication Technologies and Development, pp. 1–10 (2007). https://doi.org/10.1109/ICTD.2007.4937388
15. Dearden, A., Matthews, P., Rizvi, H.: Kheti: mobile multimedia in an agricultural co-operative. Pers. Ubiquitous Comput. 15(6), 597–607 (2011). https://doi.org/10.1007/s00779-010-0335-3
16. Riaz, W., Durrani, H., Shahid, S., Raza, A.A.: ICT intervention for agriculture development: designing an IVR system for farmers in Pakistan. In: Proceedings of the Ninth International Conference on Information and Communication Technologies and Development (ICTD'17). (2017). https://doi.org/10.1145/3136560.3136598
17. Knoche, H., Rao, S., Jamadagni, H. S., Huang, J.: Actions and advice in coli: a mobile social network to support agricultural peer learning. In: Proceedings of the 17th International Conference on Human-Computer Interaction with Mobile Devices and Services Adjunct (MobileHCI '15), pp. 1191–1198 (2015). https://doi.org/10.1145/2786567.2801608
18. Medhi-Thies, I., Ferreira, P., Gupta, N., O'Neill, J., Cutrell, E.: KrishiPustak: a social networking system for low-literate farmers. In: Proceedings of the 18th ACM Conference on Computer Supported Cooperative Work and Social Computing (CSCW '15), pp. 1670–1681 (2015). https://doi.org/10.1145/2675133.2675224
19. www.farmer.gov.in
20. Ninsiima, D.: Buuza Omulimisa (ask the extension officer): text messaging for low literate farming communities in rural uganda. In: Proceedings of the Seventh International Conference on Information and Communication Technologies and Development (ICTD) Singapore, ACM, New York, pp. 15–18 (2015)
21. Fue, K., Geoffrey, A., Mlozi, M.R.S., Tumbo, S.D., Haug, R., Sanga, C.A.: Analyzing usage of crowdsourcing platform 'Ushaurikilimo' by pastoral and agro-pastoral communities in Tanzania. Int. J. Instr. Technol. Distance Learn. 13(12), 3 (2016)
22. Jain, M., Kumar, P., Ishita Bhansali, Q., Liao, V., Truong, K., Patel, S.: FarmChat: a conversational agent to answer farmer queries. Proc. ACM Interact. Mob. Wearable Ubiquitous Technol. 2(4), 1–22 (2018). https://doi.org/10.1145/3287048
23. Call Center: https://dackkms.gov.in/account/login.aspx
24. Yashaswini, D., Hemalatha, D., Niveditha, G.: Smart chatbot for agriculture. Int. J. Eng. Sci. Comput. 9(5), 22203–22205 (2019)
25. Arora, B., Chaudhary, D.S., Satsangi, M., Yadav, M., Singh, L., Sudhish, P.S.: Agribot: a natural language generative neural networks engine for agricultural applications. In: IEEE International Conference on Contemporary Computing and Applications (IC3A), pp. 28–33 (2020). https://doi.org/10.1109/IC3A48958.2020.233263
26. Vamsi, G., Rasool, A., Hajela, G.: Chatbot: A deep neural network-based human to machine conversation model. In: Proceeding of 11th International Conference on Computing, Communication and Networking Technologies (ICCCNT), (2020). https://doi.org/10.1109/ICCCNT49239.2020.9225395

27. Kiruthika, U., Subramanian, K.S.R., Balaji, V., Raman, C.J.: E-Agriculture for direct marketing of food crops using chatbots. In: International Conference on Power, Energy, Control and Transmission Systems (ICPECTS) (2020). https://doi.org/10.1109/ICPECTS49113.2020.9337024

28. Manimala, M.J., Satya Nandini, A., Ganesh Kumar, R.: AgriApp: Enabling social change through technology. In: Poonamallee, L., Scillitoe, J., Joy, S. (eds.) Socio-Tech Innovation, pp. 163–177. Springer, Cham (2020). https://doi.org/10.1007/978-3-030-39554-4_9

29. Etim, N.A.A.: Adoption of inorganic fertilizer by urban crop farmers in Akwa Ibom State, Nigeria. Am. J. Exp. Agric. 5(5), 466–474 (2015)

30. Malik, A., Suresh, S., Sharma, S.: Factors influencing consumers' attitude towards adoption and continuous use of mobile applications: a conceptual model. Procedia Comput. Sci. 122, 106–113 (2017). https://doi.org/10.1016/j.procs.2017.11.348

31. Vijayalakshmi, K.: Agriculture Talk BOT using AI. Int. J. Recent Technol. Eng. 8(2S5), 186–190 (2019). https://doi.org/10.35940/ijrte.B1037.0782S519

32. Zaid, A., Wissam, K., Laith, M.: Adopting text similarity methods and cloud computing to build a college Chatbot model. J. Educ. Sci. 30(1), 117–125 (2021)

Urban Data: Sources and Targeted Applications for Urban Planning Indicators Modelling

Stéphane Cédric Koumetio Tékouabou[1]([✉]), Jérôme Chenal[1,2],
Rida Azmi[1,2,3,4], El Bachir Diop[1,2,3,4], and Hamza Toulni[3,4]

[1] Center of Urban Systems (CUS), Mohamed VI Polytechnic University (UM6P), Hay Moulay Rachid, 43150 Ben Guerir, Morocco
ctekouaboukoumetio@gmail.com
[2] Urban and Regional Planning Community (CEAT), Ecole Polytechnique Federale de Lausanne (EPFL), Lausanne, Switzerland
[3] LIMSAD Laboratory, Faculty of Sciences Ain Chock, Hassan II University, 20100 Casablanca, Morocco
[4] EIGSI, 282 Route of the Oasis, Mâarif, 20140 Casablanca, Morocco

Abstract. Urban data strongly favored by urban digitization and web 2.0 constitute the raw material whose sources often diverge. However, as far as we know, little or no work has been done to explore the sources and targeted applications for urban planning indicators modelling. We aim to guide neophytes who seek to integrate smart data-driven applications into urban planning processes with greater clarity and credibility. For this purpose, we used test mining to analyze 250 (out of more than 750) relevant papers in the Scopus database and applied ML to an urban planning problem. We found that the data comes broadly from two main categories of sources, namely sensors and statistical surveys (including social network data). Data sources are highly correlated with their structure and the potential planning issues addressed. We conclude our work by discussing the potentialities, emerging issues, and challenges that urban data sources should face to better catalyze intelligent planning.

Keywords: Urban data · Data source · Urban planning · Smart cities · Machine Learning · Urban planning indicators · Urban modelling

1 Introduction

Machine learning algorithms are fed with the best possible data to better adapt to the target task [1,2]. In the field of urban planning, these data often come from various sources depending on the issues and indicators targeted [3]. To deduce patterns associated with urban form indicators using ML techniques, researchers have relied on various data sources. These sources are often correlated to the issues studied and range from the most classical in urban science

F. Ortiz-Rodríguez et al. (Eds.): EGETC 2022, CCIS 1666, pp. 212–226, 2022.
https://doi.org/10.1007/978-3-031-22950-3_16

(satellite data and institutional surveys) to the most recently emerging ones such as ubiquitous data [4]. These come from devices used massively by the populations and present almost everywhere in a city. With the advent of the IoT and the smart city, ubiquitous data is increasingly used to better understand the behaviour of certain indicators associated with the city [5]. This emergence of urban data favourable to the training of powerful ML algorithms has made it possible to provide more intelligent solutions to the current challenges of cities, such as "sustainable planning, smart city, digitalization, resilience, developing better strategies and studying the impact of new urban development projects" [3]. Globally, urban data collection sources include two main categories: data from sensor-based technologies and data from institutional surveys [4].

Seemingly, it is very difficult to find an exhaustive categorization of urban data sources which are now very divergent. This categorization varies from author to author, depending on the field of study and the context. Some authors speak of opportunistic and non-opportunistic data (categorization based on the means of network communication [6]) or even yet opportunistic or participatory data depending on whether or not the participants are known and notified in advance [7]. However, this initially very logical categorization (based on the Internet acquisition protocol) is now adapted to physical resources or both in some cases [8]. On the other hand, other authors discuss vectorized (spatial) or attribute data (categorization based on the structure of the data) [9]. Some specialists simply discuss sensing data, making it seem as if all urban data comes from dedicated sensors [9,10]. But what is the initial source of this data? The word "source" refers to the "origin", or the "place where something comes from". Thus the data is first collected (captured/detected) from somewhere for a well-defined geographical area (called the "study area") by a fixed or mobile onboard currency before being routed in real time or otherwise to the storage and processing base [10]. In addition to sensor data, statistical surveys are another important source of urban data to explore information on several indicators [4]. The information describing the data from these two sources allow the generation of urban metadata which is often useful for several studies [11]. Whether this urban data comes from sensors or statistical surveys, it is shared under open access or licensed platforms, as discussed in Sect. 3.3.

In the rest of this study, we discuss urban data sorted by their sources and structures related to applications for modelling urban form indicators in planning. Data related to intelligent urban planning decision support systems and tools are also included. To this end, we have addressed the same research methodology presented by [3] to better circumscribe the relevant work in the literature. We refer from time to time to these targeted state-of-the-art papers as well as to some related works to justify our proposals. As a result, the context (structural setting, GIS, etc.) of urban data. After that, we'll look at urban data sources in Sect. 3. Then, in Sect. 4, we'll summarize the analysis of urban data sources according to urban planning indicators. Finally, we'll have an overall discussion, followed by, wrapping up our work in Sect. 5.

2   Research Methodology

The literature research method adopted in this article is a continuation of the one used in the paper [3] of which this paper is complementary. Similarly, we first performed a literature search on the SCOPUS database by entering a search query combining keywords. It allowed us to retrieve 751 raw articles and 723 after deleting reviews, conference reviews, and letters. To obtain targeted documents clearly mentioning the description and thus the source of the urban data involved, we have adapted the search elements after several filterings based on data analysis techniques thanks to the ORANGE tool [12, 13]. However, several related articles that are recognized as relevant and that would not have been retained following the previous steps were added manually. Therefore, we reach the 250 most relevant articles that were taken into consideration in the analysis of the following sections.

3   Urban Data Analysis

The overall result in terms of urban data sources involved in selected papers from our literature survey conducted according to the queries proposed in Sect. 2 is shown in Fig. 1. It shows that 58% of the works applying machine learning use data coming exclusively from sensors while 33% use hybrid data (sensors and surveys) and finally 9% use surveys exclusively. These sources of data give an idea of their reliability according to the desired study and the real impact of the results obtained.

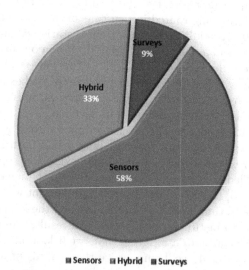

Fig. 1. Distribution of urban data sources in accordance to the queries from [3], which we have altered for our research.

In addition to the results given in Fig. 1, Table 1 summarises a comparative analysis of urban data sources for ML modelling. It discusses the different mobile and fixed techniques that can be used to collect data and transmit them to the storage and processing centre in real or delayed time.

3.1   Urban Sensor Data

Sensing is the most important step in acquiring most of the urban data [10]. It is done by using onboard sensors that are fixed somewhere to cover an area of a smaller spatial scale or carried in a mobile device [29] whose speed reflects the area covered and the accuracy of the data collected. The surveys conducted show that more than 58% of the urban data used to train the Ml algorithms comes from sensors while 33% is hybrid data and 9% is survey data and institutional statistics [3]. This proportion would be around 51.9% for OGDs according to the work of [40]. Nowadays, vast volumes of highly diversified sensor data are generated, and this amount is growing exponentially [10]. Most often, they are far from their target, this is why it is called *"remote sensing"* which is the most commonly used technique for collecting urban data. Considering the sources of data based on sensors, we can divide them about the transport technologies used which reflect the spatial extent of the territory covered and the scale of precision of the data [3]. In this sense, we distinguish several types of data depending on the type of carrier device (satellite, land, air, water, fixed, ubiquitous, ...).

a. Satellite Urban Data

Satellite data are often referred to as "satellite imagery" and are generated by remote sensing technologies. It is broadly information about the Earth and other planets in space, collected by sensors embedded in these artificial satellites in their orbit. Earth Observation (EO), which provides information on the surface and weather changes of planet Earth, is the most prevalent application of satellite data. For governments and organizations, this includes being able to act quickly in the case of natural catastrophes or criminal activity. For companies, it means the development of completely new and improved services. The special feature of this data is that it can cover a relatively larger area but with relatively lower accuracy [41]. It remains one of the most widely used applications of ML algorithms for modelling urban planning indicators due to its high availability. Five constellations are most often used, including: Lansat [21,41,42], Sentinel [16], MODIS [43], ASTER [44], etc. From a structural point of view, they consist mostly of vector images with spatial components that are a bit more complex to process. These data are also more expensive to gather, but they enable the extraction of a significant quantity of data (land, buildings, streets, landscapes, infrastructure, and so on) that may help with improved urban planning. The different constellations of data from the Lansat and Sentinel satellites have been the most widely used in the work explored. Among the most targeted indicators are indicators associated with the physical aspect of the city: urban growth [41], land use/cover [42,45], building [15–18], pollution [19–21], slums [37], Traffic

Table 1. Comparative summary of urban data sources for ML modelling. All mentioned devices can collect data and transmit them to the storage and processing centre in real or delayed time.

DS	Device type	Description	Application in urban modelling
Sensors	Satellite/radars	Data generated by remote sensing technologies using sensors carried by satellites	LST [14], building [15–18], pollution [19–21]
	Drône/plane	Data from sensors built into air vehicles (planes, drones, helicopters, etc.)	Land cover/use/zoning [22, 23], landscape [24], buildings structures [25, 26]
	Bikes/Cars /Motos	Data from sensors on or integrated into ground transporters (bicycles, motorbikes, buses, taxis, trains, etc.)	Urban mobility [27, 28], climate pollution [29, 30]
	Ubiquitous mobile devices	Data from sensors embedded in any mobile device or any other connected device of daily use (phones, watches, smart homes/infrastructures, etc)	Traffic flow [5], Heating & cooling [31]
	Fixed devices	Data from sensors either embedded in a dedicated fixed device or in any other device opportunistically (e.g. camera, street lights, ...)	Security/disasters [32, 32], pollution [31, 33], mobility [34, 35]
Survey & institutional Statistics	Social Networks/medias	Emerging data from the social networks (including web surveys) such as Facebook, Twitter, etc.	Road traffic crash location [36], slums [37]
	Crowd-sourcing	Data from a large group of people on a study area, who submit (voluntarily) their data via the internet, social media, or smartphone applications	Land use [38], mobility slums [5]
	Interviews	Data from interviews on urban issues that can be conducted offline or online via social media	Environment changes [39]
	Institutional statistics	Data from governmental and non-governmental institutions' statistics	Pollution [19, 21], slums [37]

flow [46], urban streets [47], ...), environment quality/changes [39,48] or climate (LST/UHI [49], Heating & cooling [31], ...). One of the inherent added values of satellite data is the availability of authentic information on the entire surface of the Earth, weather, and other incidents. The cumulative data it contains helps to locate and understand long-term trends and the point data helps to act quickly on detected problems. The number of applications for satellite data is limitless, offering many benefits on a global and local scale.

b. Aerial Remote Sensing Data

Although satellite data are the majority and have long dominated the main source of large-scale spatialized urban data, new technologies have favoured the emergence of new sources of aerial remote sensing data from drones, unmanned aerial vehicles (UAVs), aircraft, airbus, helicopters, etc. [22–26,50]. These aerial technologies sources currently provide large amounts of data to explore cities [29]. Aerial remote sensing data covers a relatively smaller spatial scale than satellite data but with greater accuracy [51]. They are being used more and more with the emergence of drones and the search for better precision in a specific study area [25]. Aerial sensing data are for example widely used to model and monitor land registry notably zoning and land cover/use [22,23], urban environment monitoring [25,50], landscape [24], the structure of buildings to prevent house collapses and disaster management [25,26], etc. This type of emerging data is mostly dedicated (non-opportunistic) because of demanding and sometimes critical missions [26]. Drones and other UAVs are increasingly used by urban managers and planners to support their missions [50,51].

c. Data from Ground-Based Sensors (Bikes, Motors, Cars, ...)

Ground carriers (valos, taxis, cars, buses, metro, motorbikes, etc.) are widely used in the remote sensing process to cover a relatively small local or regional territorial scale compared to satellites or other air carriers [28,28,30]. [29] has shown that the use of on-board sensors in buses can helped to acquire opportunistic data on urban activity such as mobility. The GPS (global positioning systems) embedded in these devices also play an important role in the acquisition of spatial data [30]. This source solves three challenges, namely maximum delivery time, minimum measurement frequency, and spatial coverage, which are important parameters for urban data acquisition. Bike sharing [27,28], cars/bus [29], taxi and motorbike taxi [30] and various other means of urban land transport have also been used to acquire urban data that is often opportunistic and therefore low cost and socially inclusive. Applications of such data have included the detection and monitoring of urban heat islands [30,52], urban mobility indicators such as transport patterns [28,29,53], air pollution [28], etc.

d. Ubiquitous Urban Sensing Data

The emergence of ubiquitous urban data is driven by the revolution in ICT and low-cost connected mobile devices, IoT, and smart cities as sources of massive data [5]. These ubiquitous devices use embedded and non-embedded sensors and sensor networks to communicate continuously with wired and/or wireless computing devices embedded in personal devices (mobile phones and all digital devices), buildings, infrastructure, etc. [52]. The IoT has thus enabled the circulation of huge amounts of data making everyday devices one of the main sources of urban data [54]. This enables ubiquitous person-to-person, person-to-object, and object-to-object communication, even if the computers or communication devices are not able to communicate with each other. These ubiquitous devices therefore improve the efficiency of urban infrastructure planning, management and use in many ways [5,52]. Thus, these devices collect huge amounts of local data such as temperature, humidity, mobility, pollution, etc. which can be transferred to storage and processing centres. The digital infrastructure also contributes to the creation of a smart, sustainable, and environmentally friendly city by making ubiquitous computing available to the public [3]. This allows it to immediately report environmental risks to the relevant authorities, for example and leads to a significant shift towards a new paradigm of urban infrastructure planning and provision [30].

e. Fixed In Situ Sensing Data

Despite the widespread dominance of remote sensing technologies among urban data collection methods, sensing by sensors or sensor networks fixed in situ is still very much used and pragmatic. This is the case of indoor sensors or detection at relatively low scale of spatial coverage with a better accuracy such as traffic monitoring in situ [54]. Fixed sensors are often either embedded in a dedicated fixed device or any other device opportunistically (e.g. camera, street lights, ...) which collect data and transmit them to the storage and processing centre in real or delayed time [32]. Like the methods discussed above, these methods produce data on urban activity in general [3]. Thus, they allow for a diversification of data sources to enhance intelligent urban planning. Urban data from fixed sensor networks have been used for air quality & pollution [33], mobility [34,35], security & disasters [32], climate (UHI, heating, cooling, ...) [31], etc.

3.2   Survey Statistical-Based Urban Data (Urban Survey Data)

Researchers use a variety of quantitative and sometimes qualitative data sets to explore urban indicator patterns [3]. Apart from the sensor-based data discussed earlier, survey (or static) data is one of the main sources of urban data. These data come from many federal, state, regional, and local government agencies, non-governmental institutions, as well as various private and proprietary sources. But for many research questions, and even more so for training machine learning algorithms, appropriate data does not exist; urban researchers must undertake their own data collection [4]. Although surveys are the primary method for generating new data, urban planning researchers have also used a range of creative data generation methods. These methods increasingly incorporate ICT and social participation [5]. Individual or grouped citizen initiatives play an important role in the collection and provision of these types of data. Therefore, we classify this category of data as those from institutional (statistical) surveys, social networks (web sensing), interviews, crowdsourcing [52,55], etc. These data are often used alone [56,57] or in combination with sensor data for more comprehensive and reliable studies [58–60]. On the other hand, they are much more opportunistic, sometimes easy to collect and process, unlike sensor data. Several authors have combined survey data and sensor data to associate a socio-functional aspect of the city with an urban form indicator [3]. This is the case of [61] who correlated the physical activity of city users (obtained by survey) to the greenness of the streets (obtained by google street view data).

a. Institutional Statistics and Surveys

Institutional data sources (e.g., national censuses, municipal records, federal mapping agencies, macroeconomic records) have historically provided the backbone for quantifying, analyzing and understanding the mechanisms that operate in a city [4,40]. Institutional statistics as data sources continue to provide valuable information, unofficial data sources are emerging in volume and availability in recent years [40]. These official statistics include data on population, business and economy, employment, crime and justice, health, household service access, socio-economic characteristics [62], etc. The majority of data from institutional statistics are shared on an open-access basis (in several countries) to encourage their re-use in order to derive value for both institutions and citizens: this is called open government data [4,40].

b. Interviews Based Survey

In urban data collection, interview techniques are often much more qualitative than quantitative approaches [63]. Interview techniques include focus groups, interviews, and observation which can be conducted by telephone, face-to-face [64], by online questionnaires using NTIC [65], etc. An appropriate interview depends on the research questions of the study and considerations such as interest in collective or individual experiences, the sensitivity of the subjects, and the time available [66]. Researchers must also take into account the level of vulnerability of human subjects as well as the resources and budget of the project. Interview methods, although classical, are still widely used in urban planning to survey population, housing, transport, and mobility [63,64], etc. While interviews have the advantages of being inexpensive and quick to deploy, a major disadvantage is that they can easily be biased by the interviewer's perception [66]. To overcome this limitation, interview data is often merged with other types of data such as institutional statistics or even sensor data [63].

c. Crowdsourcing and Social Medias' Urban Data

In our context, crowdsourcing consists of obtaining information or opinions from a large group of people in a study area, who submit (voluntarily) their data via the internet, social media or smartphone applications. It is a data acquisition mechanism with high geographical proximity that allows for the undertaking of citizen e-participation in the target area [67]. Mobile devices, social media, smart cities and the underlying telecommunications infrastructure have fostered a global trend where individuals are increasingly volunteering to collect and share observations about the world around them [68]. Crowdsourced urban data can be in the form of images, text, time, and location, and is an invaluable resource as it provides continuous spatial and temporal observations that would otherwise not be recorded [34]. In this sense, new associated concepts will emerge concerning urban data such as VGI (volunteered geographical information) [69], network sensing [29], social media [36], citizen as a sensor [69] etc. The strong trend of crowdsourcing results in increased volumes of such data making it difficult for the scientific community to ignore them, even if they are viewed with scepticism about their scientific validity [67]. For example, traffic applications such as Waze encourage drivers to report accidents and other incidents on the road in order to provide up-to-date information in real-time to the application's users [34]. The exploration of these data is very important for optimal urban traffic planning and accident avoidance in urban mobility [3,53]. The urban scope of crowdsourcing as a source of urban data is important for a range of applications related to urban planning and governance, such as risk management, food security, health, and climate change [67].

3.3 Urban Data-Sharing Platforms

Several studies classify urban data sources according to accessibility i.e. the storage and sharing platform from which users can access the data. Most often, it is not always raw data but semi-structured or structured data in a format more suitable for potential applications. Some platforms, such as Google Eart, go so far as to offer a tool (GEE [70]) for manipulating this data directly online, thus limiting the technical and algorithmic complexity [71]. If in the past, access to data was still subject to payment and even highly protected, current trends are more towards open source platforms allowing scientific research to be boosted [4]. Several states, such as the UK, have lifted the taboo on institutional data, for example, and regularly publish data [27]. Given the diversity of sources and the typology of urban data, it can be found in several data repositories for machine learning such as UCI machine learning repository, Kaggle, KDD, government websites, etc. However, some initiatives are currently taken as reliable sources of city exploration data in several studies.

4 Urban Planning Issues According to the Urban Data Source

In the Sect. 3 we have extensively discussed the urban data sources, and relative use of ML methods for urban planning problems. Figure 2 illustrates the urban planning problems addressed by the data sources.

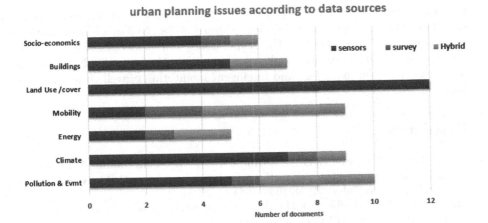

Fig. 2. Urban planning issues by urban data source

From Fig. 2, it is clear that the land use/cover issue, which is assimilated to the whole of classical urban planning, is the most addressed urban planning issue using ML methods and only through sensor data, more precisely satellite data. The main indicators targeted in this problematic include land use [42,72,73], land cover [45,74,75], urban growth [41,76], land values [58], etc. Then comes the issues of pollution and environment and climate and mobility for which different data sources have been involved. These are followed by issues of constructions for which the data of sensors and hybrids have been involved. In the end come the socio-economic and energetic urban issues for which the three data sources have been used. For these different problems, we can refer to [3] for more details on the associated indicators.

5   Summary and Conclusion

Throughout our study, we have addressed the elements related to urban data for better use in training machine learning methods for supporting intelligent urban planning. We have addressed in turn: a) urban data structures which in almost all cases are indexed including vector data and attribute tables; b) the acquisition process distinguishing between opportunistic and non-opportunistic data and c) urban data sources which recall the very origin where they provide and the values they contain. Globally urban data sources are either sensors or statistic surveys which include the emerging user-generated content which ultimately amount to statistics [4]. We found that 58% of the works applying machine learning use data coming exclusively from sensors while 33% use hybrid data (sensors and surveys) and finally 9% use surveys exclusively [3]. These data are accessible from various digital platforms which are either free of charge or under a paying licence with an emerging trend towards open data and open source. These increasingly numerous platforms can come from governments, non-governmental organisms (associations, citizen groups, NGOs, etc.) or private companies (e.g. Google Earth). The scope, issues and challenges of urban data sources for machine learning application to urban planning clearly points to our future work on modelling and intelligent monitoring of well-chosen related indicators.

References

1. Al-Garadi, M.A., Mohamed, A., Al-Ali, A.K., Du, X., Ali, I., Guizani, M.: A survey of machine and deep learning methods for internet of things (IoT) security. IEEE Commun. Surv. Tutor. **22**(3), 1646–1685 (2020)
2. Jordan, M.I., Mitchell, T.M.: Machine learning: trends, perspectives, and prospects. Science **349**(6245), 255–260 (2015)
3. Tekouabou, S.C.K., Diop, E.B., Azmi, R., Jaligot, R., Chenal, J.: Reviewing the application of machine learning methods to model urban form indicators in planning decision support systems: potential, issues and challenges. J. King Saud Univ.-Comput. Inf. Sci. (ARTICLE) (2021)
4. Mainka, A., Hartmann, S., Meschede, C., Stock, W.G.: Mobile application services based upon open urban government data. In: iConference 2015 Proceedings (2015)
5. Niu, H., Silva, E.A.: Crowdsourced data mining for urban activity: review of data sources, applications, and methods. J. Urban Plann. Dev. **146**(2), 04020007 (2020)
6. Leguay, J., Lindgren, A., Scott, J., Friedman, T., Crowcroft, J.: Opportunistic content distribution in an urban setting. In: Proceedings of the 2006 SIGCOMM workshop on Challenged networks, pp. 205–212 (2006)
7. Lane, N.D., Eisenman, S.B., Musolesi, M., Miluzzo, E., Campbell, A.T.: Urban sensing systems: opportunistic or participatory? In: Proceedings of the 9th workshop on Mobile computing systems and applications, pp. 11–16 (2008)
8. Llaguno, M.: Opportunistic mobile urban sensing technologies. In: American Meteorological Society (2020)
9. Xu, B., Chen, J., Yu, P.: Vectorization of classified remote sensing raster data to establish topological relations among polygons. Earth Sci. Inf. **10**(1), 99–113 (2017)
10. Sagl, G., Blaschke, T.: 14 integrated urban sensing in the twenty-first century. Glob. Urban Monit. Assess. Through Earth Observ. 269 (2014)
11. Ozguven, E.E., et al.: Metadata-based needs assessment for emergency transportation operations with a focus on an aging population: a case study in florida. Transp. Rev. **36**(3), 383–412 (2016)
12. Demšar, J., Zupan, B., Leban, G., Curk, T.: Orange: from experimental machine learning to interactive data mining. In: Boulicaut, J.-F., Esposito, F., Giannotti, F., Pedreschi, D. (eds.) PKDD 2004. LNCS (LNAI), vol. 3202, pp. 537–539. Springer, Heidelberg (2004). https://doi.org/10.1007/978-3-540-30116-5_58
13. Demšar, J., et al.: Orange: data mining toolbox in python. J. Mach. Learn. Res. **14**(1), 2349–2353 (2013)
14. Waleed, M., Sajjad, M.: Leveraging cloud-based computing and spatial modeling approaches for land surface temperature disparities in response to land cover change: evidence from Pakistan. Remote Sens. Appl. Soc. Environ. 100665 (2021)
15. Milojevic-Dupont, N., et al.: Learning from urban form to predict building heights. Plos One **15**(12), e0242010 (2020)

16. Geiß, C., Schrade, H., Pelizari, P.A., Taubenböck, H.: Multistrategy ensemble regression for mapping of built-up density and height with sentinel-2 data. ISPRS J. Photogram. Remote Sens. **170**, 57–71 (2020)

17. Hecht, R., Meinel, G., Buchroithner, M.: Automatic identification of building types based on topographic databases-a comparison of different data sources. Int. J. Cartogr. **1**(1), 18–31 (2015)

18. Wurm, M., Droin, A., Stark, T., Geiß, C., Sulzer, W., Taubenböck, H.: Deep learning-based generation of building stock data from remote sensing for urban heat demand modeling. ISPRS Int. J. Geo Inf. **10**(1), 23 (2021)

19. Lee, C.: Impacts of urban form on air quality: emissions on the road and concentrations in the us metropolitan areas. J. Environ. Manage. **246**, 192–202 (2019)

20. Deters, J.K., Zalakeviciute, R., Gonzalez, M., Rybarczyk, Y.: Modeling pm2. 5 urban pollution using machine learning and selected meteorological parameters. J. Electr. Comput. Eng. **2017** (2017)

21. Choung, Y.-J., Kim, J.-M.: Study of the relationship between urban expansion and pm10 concentration using multi-temporal spatial datasets and the machine learning technique: case study for Daegu, South Korea. Appl. Sci. **9**(6), 1098 (2019)

22. Jenkins, N.A.L.: An application of aerial drones in zoning and urban land use planning in Canada. Ryerson University (2015)

23. Norzailawati, M.N., Alias, A., Akma, R.S.: Designing zoning of remote sensing drones for urban applications: a review. Int. Arch. Photogram. Remote Sens. Spat. Inf. Sci. **41** (2016)

24. Iizuka, K., Itoh, M., Shiodera, S., Matsubara, T., Dohar, M., Watanabe, K.: Advantages of unmanned aerial vehicle (UAV) photogrammetry for landscape analysis compared with satellite data: A case study of postmining sites in Indonesia. Cogent Geosci. **4**(1), 1498180 (2018)

25. Gallacher, D.: Drone applications for environmental management in urban spaces: a review. Int. J. Sustain. Land Use Urban Plann. **3**(4) (2016)

26. Erdelj, M., Natalizio, E., Chowdhury, K.R., Akyildiz, I.F.: Help from the sky: leveraging UAVs for disaster management. IEEE Pervasive Comput. **16**(1), 24–32 (2017)

27. Abdellaoui, E.A.A., Tekouabou, S.C.K.: Intelligent management of bike sharing in smart cities using machine learning and internet of things. Sustain. Urban Areas **67**, 102702 (2021)

28. Cai, H., Wang, J., Sun, Y.: Dynamic management of environmental risk of urban traffic exhaust pollution based on taxi trail big data. In: Proceedings of the 4th World Congress on Civil, Structural, and Environmental Engineering (CSEE 2019), pp. ICEPTP 151 1–8. IEEE (2019)

29. Caminha, P.H.C., Costa, L.H.M.K., de Souza Couto, R.: A bus-based opportunistic sensing network. In: Anais Estendidos do XXXIX Simpósio Brasileiro de Redes de Computadores e Sistemas Distribuídos, pp. 57–64. SBC (2021)

30. Zhou, B., Chen, L., Zhao, S., Zhou, F., Li, S., Pan, G.: Spatio-temporal analysis of urban crime leveraging multisource crowdsensed data. Pers. Ubiquit. Comput. 1–14 (2021)

31. Koschwitz, D., Frisch, J., Van Treeck, C.: Data-driven heating and cooling load predictions for non-residential buildings based on support vector machine regression and NARX recurrent neural network: a comparative study on district scale. Energy **165**, 134–142 (2018)

32. Ufuoma, G., Sasanya, B.F., Abaje, P., Awodutire, P.: Efficiency of camera sensors for flood monitoring and warnings. Sci. Afr. **13**, e00887 (2021)

33. de Souza, P.: Air pollution in Kenya: a review. Air Qual. Atmos. Health **13**(12), 1487–1495 (2020)
34. Tampubolon, H., Yang, C.-L., Chan, A.S., Sutrisno, H., Hua, K.-L.: Optimized capsnet for traffic jam speed prediction using mobile sensor data under urban swarming transportation. Sensors **19**(23), 5277 (2019)
35. Saiqun, L., Zhang, Q., Chen, G., Seng, D.: A combined method for short-term traffic flow prediction based on recurrent neural network. Alex. Eng. J. **60**(1), 87–94 (2021)
36. Milusheva, S., Marty, R., Bedoya, G., Williams, S., Resor, E., Legovini, A.: Applying machine learning and geolocation techniques to social media data (twitter) to develop a resource for urban planning. PLoS One **16**(2), e0244317 (2021)
37. Ibrahim, M.R., Titheridge, H., Cheng, T., Haworth, J.: predictSLUMS: a new model for identifying and predicting informal settlements and slums in cities from street intersections using machine learning. Comput. Environ. Urban Syst. **76**, 31–56 (2019)
38. Gervasoni, L., Bosch, M., Fenet, S., Sturm, P.: A framework for evaluating urban land use mix from crowd-sourcing data. In: 2016 IEEE International Conference on Big Data (Big Data), pp. 2147–2156. IEEE (2016)
39. Chan, J.C.-W., Chan, K.-P., Yeh, A.G.-O.: Detecting the nature of change in an urban environment: a comparison of machine learning algorithms. Photogramm. Eng. Remote Sens. **67**(2), 213–226 (2001)
40. Nikiforova, A.: Smarter open government data for society 5.0: are your open data smart enough? Sensors **21**(15), 5204 (2021)
41. Gómez, J.A., Patiño, J.E., Duque, J.C., Passos, S.: Spatiotemporal modeling of urban growth using machine learning. Remote Sens. **12**(1), 109 (2020)
42. Okwuashi, O., Ndehedehe, C.E.: Integrating machine learning with Markov chain and cellular automata models for modelling urban land use change. Remote Sens. Appl. Soc. Environ. 100461 (2020)
43. Kabano, P., Lindley, S., Harris, A.: Evidence of urban heat island impacts on the vegetation growing season length in a tropical city. Landsc. Urban Plan. **206**, 103989 (2021)
44. EOS. Advanced spaceborne thermal emission and reflection radiometer (1999)
45. Kafy, A.-A., et al.: Cellular automata approach in dynamic modeling of land cover changes using RapidEye images in Dhaka, Bangladesh. Environ. Challenges 100084 (2021)
46. Fu, R., Zhang, Z., Li, L.: Using LSTM and GRU neural network methods for traffic flow prediction. In: 2016 31st Youth Academic Annual Conference of Chinese Association of Automation (YAC), pp. 324–328. IEEE (2016)
47. Middel, A., Lukasczyk, J., Zakrzewski, S., Arnold, M., Maciejewski, R.: Urban form and composition of street canyons: a human-centric big data and deep learning approach. Landsc. Urban Plan. **183**, 122–132 (2019)
48. Liu, L., Silva, E.A., Wu, C., Wang, H.: A machine learning-based method for the large-scale evaluation of the qualities of the urban environment. Comput. Environ. Urban Syst. **65**, 113–125 (2017)
49. Gao, S., Zhan, Q., Yang, C., Liu, H.: The diversified impacts of urban morphology on land surface temperature among urban functional zones. Int. J. Environ. Res. Public Health **17**(24), 9578 (2020)
50. Peleshko, D., Rak, T., Noennig, J.R., Lytvyn, V., Vysotska, V.: Drone monitoring system dromos of urban environmental dynamics. In: ITPM, pp. 178–193 (2020)

51. Provost, E.J., et al.: Quantifying human use of sandy shores with aerial remote sensing technology: the sky is not the limit. Ocean Coast. Manag. **211**, 105750 (2021)
52. Boulos, M.N.K., et al.: Crowdsourcing, citizen sensing and sensor web technologies for public and environmental health surveillance and crisis management: trends, OGC standards and application examples. Int. J. Health Geogr. **10**(1), 1–29 (2011)
53. Elmandili, H., Toulni, H., Nsiri, B.: Optimizing road traffic of emergency vehicles. In: 2013 International Conference on Advanced Logistics and Transport, pp. 59–62. IEEE (2013)
54. Mondal, M.A., Rehena, Z.: An IoT-based congestion control framework for intelligent traffic management system. In: Chiplunkar, N.N., Fukao, T. (eds.) Advances in Artificial Intelligence and Data Engineering. AISC, vol. 1133, pp. 1287–1297. Springer, Singapore (2021). https://doi.org/10.1007/978-981-15-3514-7_96
55. Boudhane, M., Nsiri, B., Toulni, H.: Optical fish classification using statistics of parts (2016)
56. Jack, E., McCormack, G.R.: The associations between objectively-determined and self-reported urban form characteristics and neighborhood-based walking in adults. Int. J. Behav. Nutr. Phys. Act. **11**(1), 71 (2014)
57. Kontokosta, C.E., Hong, B., Johnson, N.E., Starobin, D.: Using machine learning and small area estimation to predict building-level municipal solid waste generation in cities. Comput. Environ. Urban Syst. **70**, 151–162 (2018)
58. Ma, J., Cheng, J.C.P., Jiang, F., Chen, W., Zhang, J.: Analyzing driving factors of land values in urban scale based on big data and non-linear machine learning techniques. Land Use Policy **94**, 104537 (2020)
59. Abrantes, P., Rocha, J., da Costa, E.M., Gomes, E., Morgado, P., Costa, N.: Modelling urban form: a multidimensional typology of urban occupation for spatial analysis. Environ. Plann. B Urban Anal. City Sci. **46**(1), 47–65 (2019)
60. Porat, I., Shach-Pinsly, D.: Building morphometric analysis as a tool for urban renewal: identifying post-second world war mass public housing development potential. Environ. Plann. B Urban Anal. City Sci. **48**(2), 248–264 (2021)
61. Yi, L.: Using google street view to investigate the association between street greenery and physical activity. Landsc. Urban Plan. **191**, 103435 (2019)
62. Mutono, N., Wright, J., Mutembei, H., Thumbi, S.M.: Spatio-temporal patterns of domestic water distribution, consumption and sufficiency: neighbourhood inequalities in Nairobi, Kenya. Habit. Int. **119**, 102476 (2022)
63. Janssens, W., Pradhan, M., de Groot, R., Sidze, E., Donfouet, H.P.P., Abajobir, A.: The short-term economic effects of COVID-19 on low-income households in rural Kenya: An analysis using weekly financial household data. World Dev. **138**, 105280 (2021)
64. Ballantyne, E.E.F., Lindholm, M., Whiteing, A.: A comparative study of urban freight transport planning: addressing stakeholder needs. J. Transp. Geogr. **32**, 93–101 (2013)
65. Hussnain, M.Q., Anjum, G.A., Wakil, K., Tharanga, P.H.T.D.: Improving efficiency in data collection for urban development plans through information and communication technology. In: International Conference on Town Planning and Urban Management (ICTPUM), Lahore (2014)
66. Nightingale, D.S., Rossman, S.B.: Collecting data in the field. Handb. Pract. Program Eval. **3**, 321–346 (2004)
67. See, L., et al.: Urban geo-wiki: a crowdsourcing tool for improving urban land cover (2013)

68. Hoseinzadeh, N., Liu, Y., Han, L.D., Brakewood, C., Mohammadnazar, A.: Quality of location-based crowdsourced speed data on surface streets: a case study of waze and bluetooth speed data in Sevierville, TN. Comput. Environ. Urban Syst. **83**, 101518 (2020)
69. Goodchild, M.F.: Citizens as sensors: the world of volunteered geography. Geo-Journal **69**(4), 211–221 (2007)
70. Mutanga, O., Kumar, L.: Google earth engine applications (2019)
71. Tamiminia, H., Salehi, B., Mahdianpari, M., Quackenbush, L., Adeli, S., Brisco, B.: Google earth engine for geo-big data applications: a meta-analysis and systematic review. ISPRS J. Photogramm. Remote. Sens. **164**, 152–170 (2020)
72. Huang, B., Zhao, B., Song, Y.: Urban land-use mapping using a deep convolutional neural network with high spatial resolution multispectral remote sensing imagery. Remote Sens. Environ. **214**, 73–86 (2018)
73. Hagenauer, J., Helbich, M.: Mining urban land-use patterns from volunteered geographic information by means of genetic algorithms and artificial neural networks. Int. J. Geogr. Inf. Sci. **26**(6), 963–982 (2012)
74. Novack, T., Esch, T., Kux, H., Stilla, U.: Machine learning comparison between WorldView-2 and QuickBird-2-simulated imagery regarding object-based urban land cover classification. Remote Sens. **3**(10), 2263–2282 (2011)
75. Schneider, A.: Monitoring land cover change in urban and peri-urban areas using dense time stacks of Landsat satellite data and a data mining approach. Remote Sens. Environ. **124**, 689–704 (2012)
76. Shafizadeh-Moghadam, H., Asghari, A., Tayyebi, A., Taleai, M.: Coupling machine learning, tree-based and statistical models with cellular automata to simulate urban growth. Comput. Environ. Urban Syst. **64**, 297–308 (2017)

Understanding KlimaDAO Use and Value: Insights from an Empirical Analysis

Miguel-Angel Sicilia[✉], Elena García-Barriocanal, Salvador Sánchez-Alonso, Marçal Mora-Cantallops, and Juan-José de Lucio

Computer Science Department, University of Alcalá, Polytechnic Building. Ctra. Barcelona km. 33.6, 28871 Alcalá de Henares (Madrid), Spain
{msicilia,elena.garciab,salvador.sanchez,marcal.mora,juan.delucio}@uah.es

Abstract. Blockchain technologies have demonstrated the potential to build decentralized finance (DeFi) protocols that are composable and interoperable. One of the envisioned applications of blockchains is that of becoming a platform for markets of greenhouse-gas emissions. KlimaDAO is one of the recently launched protocols that attempts to bridge existing voluntary carbon markets to DeFi by means of building incentive mechanisms on top of tokenized carbon assets. That approach may eventually bring benefits to carbon markets in terms of liquidity and transparency and address a wider audience. Here we report the analysis of the early status of that initiative in an attempt to get insights in its actual functioning and value, and on the extent to which they are currently addressing the original goals and potential benefits of this kind of protocols.

Keywords: KlimaDAO · Carbon markets · Decentralized finance · Tokens · Blockchain

1 Introduction

Since the adoption of the Paris Agreement under the United Nations Framework Convention on Climate Change (UNFCCC) in December 2015 [12], there has been an increase in the interest of organizations to reach low or net zero emissions of greenhouse gases (GHG). Carbon markets aim at reducing GHG sent to the atmosphere by setting limits on emissions and/or enabling the trading of emission units as a kind of environmental financial instrument [13]. Trading those units enables organizations that can reduce emissions at lower cost to be paid to do so by higher-cost emitters, or fund projects that aim at reducing emissions.

One type of those markets are emission trading systems (ETS) that trade pollution permits or *allowances*. In addition to the EU emissions trading system (EU ETS), national or sub-national systems are operating or under development in Canada, China, Japan, New Zealand, South Korea, Switzerland and the

F. Ortiz-Rodríguez et al. (Eds.): EGETC 2022, CCIS 1666, pp. 227–237, 2022.
https://doi.org/10.1007/978-3-031-22950-3_17

United States. But the type of market in which we are interested here is that of voluntary carbon markets. These markets allow buying carbon credits issued by privately organized certification schemes to voluntarily offset the carbon footprint of organizations (linked to some potential market penalties on firm value related to emissions [10]), or more broadly, of human activities.

While voluntary carbon markets nowadays face significant challenges, especially at the supply side [9], different initiatives in the last years have emerged that attempt to solve problems of those markets [7] [14]. In spite of the underlying narratives [3] for these markets and related controversies, we can expect an increase of those in the coming years.

In the emerging space of decentralized finance (DeFi) [11], carbon markets have been considered to complement existing ones, with several initiatives that attempt to combine DeFi with those markets with the added benefits of composability and decentralization. Here we focus on KlimaDAO, a decentralized autonomous organization (DAO) and DeFi protocol created with the aim of acting as a bridge between Web3 and established carbon offset markets, using smart contracts to securely and transparently govern transactions, and experimenting with incentives mechanisms. In their manifesto, written by a pseudoanonymous team, KlimaDAO self-portraits as "a network coordinating the delivery of climate finance toward high-impact and validated sustainability projects which produce tangible environmental benefits".

KlimaDAO attempts to address problems of iliquidity (since carbon credits come in different forms), opacity (lack of open access to markets) and inefficiency (costs of transaction). These stated objectives are partially overlapping with the assessment of the potential of blockchain technologies by Kotsialou et al. [8] that mention improved verifiability, reduced transaction costs and, to a lesser degree, aid in addressing additionality and permanence concerns. Here we report an empirical analysis of the actual use of the protocol, in an attempt to gain insights on its state of development so far, and considering how the current status aligns with the aims and potentials stated by the founders and others.

The rest of this paper is structured as follows. Section 2 briefly surveys existing initiatives in the domain of blockchain-based carbon offset markets and discusses the principal features of KlimaDAO. Then, Sect. 3 describes and discusses the actual bridging of carbon assets into KlimaDAO via the Toucan Protocol. Section 4 provides the analysis of the transactions in KlimaDAO associated to existing carbon pools. Finally, conclusions and outlook are provided in Sect. 5.

2   Background

2.1   Carbon Offset Markets and Blockchains

Franke et al. [4] compare public and private blockchain designs for a "Paris agreement market carbon market mechanism" and mention transparency in the public, permissionless case as a clear advantage, together with the possibility of developing further applications for participation. This latter aspect is related to the *composability* of DeFi protocols, that has the potential of increasing liquidity and usage in general. Hartmann and Thomas [6] recommended Australian carbon market blockchain design (ACMBD) as a partially decentralised, private blockchain. That ACMBD represents a different approach to the kind of decentralized options that we focus on here, but similarly to them, justifies its deployment chiefly in terms of transparency, liquidity and market effectiveness as overall aims.

Howson et al. [7] discuss several blockchain initiatives as potential fixes for limitations of the REDD+ programme, concluding that those projects have so far proved of limited critical concern. Woo et al. [14] provide a review of some existing initiatives in carbon markets supported by blockchain networks. Concretely, they mention Nori built on Ethereum, and Veridium and Poseidon built on top of Stellar. In a more detailed discussion, Kotsialou et al. [8] that mention improved verifiability, reduced transaction costs and, to a lesser degree, aid in addressing additionality and permanence concerns.

As evidenced by the discussion above, the scarce and scattered scholarly literature on the topic has yet not explored and analyzed the actual use of carbon market-related blockchain projects, and the implications that decentralization may have in the promises made by those initiatives from an empirical perspective. This is why we focus here on initiatives that aim at public, permissionless networks that have support for smart contracts, since that support is fundamental for building integration with other DeFi protocols. At the time of this writing, the Stellar network is still in research phase for its smart contract implementation, so that we discarded projects on top of Stellar. Another relevant project is the Regen Network[1], a layer-1 blockchain in the COSMOS interchain ecosystem, so that the network has its own governance instead of having a DAO on top of an existing blockchain. Regen Network includes in its plans registries and tokenization of carbon assets, along with other plans in a longer term roadmap.

Also at the time of this writing, Nori[2] has still not launched its token, and the Regen network has just recently launched their mainnet Regen Ledger. This leaves us with KlimaDAO as the target for empirical study having. It should be noted that Nori and the Regen Network have a concept similar to KlimaDAO in tokenization of offsetting assets, but currently they do not consider other DeFi mechanisms as staking and bonding, which are built-in for KlimaDAO. In consequence, these different protocols may not be considered as equivalent and would in the future need to be studied separately.

2.2   KlimaDAO

The fundamental building block of KlimaDAO is the KLIMA token, a fungible (ERC20 standard compliant) token backed by at least 1 tonne of tokenized verified carbon offsets locked in the KlimaDAO treasury. The token in addition is used as a governance token, so that holders of KLIMA have the ability to vote

---

[1] https://www.regen.network/.
[2] https://nori.com/.

on KlimaDAO policy. In consequence, KlimaDAO is conceptualized by their proponents as a "de-central" bank governing the monetary policy of KLIMA.

KlimaDAO incentivizes new supply of Tokenized Carbon Tonnes (TCT) on the blockchain through the KLIMA token, and disincentivizes companies wanting to offset their carbon footprint with only carbon credits, and forces them to perform environmentally friendly actions.

Users of tokens may have different incentives including as discussed by Freni et al. [5] namely access, discounts, revenues, rewards, earnings, appreciation, reputation and participation in governance. To fully understand the current proposition of KlimaDAO, its roots and inspiration from the OlympusDAO protocol should be considered, that revolve around building a treasury by the complementary mechanisms of *bonding* and *staking* in a game theoretic setting that is hypothesized to stabilize prices [2].

Staking. Staking is designed to incentivise longer-term holding of KLIMA, and to give market participants exposure to the climbing price of carbon. The longer participants hold the tokens and stake, the more they receive compounded rewards.

Bonding. Any address can purchase discounted KLIMA tokens over a vesting period of several days using bonds. The more bonds there are (more demand), the higher the premium and the lower the discount is and viceversa.

2.3 Bridging Offset Assets

Currently in KlimaDAO, BCTs (Base Carbon Tonne) and MCO2s (Moss Carbon Credit Token) are the main TCTs within the KlimaDAO treasury, and both represent real-world Verified Carbon Units (VCUs) from a registry such as Verra. BCT can be created via the Toucan Protocol's public bridge while MCO2 is a centrally managed product of Moss[3]. The protocol currently accepts also UBO (Universal Base Offset) and NBO (Nature Base Offset).

Toucan has built the infrastructure to bridge, fractionalize and pool carbon credits from legacy markets so they can be utilized in web3 markets. Every TCO2 represents a unique carbon offset brought on-chain using the Toucan Carbon Bridge. Currently, the documentation of the Toucan Protocol describes how in the process of tokenizing access, it requires "to be approved by a Toucan Verifier, a trusted member of the Toucan community". This is a point of centralization of control that may in the future be changed with other mechanisms used for creating synthetic assets in the blockchain as decentralized oracles [1]. In the current setting, the quality and trust associated to the projects is reliant on the already existing external centralized registries, not bringing any additional benefit in that aspect.

---

[3] https://moss.earth/.

3 Carbon Assets in KlimaDAO

Here we analyze the actual historical activity of incoming carbon assets into KlimaDAO, focusing on those coming from the Toucan Protocol, since it is currently the only partially decentralized bridge available (C3.app was just incorporated recently), so that it reflects the activity of users tokenizing assets.

In the Toucan Protocol, the Carbon Bridge (CB) allows anybody to tokenize carbon credits, linking legacy carbon registries with the Toucan Registry (TR) on the Polygon network. Double counting is avoided by making the process one-way, so that users have to retire the credits from the source registry.

The process starts with the creation of a `BatchNFT` that contains an associated `Reference-ID`. That identifier is required to be associated to the retirement of credits in a legacy registry. This entails the users doing the retirement and adding the identifier to the process, e.g. including it in the retirement notes on Verra. Then, some identifier from the legacy registry, e.g. a Verra serial number, is updated in the `BatchNFT`, establishing a bidirectional association. After this is done, the NFT is pending approval, and eventually a Toucan Verifier checks it is correct.

The `CarbonOffsetBatches` contract was deployed on Polygon mainnet October 10th 2021. The projects tokenized using the CB are described in a `NFTData` struct[4] defined as follows, containing data to trace to the project, status and eventually, comments about that status.

```
uint256 projectVintageTokenId;
string serialNumber;
uint256 quantity;
RetirementStatus status;
string uri;
string[] comments;
address[] commentAuthors;
```

At the time of this writing in June 2022, there is a total of 1252 `BatchNFTs` minted. However, of those only 836 are with *confirmed* status, with 47 *rejected* and the remaining 369 pending. Looking at the data, this large amount of pending ones appears to be attributable to failed or incomplete mints, since for most of them in that status their `serialNumber` is empty. The quantities retired are non normal, with a mean of 1.13, but a median of 10,000, showing a long tailed distribution.

Looking at the transactions, there are 829 calls to `fractionalize`, which represent successful conversion to TCO2 ERC20 tokens of most of the confirmed NFTs.

Figure 1 shows transactions over time, with an initial peak phase of mints followed by a plateau that indicates a constant activity of bridging carbon assets. With regard to decentralization in the tokenization, there are 300+ addresses

---

[4] Smart contract source code is available at https://github.com/ToucanProtocol/contracts/.

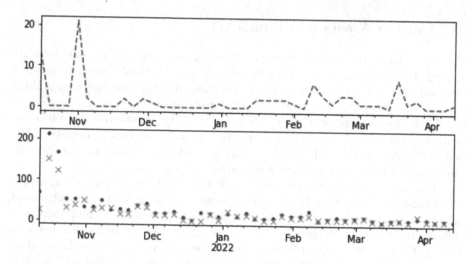

Fig. 1. Transactions over time. The upper plot shows "Mint Empty Batch" transactions, the lower shows "fractionalize" transactions (crosses) and "reject" transactions (points) respectively

as origin of transactions, however, since addresses cannot be linked to actual individuals or organizations, we cannot reliably conclude on that aspect.

4   KlimaDAO Activity

Albeit all of them represent a carbon credit with a value of 1 tCO2e, TCO2 tokens are project-specific and consequently heterogeneous across project types, countries and other factors. These makes them be traded as differentiated products rather than as commodities, and typically most transactions happen over-the-counter (OTC). There is an additional step required to make those tokens more easily tradeable, which is know as pooling. After assets are pooled, they can be considered as being part of a completely fungible token.

4.1   Carbon Pools

The idea is that a carbon pool specifies a number of attributes or requirements on the TCO2 tokens it aggregates. Those attributes may be project type, vintage or country. It is expected that these pools can be created in the future by anyone, allowing for curated or specialized carbon pools.

Here we examine the Base Carbon Tonne (BCT) ERC20 token coming from a pool arranged as a collaboration of KlimaDAO and Toucan for TCO2 tokens that are Verra VCUs and have a vintage of 2008 or later. TCO2 tokens that met those requirements can be locked in the base carbon pool and the depositor receives an equal amount of BCT. Currently, the Nature Carbon Tonne (NCT) is another tool for a number of Verra methodologies and earliest vintage 2012, targeting higher-quality credits "including ecological co-benefits (soil quality, water quality, air quality), habitat preservation, species protection, social and economic benefits for communities who engage in carbon credits projects".

4.2   Retirement of Carbon Assets

KlimaDAO currently lists smart contracts for bridge-specific retirements (Toucan and Moss) but also an aggregator. We have examined transactions sent to this aggregator, which accepts a number of tokens (including USDT, KLIMA and sKLIMA) to retire from BCT or MCO2. That aggregator was deployed March 2022 and has only 550 transactions of type `retireCarbon`[5] at the time of this writing. All the transactions but two were expressed in carbon as indicated in the `amountInCarbon` data field.

The actual amount of carbon retired is according to the documentation expressed in the number of decimals for the used token. Following that convention, total retirements by token are summarized in the following Table.

Table 1. Retirement activity per token pool in the aggregator

Token	txn-#	Amount retired	address-#	Main retirement token
UBO	15	257.4	13	KLIMA (92%)
BCT	399	102,631,6	187	BCT (94%)
NBO	11	60,6	11	sKLIMA (45%)
MCO2	92	5,370.2	58	MCO2 (88%)
NCT	31	1,149.0	26	NCT (94%)

Retirements median is 1.0 and mean around 200 (it should be noted that these are not the total figures since these count only regular retirements via the aggregator). The number of transactions relative to addresses point out to a highly decentralized process, but this has to been taken cautiously as there is no reliable way to connect addresses to actual organizations or individuals. Retirements have also some free text in the `beneficiaryString` and `retirementMessage` fields, however there is no relevant information as there are very few repeated beneficiary strings, except `luminimul` with 99 retirements of small amounts (50Kg) of eCO2 and a repeating message.

Table 1 also provides the main source token burnt for the retirement that happens to be the same token retired except for the cases of UBO and NBO. However, the latter have relatively small quantities since they are more recent additions, so that it may change in the future. There are also retirements using the USDC stablecoin for several of the pools, but in lower amounts.

---

[5] It should be noted that there are also a much lower volume of transactions using `retireCarbon_specific`.

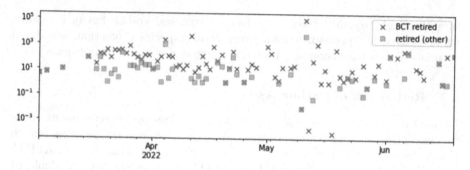

Fig. 2. Daily retirements from the aggregator in logarithmic scale, comparison of BCT versus the rest of pooled assets

Figure 2 shows the daily retirements in the KlimaDAO aggregator, comparing BCT with the rest of pooled assets. No obvious trend can be appreciated, so that no preferences can be inferred. In any case, the time span covered is short and additional pooled assets have only be recently included, so that more time is required to understand differences.

4.3 KLIMA Token, Staking and Bonding

KLIMA is backed by at least 1 tonne of tokenized verified carbon offsets locked in the KlimaDAO treasury. Staking and bonding are the mechanisms used in KlimaDAO for building a treasury. The analysis of the treasury approach [2] is complex and not our focus here. Comprehensive metrics can be found in an open Dune Analytics dashboard[6].

Overall, the relation of KLIMA and its cryptoeconomic mechanisms and their contribution or connection with carbon retirement incentives are difficult to assess. The fact that carbon offsets can be retired using tokens different than KLIMA may lead to some disconnect, so that users might use other tokens — possibly stablecoins — to retire offsets, staying unrelated to the overall KlimaDAO mechanisms. However, to date, as discussed above, most retirements are done in the TCT tokens themselves.

If we look at the overall market value of the BCT carbon pool in Fig. 3, it is apparent that it is related to overall financial market conditions that have deteriorated lately due to the macroeconomic context, and has only some disconnect in the month of June from reference cryptoassets BTC and ETH. This complicates the comparison with off-chain carbon prices as those of GEO and NGEO prices.

The amount of KLIMA not staked and not in liquidity pools remains below 1%, which is coherent with the aims of the protocol.

---

[6] https://dune.com/Cujowolf/Klima-DAO.

Fig. 3. Price of BCT in US dollars (blue), BTC (yellow) and ETH (red) (from Coingecko) (Color figure online)

5   Conclusions and Outlook

Different blockchain-based projects have attempted to address perceived limitations or pitfalls of carbon markets in the last years. The differ in the technology used, the approach to tokenizing carbon assets and their integration with other DeFi primitives. In any case, the actual usage of those protocols is nowadays mostly unexplored. Here we have discussed empirical insights on the initial phase of the KlimaDAO project, which is arguably the most sophisticated and flexible project in this domain since it combines several DeFi primitives with carbon asset tokenization and pooling mechanisms.

The analysis of the protocol should take separately the tokenization, pooling, and then cryptoeconomic phases. The two first ones are in KlimaDAO done in conjunction with bridges as Toucan, and show a potential to steadily on-ramp off-chain assets into blockchains, clearly contributing to make them more liquid. That tokenization, and foremost its pooling under criteria that may result in asset classes for different user preferences or quality in the methodologies used to value the projects. The fact that these pools can be created by anyone and they are transparent in gating criteria and composition clearly fulfills the objective of increased transparency. With regards to other potentials, the approach for tokenizing assets is not contributing to additionality and permanence [8] or any other confidence issue in a clear way, since the current approach is semi-automated proof of tokenization of existing assets that is to date not even completely decentralized.

The amount of tokenized carbon units to date when compared to off-chain availability is small (for Verra around a 3% of assets have been tokenized at the time of this writing), but given that the protocols involved are relatively recent, it shows potential as a substantial future on-chain market. Further, the current use of bridges show an steady process of tokenization and specialized or alternate bridges have recently appeared.

The analysis of the actual KlimaDAO bonding and staking mechanisms in the overall on-chain market are difficult to assess due to its short lifespan and the fact that DeFi markets and usage are influenced by the overall volatility of cryptocurrency markets and more in general, with macroeconomic terms. However, the potential benefits of these mechanisms as incentives to increased carbon tokenization deserve attention from policy makers.

Since there are several emerging initiatives in the blockchain space that address environmental finance and more concretely, offset markets, future work should assess and compare them against their stated objectives and potential. Also, pooling in different asset classes deserve future attention to understand preferences and complementarities. Finally, the systemic effects of integrating tokenized carbon assets into DeFi are still yet to be explored as protocols as KlimaDAO mature.

References

1. Al-Breiki, H., Rehman, M.H.U., Salah, K., Svetinovic, D.: Trustworthy blockchain oracles: review, comparison, and open research challenges. IEEE Access **8**, 85675–85685 (2020)
2. Chitra, T., Kulkarni, K., Angeris, G., Evans, A. Xu, V.: DeFi liquidity management via Optimal Control: Ohm as a case study (2022)
3. Dalsgaard, S.: Tales of carbon offsets: between experiments and indulgences? J. Cult. Econ. **15**(1), 52–66 (2022)
4. Franke, L., Schletz, M., Salomo, S.: Designing a blockchain model for the Paris agreement's carbon market mechanism. Sustainability **12**(3), 1068 (2020)
5. Freni, P., Ferro, E., Moncada, R.: Tokenomics and blockchain tokens: a design-oriented morphological framework. Blockchain: Res. Appl **3**(1), 100069 (2022)
6. Hartmann, S., Thomas, S.: Applying blockchain to the Australian carbon market. Econ. Pap. J. Appl. Econ. Policy **39**(2), 133–151 (2020)
7. Howson, P., Oakes, S., Baynham-Herd, Z., Swords, J.: Cryptocarbon: the promises and pitfalls of forest protection on a blockchain. Geoforum **100**, 1–9 (2019)

8. Kotsialou, G., Kuralbayeva, K., Laing, T.: Blockchain's potential in forest offsets, the voluntary carbon markets and REDD+. Environ. Conserv. 1–9 (2022)
9. Kreibich, N., Hermwille, L.: Caught in between: credibility and feasibility of the voluntary carbon market post-2020. Clim. Policy **21**(7), 939–957 (2021)
10. Matsumura, E.M., Prakash, R., Vera-Munoz, S.C.: Firm-value effects of carbon emissions and carbon disclosures. Account. Rev. **89**(2), 695–724 (2014)
11. Meyer, E., Welpe, I. M., Sandner, P.: Decentralized Finance-A Systematic Literature Review and Research Directions. ECIS 2022 Research Papers, vol. 25 (2022)
12. Rajamani, L.: The 2015 Paris agreement: interplay between hard, soft and non-obligations. J. Environ. Law **28**(2), 337–358 (2016)
13. Tao, H., Zhuang, S., Xue, R., Cao, W., Tian, J., Shan, Y.: Environmental finance: an interdisciplinary review. Technol. Forecast. Soc. Chang. **179**, 121639 (2022)
14. Woo, J., Fatima, R., Kibert, C.J., Newman, R.E., Tian, Y., Srinivasan, R.S.: Applying blockchain technology for building energy performance measurement, reporting, and verification (MRV) and the carbon credit market: a review of the literature. Build. Environ. **205**, 108199 (2021)

Author Index

Abdellatif, Tamer Mohamed 49
Al Mehairi, Alya 49
Anitha, J. 1
Asuquo, Daniel E. 192
Averyanova, Yuliya 64
Azmi, Rida 212

Banerjee, Sourav 25
Biswas, Utpal 25
Butt, Saad 117

Carbonaro, Antonella 109
Cepero, Teresa 176
Chenal, Jérôme 212
Conchon, Emmanuel 49

Das, Debashis 25
de Lucio, Juan-José 227
Deepak, Gerard 81
Diop, El Bachir 212

Eunice, R. Jennifer 12

Fernandez-Cortez, Vanessa 141

García-Barriocanal, Elena 227
Goyal, Mukta 36

Haldar, Paranjay 25
Hemanth, D. Jude 1, 12

James, Otobong R. 192
Jothi, E. Smily Jeya 1

Kumar, Shipra Ravi 36

López-Chau, Asdrúbal 141

Maestre-Góngora, Gina Paola 176
Montané-Jiménez, Luis G. 176
Mora-Cantallops, Marçal 227

Nikiforova, Anastasija 161

Osypova, Olha 95

Palvannan, S. 81
Phukan, Orchid Chetia 117
Priyadharshini, Jemima 1

Rojas-Hernández, Rafael 141
Roy, Rajdeep 25

Sánchez-Alonso, Salvador 227
Sicilia, Miguel-Angel 227
Singh, Ghanapriya 117
Skitsko, Volodymyr 95, 126

Tékouabou, Stéphane Cédric Koumetio 212
Tiwari, Sanju 117
Toulni, Hamza 212

Udo, Edward N. 192
Usip, Patience U. 192

Valle-Cruz, David 141
Voinikov, Mykola 126

Zgheib, Rita 49
Znakovska, Yevheniia 64

Author Index

Printed in the United States
by Baker & Taylor Publisher Services